THE LORD OF THE RINGS

THE RETURN OF THE KING

From the ashes a fire shall be woken,
A light from the shadows shall spring;
Renewed shall be the sword that was broken:
The crownless again shall be king.

CONTENTS

Good Warriors

FORCES OF DARKNESS

Heroes

Evil Warriors

Scenarios

THE WAR OF THE RING
Good Heroes

Good Warriors

The Miniatures

Painting the Models

Making Terrain

The Gaming Hobby

Appendix

THE RETURN OF THE KING

by
Alessio Cavatore

Original Game Design
Rick Priestley

The War of the Ring section
Matthew Ward

Book Design
John Blanche & Markus Trenkner

Illustration & Graphics
David Gallagher & Nuala Kennedy

Production/Design Management
Jim Butler, Gordon Davidson & Simon Smith

Production & Photography
John Michelbach, Talima Fox & Michelle Barson

Citadel Miniatures Designers
Alan Perry and Michael Perry, Gary Morley,
Trish Morrison & Brian Nelson

Scenic Model Makers
Dave Andrews & Mark Jones

Miniatures Painters
Kevin Asprey, Tammy Haye, Neil Green,
Neil Langdown, Darren Latham, Keith Robertson,
Sebastien Perbet & Kirsten Williams

Reprographics
Simon Burton, Sean Cutler,
Marc Elliott, David Musson,
Ian Strickland & Lee Sanderson

Game Development
Rob Wood, Chris Harbor,
Mark Scard, Mark Bedford, Mark Latham,
Darron Bowley, Steve Hammatt, Rob Broom,
Conrad Gonsalves, Adrian Champion,
Kevin Barraclough & David Smith

Special thanks to
Peter Jackson, Richard Taylor
and everybody at Weta,
John Mayo and David Imhoff (New Line Cinema),
Laurie Battle (Tolkien Enterprises) & Andy Jones

PRODUCED BY GAMES WORKSHOP
Second Printing Dec 2003

Games Workshop Lord of the Rings website:
www.games-workshop.com/lotr/

Games Workshop website:
www.games-workshop.com

UK
Games Workshop,
Willow Rd,
Lenton,
Nottingham, NG7 2WS

US
Games Workshop,
6721 Baymeadow Drive,
Glen Burnie,
Maryland 21060-6401

Australia
Games Workshop,
23 Liverpool Street,
Ingleburn
NSW 2565

Canada
2679 Bristol Circle
Units 2 & 3,
Oakville,
Ontario L6H 6Z8

 NEW LINE CINEMA
An AOL Time Warner Company

Lord of the Rings website:
www.lordoftherings.net

 AOL keyword:
Lord of the Rings

Tolkien Enterprises

THE LORD OF THE RINGS BATTLE GAME

Welcome to The Return of The King edition of Games Workshop's The Lord of The Rings battle game – the game of adventure and battles in the world of Middle-earth.

To those of you who already own previous editions of our game, I'd especially like to say thank you for your support and enthusiasm – and not least for taking the plunge and adding The Return of The King to your collection. This new rules manual is completely compatible with your existing manuals, adding new characters and scenarios from The Return of The King, as well as an up-to-date rules set with various new features. In order to make our game complete, we have repeated the core game rules from the earlier editions – this takes up only a relatively small part of the manual and is essential for the sake of players who are new to the game. We have, of course, taken the opportunity to work some improvements and corrections into the rules, so you'll find it is worthwhile reading them through even if you are already familiar with the game.

Also, this edition of the game features the completely new War of the Ring section. This expands the scope of our game beyond the contents of the film and into the vast realm of The Lord of The Rings book, allowing players to explore the rich history and fascinating lands of Middle-earth.

If you have never played a tabletop battle game before, then do not be put off by the length or apparent complexity of this manual. The core rules are relatively easy to learn, whilst many of the special or detailed rules only apply in rarefied situations and can be safely ignored to begin with. Similarly, don't be daunted by the prospect of painting all those miniatures – you don't have to paint all your models to enjoy using them on the battlefield.

If you're an experienced tabletop gamer but new to The Lord of The Rings strategy battle game, don't be put off by what is a relatively short set of rules compared to other games. Although the basic game system might seem beguilingly simple, you'll find it requires considerable skill to employ it effectively. Players who yearn for more detail (and who doesn't!) will find a growing body of supplementary material already available, with the promise of yet more to come in the future.

This manual is divided into sections, as you will see if you leaf through the pages to get an overall impression of what it is all about. There is no need to read the whole manual through from start to finish – each section can be consulted as the need arises. For those who want an immediate taste of how the game works without reading the complete rules, turn to page 174 for an example encounter.

For all the latest news about The Lord of The Rings battle game and recent model releases, see Games Workshop's monthly games supplement White Dwarf or check out our website at www.games-workshop.com.

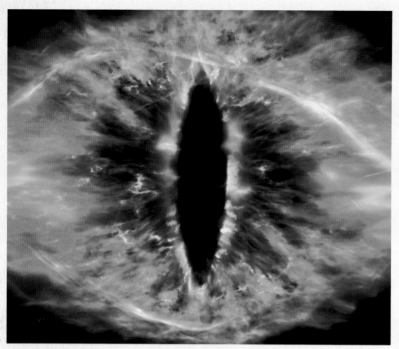

Concealed within his fortress, the Lord of Mordor sees all.

ᴥ ᴥ ᴥ ᴥ

Three Rings for the Elven-kings under the sky,

Seven for the Dwarf-lords in their halls of stone,

Nine for the Mortal Men doomed to die,

One for the Dark Lord on his dark throne,

In the land of Mordor, where the Shadows lie.

One Ring to rule them all, One Ring to find them,

One Ring to bring them all, and in the darkness bind them,

In the land of Mordor, where the Shadows lie.

ᴥ ᴥ ᴥ ᴥ

THE MISTY MOUNTAINS

The Misty Mountains lie between the regions of Eriador and Rhovanion, a rocky spine that splits Middle-earth in twain. These ageless peaks have seen much. It is here that the Dwarves and Goblins have waged their underground war for many centuries, and it is on the foothills of these mountains that the land of Hollin, where Celebrimbor forged the Rings of Power, once lay.

Gandalf leads the Fellowship onto the slopes of Caradhras.

Far below the surface of the world, a bitter struggle rages.

Let them come! There is one Dwarf yet in Moria that still draws breath!

Goblin Shaman

Durbûrz

Moria Goblin Drummers

"When winter first begins to bite
and stones crack in the frosty night,
when pools are black and trees are bare
'tis evil in the Wild to fare."

- The Fellowship of The Ring

Daren Parwood's Balrog in all its illuminated glory!

INTRODUCTION
TO THE GAME RULES

The rules of the game are explained in a conversational style with examples throughout. We have tried to describe rules in a way that enables new players to learn the game as quickly as possible. Once familiar with the rules, the majority of players will find the reference pages are all that are needed during most games.

WHAT YOU WILL NEED

In order to play you will need a few basic items in addition to this rules manual:

Dice

You will need a number of ordinary six-sided dice to play this game – at least a couple will do but preferably a half dozen or so.

Measure

The movement of models and shooting of weapons requires the use of a measure marked in inches or centimetres. A measuring stick, tape measure or ruler will do just fine.

Record sheet

It is useful to have some means of recording details of the warriors which you can refer to throughout the game. You can do this using a sheet of paper or by copying the record sheet from the back of this book. You will need a pen or pencil to note sundry details.

Somewhere to play

Any reasonably flat surface will do – a kitchen table, table tennis table, or even the floor.

Warriors

Any number of model warriors can take part in a battle – from a handful to many hundreds. It is best to start with about five or six models a side and familiarise yourself with the rules before attempting a huge battle.

Scenery

Strictly speaking you don't need scenery for your playing area at all – but a featureless, flat expanse is a bit dull! A few tumbled ruins, rocks, and trees will help to set the scene. These can be made at home, purchased separately, or improvised from pieces of card or modelling clay.

ADVANCED & SPECIAL RULES

To make the game quicker to learn we have divided the Advanced and Special rules from the rest of the text.

Advanced rules introduce extra detail into the game. If you are just starting out, we recommend that you ignore them. Advanced rules are included at the end of each section where appropriate, or gathered together in the Advanced Rules section which starts on page 44.

Special rules apply only to specific types of creature – they are special to that individual or race.

MEASURING

Throughout these rules you'll often be asked to measure how far a model moves or shoots, etc. Players are allowed to measure at any time they wish – a player might wish to measure before deciding where to move a warrior, for example.

The distance between two models is measured 'base to base' (ie, from the edge of the first model's base to the edge of the other model's base).

All distances have been given in both inches and centimetres. A game can be played using either system – but you can't mix the two systems together. Decide whether you want to play in inches or centimetres and stick to the one method. Note that distances are not exact translations of one system or the other as that would be extremely inconvenient – for example, centimetres have been rounded to whole even numbers to facilitate easy halving of distances for movement penalties.

ROLLING DICE

When you roll a dice it is sometimes necessary to add or subtract bonuses from the roll – so a roll of 4 with a +1 bonus is a score of 5. Easy enough!

The only thing you need to remember is that the minimum score is always 1 and the maximum score is always 6 – regardless of any bonus or penalty you cannot score better than 6 or worse than 1.

D6 OR D3

Sometimes the abbreviation D6 is used instead of the word 'dice'. These mean exactly the same.

At other times you can find the phrase 'roll a D3'. This means to roll a dice and divide the result by two, rounding up. So, if you roll a 1 or 2 your result will be 1, if you roll a 3 or 4 your result will be 2, and if you roll a 5 or 6 your result will be 3.

RE-ROLLS

Sometimes the rules allow you to 're-roll' the dice. This is exactly as it sounds – pick up the dice you wish to re-roll and roll it again. The second result always counts even if it is worse than the first, and no dice can be re-rolled more than once regardless of the source of the re-roll.

STARTING A GAME

Each game represents a conflict between two opposing sides. This might be anything from a small encounter involving a handful of warriors to a huge clash between two armies.

1) PICK A SCENARIO

Start by picking a scenario from the Scenarios section (see pages 98-113). The scenarios represent different kinds of battles both large and small. We suggest players begin with the smaller encounters as these involve fewer models and are relatively quick to resolve.

2) SELECT YOUR FORCES

All models are allotted a points value which reflects their effectiveness in the game. Powerful warriors are worth more points than weak warriors. The rules for each scenario explain how many points you can spend on your force, as well as any special conditions that apply.

3) DEPLOY YOUR FORCES

The models are placed on the tabletop in their starting positions according to the instructions for the scenario.

4) PLAY THE GAME

The rules for play are described on the following pages.

5) THE END OF THE GAME

The rules for each scenario specify when the game ends. This will usually be after a set number of turns or once some special objective has been fulfiled. Once the requisite number of turns have been played or the objective achieved, the game is over. The players can then work out which side has won.

A bitter fight breaks out in the streets of Osgiliath.

CHARACTERISTICS

Because we recognise that all combatants are not the same we must make allowances for their differences. This is achieved by what we call 'characteristics'. There are six different characteristics that define each warrior's abilities. These are Fighting, Strength, Defence, Attacks, Wounds, and Courage. Each of these has a value written in the form of a characteristic profile like this:

	F	S	D	A	W	C
Warrior of Minas Tirith	3/4+	3	5	1	1	3

Example: This is the characteristic profile for a Warrior of Minas Tirith armed with a bow. His characteristic values are typical for a Man. Whilst most ordinary Men have similar characteristic values, Heroes and other individuals have greater values to represent their superior abilities.

Fighting

A warrior's Fighting value (F) consists of two numbers divided by a slash. The first number represents his martial skill in hand-to-hand fighting – the greater this is, the better fighter the warrior is. The second number is the Shooting value and this indicates the minimum dice roll the warrior needs to score a hit with a bow or other long ranged weapon. If a warrior does not carry a long ranged weapon it is convenient to miss out the Shooting value or replace it with a dash (-). A value of 3 is about average for hand-to-hand fighting and 4+ (ie, a roll of 4, 5 or 6) is average for shooting.

Strength

A warrior's Strength value (S) indicates how strong he is and how powerfully he can strike his enemies. For example, a big creature such as a Cave Troll is very strong compared to a Man. A value of 3 is about average for a man-sized creature.

Defence

A warrior's Defence value (D) indicates how tough or resilient he is. Many monstrous creatures are especially tough, whilst armour and shields all increase a warrior's resilience to a blow. A value of 3 is about average for a man-sized creature without armour; 6 would be about average for the same warrior fully armoured for battle.

Attacks

The Attacks value (A) indicates how many strikes a warrior makes when he wins a fight. Most warriors can strike once per turn and so have a value of 1. Heroic individuals and some big monsters can strike two, three or more times, making them very dangerous in close combat.

Wounds

The Wounds value (W) indicates how many wounds a warrior can suffer before he is slain. In the case of most man-sized creatures this value is 1 – a single wound is sufficient to kill. Some Heroes and monstrous creatures can sustain injuries that would incapacitate an ordinary man – they have 2, 3 or more wounds to represent this.

Courage

The Courage value (C) shows how brave and determined the warrior is. A value of about 3 is average, a warrior with Courage of 5 or more is very brave, and a warrior with a value of less than 3 is rather timid.

Warrior of Minas Tirith with bow	F	S	D	A	W	C
	3/4+	3	5	1	1	3

Warrior of Rohan with with sword and shield	F	S	D	A	W	C
	3/-	3	5	1	1	3

Dwarf Warrior with axe & shield	F	S	D	A	W	C
	4/4+	3	7	1	1	4

Mordor Orc with bow	F	S	D	A	W	C
	3/5+	3	4	1	1	2

Mordor Orc with sword & shield	F	S	D	A	W	C
	3/-	3	5	1	1	2

Mordor Uruk-hai with sword	F	S	D	A	W	C
	4/-	4	5	1	1	3

THE GAME TURN

TURNS

The game is divided into turns. During each turn models can move, shoot with ranged weapons, and fight each other in hand-to-hand combat.

SIDES

There are always two sides in a The Lord of The Rings battle. One side commands the forces of Good and the other the forces of Evil.

Each side is represented by a number of models controlled by one or more players. See the Scenarios section for rules about choosing models (see pages 98-113).

There must be at least one player on each side. If there are more players taking part, each controls a portion of the models. The bigger the game the more useful it is to have extra players to help with such things as movement and rolling dice.

The Men of Minas Tirith clash with Orcs in furious mêlée.

THE TURN SEQUENCE

During each turn both sides move, shoot, and fight in the order given below. This is called the 'Turn Sequence'. Each part of the sequence is called a 'phase'.

Phase

1   Priority
   Both sides roll a dice to establish which side has priority that turn.

2   Move
   Both sides move their models. The side with priority moves its models first. Once the side with priority has made its moves, the other side moves.

3   Shoot
   Both sides shoot. The side with priority shoots first. Once the side with priority has finished its shots, the other side shoots.

4   Fight
   Both sides fight hand-to-hand combats. The side with priority decides the order in which combats are fought.

5   End
   The turn is over. Begin another turn starting with Phase 1 – Priority.

THE PRIORITY PHASE

In the first turn, priority automatically goes to the Good side unless the scenario calls for an exception. This means the Good side will normally move and shoot first in the first turn.

In subsequent turns both sides roll a dice in the Priority phase at the start of the turn. The side that scores highest has priority for that turn. If the dice rolls are equal, priority automatically changes from one side to the other – the side that had priority in the previous turn will always lose it on a tie.

It is important to remember which side has priority each turn. You can use a token such as a coin or a distinctive model, passing it from one side to the other to indicate which has priority.

There are a few exceptions to the Priority rules – but these need not concern us right now. In some scenarios the Good side does not necessarily go first, for example. Also, in the section on Heroes we will be discussing rules that occasionally allow Heroes to override the normal priority and move, shoot or fight before other warriors. These exceptions will be explained in due course.

THE MOVE PHASE

Once priority has been established the turn proceeds to the Move phase. During the Move phase, each side gets to move its models up to the maximum distance as shown on the chart below. Models do not have to move the full distance – they can move less or not at all if the player prefers.

The distance a model is allowed to move depends upon its race. Some races are faster than others. The following Movement chart summarises the Move distances for each race. If you own the original The Fellowship of The Ring or The Two Towers editions of the game you will notice we have included creatures from those games for reference.

WHICH SIDE MOVES FIRST?

The side that has priority that turn moves all of its models first. Once all of the first side's moves are complete, the other side gets to move all of its models.

MOVING THE MODELS

Each player can move his models in any order.

Measure the distance each model moves using a measuring tape or ruler. Models don't have to move in a straight line, they can move in curving paths or however you like so long as they move no further than their maximum permitted distance.

The warrior moves forward 6"/14cm.

MOVEMENT CHART

Type	Maximum move over open terrain	
	Inches	**Cms**
MAN/WOMAN/WIZARD	6"	14cm
HIGH ELF/WOOD ELF	6"	14cm
GWAIHIR	12"	28cm
ENT	6"	14cm
HOBBIT	4"	10cm
DWARF	5"	12cm
GOLLUM	5"	12cm
ORC	6"	14cm
MORIA GOBLIN	5"	12cm
URUK-HAI	6"	14cm
CAVE TROLL	6"	14cm
BALROG	6"	14cm
RINGWRAITH	6"	14cm
SAURON	6"	14cm
SHELOB	10"	24cm
FELL BEAST	12"	28cm
WARG RIDER	10"	24cm
HORSE RIDER	10"	24cm

As you can see distances are given in both inches and centimetres as they are throughout this rules manual. Either system can be used but stick to one or the other, don't mix them in the same game as the distances have been rounded for convenience.
Note: *The Move rate for Orcs has increased from 5" to 6" from the previous editions of the game.*

Models cannot move through other models whether friends or foes, so leave gaps for models to pass where necessary. The model's base conveniently defines the space it needs to move and fight – so gaps must be at least as wide as a model's base for a friendly warrior to move through.

When friendly models move past each other there must be room for their bases to pass without overlapping.

A model can only move to within 1" or 2cm of an enemy model that it wishes to charge (a charge is a move into contact as described overleaf). In effect, this allows models to block the movement of enemies. This known as the Control Zone rule.

Once a charger has moved to within 1"/2cm of his target he must complete his move into contact against the target model/models – he will ignore the control zone of other enemies nearby.

Once the charger has moved within 1"/2cm of his target, he ignores other models' control zones.

There are three exceptions to the Control Zone rule that are worth pointing out right away. Firstly, models already touching an enemy have no control zone – they are already engaged in fighting. An enemy model can therefore move to within 1"/2cm in this case. The second exception is that models are sometimes obliged to move within 1"/2cm because of a rule they have no say over. Where movement is because of another rule, rather than a deliberate move by the player, a model can move within an enemy's control zone without charging. In this case, models must be clearly separated by a reasonable distance to make it clear they are not touching once the move is complete. The third exception is that models can sometimes begin their move already within 1"/2cm of an enemy for some reason. In this case, the intruder cannot move closer to the enemy unless he intends to move into touch but can move around without moving closer if he wants.

1. A model cannot move within 1"/2cm of an enemy control zone unless it is moving into touch. In this situation, the Warrior of Minas Tirith armed with a sword can move into touch with either of the closest Orcs but it cannot move between them to get at the Orc behind.

2. Now that the other Man has charged, the Orc he touches no longer prevents movement within 1"/2cm, allowing the sword-armed Man to move past to attack the Orc behind.

Models can be turned to face any direction at any time during the game – not just in the Move phase. Rotating a model on the spot does not count as movement.

Models are not allowed to move off the gaming table unless they are retreating from the battle as described in the rules for Courage (see page 44) or if the scenario requires it – as discussed in the Scenario section.

CHARGES

A model can only fight an enemy it is touching base-to-base. If a player wants a model to attack an enemy, the model must be moved into touch. This is called a 'charge move' or just a 'charge'.

Once a model has moved into touch with an enemy neither can move further in that Move phase. A model that is charged before it gets a chance to move is therefore unable to do so – it is already engaged in a fight.

A model can only fight an enemy it is touching base-to-base.

There is nothing to stop a model moving into touch with several enemies at the same time if it can do so. This is entirely up to the player.

WHO CAN CHARGE?

A warrior can charge any enemy model he can see at the start of his own move and which he can reach. It does not matter if he can see his enemy at the start of the Move phase or previously in the phase – only at the start of his own move. A warrior cannot charge an enemy model he can't see when he starts his own move. If a warrior can't see an enemy at the very start of his own move, the model cannot move into touch. A move into touch is a charge by definition.

This is quite an important rule because it prevents warriors charging enemies they couldn't see or react to in a real-life situation. Imagine an enemy is on the other side of a hill, inside a building, or behind a high wall – in these situations a real warrior has no idea where his enemy is.

CAN I SEE?

The easiest way to decide if a model can see another is by bending over the tabletop for a 'model's eye view' of the action. A warrior can turn freely to look in any direction at any time so the model's eye view automatically extends all the way round the model in all directions.

If the enemy is visible from the model's eye view, then the warrior can see it. In many cases you'll be able to see bits of an enemy model but not all of it – in that case the warrior can see so long as part of the enemy's body is clearly visible.

If you can't see any part of a model's body, but you can see the tip of a weapon, back pack, or a piece of equipment or decoration we assume the model can't be seen. In principle, the small area of cloth, metal or wood that is visible is not noticed. This is a fair rule because otherwise models with tall or projecting spears would always be seen as it is virtually impossible to position them without their spears poking out somewhere! In reality, the warrior would lay the spear close to the ground or hold it close to his body as he moved – but our models are not that flexible.

Sometimes it can be hard to tell if a warrior can see or not – that's a fact of tabletop gaming life. If you really can't tell then the situation is obviously fairly marginal. In such a case, the best and fairest way to decide is to make a 'random' test. Roll a dice. If a 4, 5 or 6 is rolled the model can see, however a 1, 2 or 3 means it can't.

Tactical note: As models are moved one at a time it is sometimes possible to clear the view for one model by moving another. Similarly, it is easy for models to get in the way of each other if moved carelessly. This can be tricky to begin with – so try to move the models in an order that allows others to see or move.

FIGHTS

At the end of the Move phase, any models that are in base contact with the enemy are paired off into individual combats.

Here there are two separate one-on-one combats to the left, a two-on-one combat in the middle, and a three-on-one combat on the right.

Sometimes you will have situations where a single warrior is faced by two, three, or more enemies. This is called a 'multiple combat'. Opponents are always paired off where possible and any other combatants join into a multiple combat against an enemy they are touching.

If a warrior could join one of several combats to create a multiple combat then the player with priority that turn decides which one he joins. Similarly, where matches can be made in one of several different ways, the player with priority decides how the combatants are matched. In both cases, all touching models must be included and any multiple combats must have one model on one side and multiples on the other (never multiples on both sides in the same fight). Always separate the models slightly to make the pairs more obvious and to see what's going on.

TERRAIN

The maximum distances given for movement assume that the going is firm and level and there is nothing to impede progress. Of course that is not always the case – all too often our warriors must struggle through areas of scrub or forest, over bog or mire, or upon rocky scree slopes. We refer to all these and comparable conditions as 'difficult terrain'.

An area of difficult terrain isn't impossible to move through – but it slows progress. To represent this, all distance moved over difficult terrain count as twice the actual distance. For example, a model that moves 6"/14cm normally will move a maximum of 3"/7cm across difficult terrain.

Sometimes a model's move will be split, partly over good ground and partly over difficult terrain. In this case, the model moves normally over the good ground and only the distance over difficult terrain is doubled. For example, a model with a 6" move might move 2" over a marsh (doubled to 4") leaving only 2" for further movement. Always round any remaining fractions of movement up to the next highest half inch or full cm – any distance that is smaller than this is much too insignificant to worry about.

Below and overleaf are some examples of difficult terrain features. You may be able to think of more circumstances that would qualify. However, it is important to make sure that all the players understand which areas are considered difficult terrain before the game begins.

SPECIAL RULE

Woodland Creatures
Wood Elves and Ents are used to travelling in woodland – they therefore don't consider these areas to be difficult terrain. A Wood Elf or Ent can move 6"/14cm in a wooded area just as if he were in the open.

EXAMPLES OF DIFFICULT TERRAIN

As difficult terrain counts as double distance, it is important to be able to tell where features begin and end. It is useful to delineate the area in some way – for example, by using a card base to define the area.

A very steep slope such as this would slow down progress and so counts as difficult terrain.

Swamps and other kinds of marshy terrain are quite tricky to cross and therefore count as difficult terrain.

These ruins count as difficult terrain.

An area of woodland or copse – a typical example of difficult terrain.

An area of rocky ground would usually be considered difficult terrain.

TYPES OF DIFFICULT TERRAIN

Very steep, rock strewn or otherwise awkward slopes

Areas of wood or forests

Areas of dense scrub

Bogs, marshes and mires

Areas of shallow water, fords or pools

Areas of ruins, rubble or debris

Areas of deep snow, mud or shifting sand.

BARRIERS AND OBSTACLES

Barriers can take many forms on the tabletop – for example, a stack of barrels, a hedgerow, a rocky outcrop, a low wall or a clump of bushes. A barrier can also be something that cuts into the landscape such as a stream or ditch. The main difference between a barrier and an area of difficult terrain is that a barrier is something you might conceivably leap over, whilst an area of difficult terrain is something you must slog your way through. A good example is a thorny hedge – a barrier you might leap over – as opposed to a whole patch of thorny undergrowth where all you can do is push your way through.

If a barrier is very low and narrow then a model can cross unhindered – the warrior simply strides over the barrier. A model can automatically cross any barrier if the barrier's height and width are less than half the height of the model. For example, if a model is 28mm tall it can cross a barrier that is less than 14mm high and less than 14mm wide.

If a barrier is very high or very wide then it cannot be crossed at all or can only be crossed by climbing as noted later. A model cannot cross or must climb any barrier that is more than twice the height of the model itself. For example, a model that is 28mm tall cannot cross or must climb a wall that is 57mm high. Note that not all barriers are considered climbable – see Climbing.

If a barrier is at least half as high or half as wide as the height of a model, but not more than twice as high or wide, then the barrier is described as an 'obstacle'. For example, a wall 28mm high would form an obstacle to a model that was 28mm tall but not to a model that was 60mm tall.

A model can attempt to cross an obstacle by jumping over it as described opposite. Sometimes a model will have to jump an obstacle in order to move beyond it as in the case of a stream, for example. On other occasions a model might be able to move around an obstacle, taking a longer route but avoiding the inconvenience of jumping the obstacle itself. Below are a few examples of barriers that might form obstacles:

TYPES OF OBSTACLE

A length of wall, hedge, barricade, fence or similar barrier

A length of ditch or escarpment

A narrow stream or fissure

A large dense bush or shrub

A substantial rock or rocky outcrop

An open ground floor window

A pile of barrels, sacks, bales, or similar

A mound of straw or dung.

A fissure such as this is a typical obstacle.

A hedge, line of scrub, or patch of bushes forming an obstacle.

This shallow stream would also form an obstacle.

A pile of barrels, sacks and debris.

JUMPING AN OBSTACLE

To get over an obstacle a model must first move up to it and must have at least enough movement remaining to reach the other side were the obstacle not there. A model that does not have enough Move distance to cross the obstacle must wait until the following turn.

A dice is rolled to see if the attempt is successful. Roll a dice. If the obstacle is taller or wider than the model's height deduct -1 from the roll. Consult the chart below:

JUMP CHART

Dice	Result
1	**Stumbles and fails** – The model does not cross and cannot move further this turn.
2-5	**Success** – The model successfully clambers over the obstacle and reaches the other side. The model is placed on the other side of the obstacle with its base touching it and cannot move further this turn.
6	**Effortlessly bounds across** – The model leaps over the obstacle and can complete its move if it has any remaining.

Example. An Elf has a move of 6"/14cm. The Elf moves 2"/4cm forward towards a wall. The wall is 1"/2cm wide and a roll is required to cross. The player rolls a dice. On a score of a 1, the Elf fails to cross and can move no further that turn. On the roll of a 2-5, the Elf crosses and is placed on the other side of the wall. On the roll of a 6, the Elf moves 4"/10cm forward, crossing the wall as he does so.

JUMPING A GAP

A gap such as a chasm, ditch, or the distance from one part of a ruined building to another, can be jumped in the same way as an obstacle. A model can jump a gap of up to double its own height.

Roll on the Jump chart as you would for jumping an obstacle. On a 1, the model does not simply fail to cross but falls down to the ground. A model falling further than twice its own height may be injured as a result – see Climbing (page 20) for details about damage from falls.

SPECIAL RULE

Moria Goblins & Jumping

The stunted crook-limbed Orcs of Moria, also known as Moria Goblins, are adapted to the underground ruins of the ancient Dwarf stronghold where they live. This allows them to bound across obstacles and gaps effortlessly.

To represent this in the game, no dice roll is required when a Moria Goblin is attempting to jump a gap or obstacle up to double its own height. The jump is made automatically just as if a 6 had been rolled on the Jump chart.

"We must... go now?"

DEFENDING A BARRIER

If a warrior is placed directly behind a wall, hedge, fence, barricade, ditch or similar linear barrier then he is especially well placed to counter any foe that tries to cross. The model is said to be 'defending' the barrier and is placed with its base touching.

To count as a defendable barrier in this way a feature must be at least half as tall or wide as an attacking enemy – otherwise the enemy can step over it without penalty.

In order to defend a barrier a model has to be able to see over it.

When a model is defending a barrier, its zone of control applies to the whole area immediately in front of the defender's base plus 1"/2cm either side. This is the part of the barrier he is defending. No enemy can move into the defender's zone of control except to fight him.

The defender's zone of control extends 1"/2cm either side of his base.

The only way to cross a barrier within the defender's zone of control is to fight the model behind it. Rules for this are covered in the Fight phase section (see pages 26-34).

ADVANCED RULES

The remainder of the Move phase section is devoted to Advanced rules – which you will find useful to apply in some circumstances but can safely ignore for most games.

If you haven't played before we recommend that you skip over the following rules for now – you can always come back to them later.

CLIMBING

In areas of ancient ruins, models often have the opportunity to climb onto old tombs, or up to the ruined upper floors of buildings. If the total ascent is not more than twice the height of the model this is accomplished in the same way as for crossing an obstacle and a Jump roll is made as described previously.

Very occasionally a tall vertical or near vertical surface will offer enough handholds so that it can be climbed steadily. In this case treat the vertical surface as difficult terrain and move the model upwards or downwards counting the distance as double the measured distance. In addition, roll a dice when the model starts to climb and at the start of each move whilst climbing.

CLIMB CHART

Dice	Result
1	**Fall** – The model slips & falls to the ground. See rules below.
2-5	**Continue to climb** – If the top/bottom is reached place the model at the edge. The model cannot move further that turn.
6	**Continue to climb** – If the top/bottom is reached the model can complete its remaining move.

A model can jump, climb or fall down a vertical drop of up to double its own height without a dice test, move penalty, hindrance, or risk of injury. Eg, a model with a move of 12cm could move 6cm to the edge of a ruined platform, jump down to the ground, and move 6cm further. No Jump roll is required to jump down in this way.

Jumping or falling down a drop more than twice the model's height is dangerous. If a model jumps/falls in this way it's automatically placed lying on the ground at the foot of the drop and suffers one Strength 3 hit for each full 1" or full 2cm of fall. So, a model that falls 4"/10cm suffers four Strength 3 hits, a model that falls 12cm suffers six Strength 3 hits, etc. See the Shooting section for how to calculate the effect of hits. Note that when jumping a drop of more than double the model's height, no Jump roll is required to make the descent no matter how far. The warrior plummets to the ground quite effortlessly! Assuming the experience does not prove fatal, the model is considered to have expended all of its movement for that Move phase.

DEFENDING ELEVATED POSITIONS

A warrior who climbs to the top of a cliff, wall or other vertical surface automatically charges the nearest enemy whose zone of control overlaps the top edge of the surface. He holds on just below the top of the vertical surface and fights the warrior on the top. If no enemy zone of control overlaps the edge of the vertical surface, the warrior can position himself on the top – but he cannot charge any other enemy on the top as they would not have been visible at the start of his move. Only defenders whose zones of control extend onto the edge are assumed to be visible as the attacker climbs up the vertical surface.

Models stood on the top of a vertical surface fight by defending its edge against attackers climbing up from below. The rules for defending elevated positions are based on the rules for defending barriers (see page 19).

A warrior on the top of a wall/cliff can be placed immediately behind its edge and can then defend the edge immediately in front of him and 1"/2cm either side of him. This is exactly the same as for defending barriers and is shown on the diagram that follows.

The defender's zone of control extends 1"/2cm either side of his base. The elevated position counts as a defended barrier.

No enemy can attempt to ascend over the edge of a vertical surface if he has to enter the control zone of a model that is defending the edge. The attacker must fight the defender and kill him in order to climb over the edge and occupy his enemy's place on the top.

The rules for defending fights are used to work out the combat. This is exactly the same as for a combat over a wall, hedge, barricade or similar defence work. The only difference is that the chargers are climbing a vertical surface and so risk falling off if they fail to get over the edge as noted below.

Falling Off

The following rules apply to warriors attacking whilst climbing vertical surfaces:

If a model is fighting in this way and is forced to back away 1"/2cm, he can only move down the vertical surface. As he backs away he risks falling. If physically unable to back away for whatever reason, the warrior still risks falling. A model making way for a friend who is backing away from a fight does not have to roll – he is not retreating in the face of the enemy.

Make a random roll to see if the warrior falls as he is beaten back. On a 4, 5, or 6, the warrior keeps his footing and backs away as required. On a 1, 2 or 3, the warrior loses his footing and falls to the ground before he can back away. He falls the full distance to the ground and suffers falling damage in the usual way. (See page 20).

If the warrior at the top of the vertical surface falls, then roll a dice for every other model that is climbing right below him. Any model that rolls a 1, 2 or 3 is also knocked from the vertical surface by their own friend. Models fall from wherever they are on the surface – so warriors that are nearer the ground suffer fewer hits. See page 20 for the rules on falling damage.

The Orcs prepare their assault.

SPECIAL RULE

Moria Goblins & Climbing

Moria Goblins are adapted to their cavernous habitat beneath the mountains and can scuttle up sheer surfaces with the aid of hooks, spines, and spikes incorporated into their armour. To represent this we allow them to climb much more efficiently than other creatures.

Moria Goblins can climb up or down vertical surfaces without making a Climb roll – in effect they always count as having rolled a 6 on the chart. However, they're still reduced to half speed whilst climbing – even Moria Goblins can move about more quickly on the ground!

MODELS ON THE GROUND

Real warriors on foot can conceal themselves from view by crouching or lying behind cover. Models can also be knocked to the ground by charging cavalry. To represent this players must lie the model down.

If no part of the model's body is visible to an enemy warrior's model's eye view it cannot be seen. Note that it is only the model's body that is taken into account – not its base, weapons, etc.

If a model is on the ground but its body is still visible in its entirety to the enemy warrior's model's eye view – with no interposing cover, terrain, or other models, the model can be seen.

If a model is on the ground and the model's eye view of its body is partially obscured by scenery, cover, or other models, then it can only be seen by an enemy if a dice is rolled and scores a 4, 5 or 6. On the roll of a 1, 2 or 3, the model can't be seen because it is too cleverly concealed. It is necessary to roll a 'spotting' dice for each enemy trying to spot the model – only enemy models that successfully spot the model on the ground will see it.

When a player gets to move a warrior he can lie the model down. This costs the model half its entire move distance.

A model that is on the ground can get up. This costs the model half of its entire movement distance. The model can then complete the rest of its move normally.

Whilst on the ground, a model does not have a control zone and is unable to charge an enemy, employ magical powers, shoot, or do anything else except for moving as described below. He also cannot use any weapon except shields, hand weapons, knives and daggers.

A lying down model's Move rate is reduced to 1" or 2cm regardless of its race. This represents the warrior crawling along on its hands and knees.

A lying down model can be jumped over by friends and foes alike, in the same way as an obstacle (though, of course, it cannot be defended like an obstacle – don't even think about it!).

If a model is lying directly behind cover, we assume the warrior is capable of peeking through or over its cover without exposing itself to view. A model lying behind cover is therefore assumed to be able to see as if the model were standing, even though the cover might be in the way of the model's eye view.

If a model is charged whilst on the ground, it cannot stand up in the Move phase, but it will attempt to stand in the Fight phase. Determine who wins the fight as normal. If the model on the ground wins the fight then it cannot strike – but automatically stands instead. If the model on the ground loses, it remains down, is pushed back 1"/2cm and counts as trapped as described in the Fight Phase section.

A model lying down behind a barrier cannot count as defending it – to defend a barrier a warrior must be on its feet ready to repel the enemy.

THE SHOOT PHASE

Once both sides have moved it is time for the Shoot phase. In this phase, models from both sides can shoot their bows, crossbows, or other ranged weapons.

The side that has priority works out all shooting first, followed by the other side. Warriors that are slain before they have a chance to shoot cannot do so. A player can shoot with his models in any order.

MISSILE CHART

Different kinds of weapons have different ranges, some shoot further than others whilst some are harder hitting and more dangerous. The chart below indicates the range of each type, its Strength value, and the proportion of the model's move it must give up in order to shoot that turn.

Weapon	Range (Inches/cm)	Strength	Move Penalty
Bow	24"/56cm	2	Half
Orc bow	18"/42cm	2	Half
Elf bow	24"/56cm	3	Half
Dwarf bow	18"/42cm	3	Half
Uruk-hai crossbow	24"/56cm	4	All
Throwing weapon	6"/14cm	3	None

A model can shoot once in the Shoot phase at a target within range that it can see. We have already discussed what is meant by what a model 'sees' in the Movement rules. The rule is exactly the same whether a model is moving or shooting. If you wish to remind yourself of the rule refer back to page 16.

The player starts by selecting the model that is to shoot and indicates the target. It is a good idea to turn the shooter to face his target – this is not strictly necessary but it looks better that way.

Not all warriors are equally good marksmen, as reflected by the Shooting value in their profile. This is the second number shown on the Fight characteristic. If a warrior does not have a weapon to shoot with it is convenient to miss out the Shooting value – this is shown by a dash (–).

The Shooting value indicates the minimum dice roll which is needed by the shooter to score a hit on its target. So, a shooter with a Shooting value of 4+ needs a dice roll of 4, 5 or 6 to score a hit, a shooter with a value of 5+ needs to roll a 5 or 6, and so on. Roll a dice and if you score a hit refer to the Wound chart below to work out if the hit inflicts a wound.

WOUND CHART

DEFENCE

STRENGTH		1	2	3	4	5	6	7	8	9	10
	1	4	5	5	6	6	6/4	6/5	6/6	–	–
	2	4	4	5	5	6	6	6/4	6/5	6/6	–
	3	3	4	4	5	5	6	6	6/4	6/5	6/6
	4	3	3	4	4	5	5	6	6	6/4	6/5
	5	3	3	3	4	4	5	5	6	6	6/5
	6	3	3	3	3	4	4	5	5	6	6
	7	3	3	3	3	3	4	4	5	5	6
	8	3	3	3	3	3	3	4	4	5	5
	9	3	3	3	3	3	3	3	4	4	5
	10+	3	3	3	3	3	3	3	3	4	4

Compare the Strength value of the shot down the left hand side of the chart with the target's Defence value across the top.

The result indicates the minimum dice roll required to inflict one wound on your enemy. A score of 6/4 or 6/5 or 6/6 means you must roll a single dice and score a 6, followed by a further dice that must score

either a 4+, 5+ or another 6. A '–' indicates the target is impossible to hurt – it is just too tough!

For example, a Moria Goblin shoots an Elf. The Goblin's bow has a Strength of 2, the Elf has a Defence of 5. The Goblin therefore requires a dice roll of 6 to inflict a wound on the Elf.

Like a storm they broke upon the line of the Men of Gondor.

CASUALTIES

If a model has 1 Wound on its characteristic profile it is slain if it suffers a wound (most warriors can only take one wound). The model is then removed from the game as a casualty.

If the shot fails to inflict a wound the target is unharmed – the shot has bounced off the warrior's armour or caused only superficial hurt that is easily ignored.

MULTIPLE SHOTS

Some Heroes can shoot more than once in the Shooting phase. If a Hero has multiple shots you must work out all of his shots before going on to shoot with another model. Work out each shot separately. The player can shoot at the same target or change targets with each shot – it's up to the player.

MULTIPLE WOUNDS

Some Heroes and larger creatures have more than 1 Wound on their characteristic profile. If a model has 2 Wounds it simply means it takes 2 wounds to kill it, 3 Wounds means it takes 3 wounds to kill, and so on. If such a warrior suffers a single wound make a note on your record sheet that its Wounds value has fallen by -1. The warrior carries on fighting. When the model loses its last wound, the warrior is slain and the model is removed from the tabletop.

MOVING & SHOOTING

A bow-armed model must give up half its permitted move distance in the Move phase in order to shoot in the Shoot phase. If the model moves further than half of its move it may not shoot that turn. Eg, a model with a potential move of 5"/12cm cannot shoot if it moves further than 2.5"/6cm.

A crossbow-armed model must give up its entire move to shoot. Such a model cannot therefore move in the Move phase and then shoot in the following Shoot phase. Crossbows are much more time consuming weapons to load and fire than bows.

A warrior armed with a throwing weapon suffers no reduction in its move on account of throwing the weapon. The model can move its entire permitted Move distance and throw its weapon.

Note that if the distance a bow-armed model moves is reduced by difficult terrain then it must still give up half of its remaining move to shoot. So, a model with a 12cm move travelling over a bog would find its permitted movement reduced to 6cm. If the model also wishes to shoot a bow, its move must be further reduced to 3cm.

A model attempting to cross an obstacle, jump, climb or mount a steed during the Move phase cannot shoot that turn. A model that fails to cross an obstacle or jump a gap (on the roll of a 1) cannot shoot as the warrior was attempting to cross even though he failed to do so. A model cannot shoot whilst it is on the ground. A thrown rider cannot shoot that turn unless it shoots before it is thrown.

Legolas surveys the wilderness.

SHOOTERS IN COMBAT

Models that are touching an enemy in the Shooting phase cannot shoot that turn. They are already busily engaged in hand-to-hand fighting using swords, daggers or whatever they have about them. Hand-to-hand combat is worked out in the Fight phase (see page 26).

TARGETS IN COMBAT

Good warriors are not allowed to shoot at enemies that are already fighting with their own friends – not even if they have a clear shot. There is a great risk of hitting an ally in the hurly-burly of close combat. Evil players are free to attempt such a shot if they wish even though their target might be partially blocked by friendly combatants (we find they usually do!).

The Orc fires into combat even though he risks hitting the other Orc.

Roll to hit the target in the usual way. If the shot misses then it misses altogether, the shot flies off hitting no-one and causing no harm.

If the shot scores a hit, roll another dice to determine which side has been hit. On a 1, 2 or 3, you have hit a warrior from your own side, on a 4, 5 or 6, you have hit your intended target.

If you hit your own side and there are two or more of your own models fighting, you will hit the nearest (but don't worry there's plenty more where he came from!).

IN THE WAY!

Often a shooter's view of the target will be partly obscured by another model or some other object that lies between the shooter and target. The model or object is in the way of the shot.

A Good warrior is not allowed to shoot at a target if another Good warrior is in the way. He wouldn't want to risk hitting a friend, after all. However, an Evil warrior can shoot if other Evil warriors are in the way (life is cheap – especially when it's not your own!).

The Man cannot shoot at the Orc – his friend is in the way.

Where a shooter's view to his intended target is partly obscured by someone or something in the way then there is a chance a shot will hit whatever is in the way instead of the target. This is worked out as follows:

First roll to see if a hit is scored as normal. If you miss, the shot flies wide and hits nothing. If a hit is scored, roll a dice on behalf of the first thing in the way of the shot.

If you roll a 1, 2 or 3, the shot has hit whatever is in the way. If this is another model work out the effect of the hit. If it is a physical object the arrow strikes it and is stopped or deflected, causing no harm.

If you roll a 4, 5 or 6 the shot has missed whatever is in the way and flies on towards its intended target. Roll for the next thing in the way, and continue rolling for each thing in the way of the shot until it hits something or reaches the intended target.

The tree and wall are both in the way of this shot.

SHOOTING FROM COVER

If a model is shooting from behind cover; a low wall or other barrier; or from behind a rock, bush, or similar object; its own cover isn't considered to be in the way of its shooting so long as the model is touching the cover and is tall enough to see over or around it.

This is one of those cases where in real life a warrior could quickly lean out or over his cover to shoot – so the model is allowed to shoot so long as its head is clear to see the target.

SHOOTING FROM BEHIND FRIENDS

If a model is shooting from behind a friendly model, this model isn't considered to be in the way of its shooting so long as the base of the shooter is touching the base of the friendly model, and the friendly model's base is of the same size as the shooter's or smaller.

This is one of those cases where in real life a warrior could take a shot from above the shoulder of a comrade who is standing in front of him.

For example, a Man shoots his bow at an Orc and scores a hit. However, the Orc is behind a wall and there is a tree in front that partly obscures the Orc from view. The Man rolls to see if the tree is hit, scoring a 5, avoiding the tree. The Man next rolls for the wall and scores a 4, avoiding that also. The arrow reaches the Orc and hits him.

Note that an Evil warrior who is fighting an enemy won't be both 'in the way' and a 'target in combat'. The warrior will just be a target in combat and only one roll is required to see if he's hit. Life is difficult enough when you're a minion of Evil so we won't penalise him further!

On the other hand, a model might wish to shoot at a target that is partially obscured by two or more models engaged in combat. Good models, as usual, cannot take this kind of shot, but Evil ones can. If the shot hits the intended target, then the fight will be treated as an obstacle 'in the way' of the shot. If a 1-3 is rolled, the arrow is stopped by the fight and the hit must be resolved in the same way as a shot directed against targets in combat (see above).

As the two Men are in base contact, the Man with the bow can shoot the Orc as if the other Man was not in the way.

The defenders of Osgilliath bravely prepare for the Orcs' onslaught.

THE FIGHT PHASE

During the Fight phase, both sides work out combat between opposing models in base-to-base contact. Enemies are only allowed to touch where one has charged the other as we have already described in the Move phase section of the rules (see page 16).

WHEN TO FIGHT

The side that has priority that turn decides the order that fights are resolved. The deciding player chooses which combat he wants to work out first, the players work out the result, then the player with priority nominates the second combat, and so on until all fights have been resolved.

WORKING OUT A FIGHT

The easiest way to explain how combat works is to consider a fight between a Warrior of Minas Tirith and an Orc. Both have 1 Attack and 1 Wound on their characteristic profile and a Fight value of 3.

Where the combatants have 1 Attack, both players roll one dice on behalf of their warrior. The highest scoring warrior wins the fight. If both warriors roll the same result, the warrior with the highest Fight value wins – if both have the same Fight value roll a dice – 1, 2 or 3 the Evil side wins; 4, 5 or 6 the Good side wins.

The Goblins rise up out of the deeps.

"Death! Ride, ride to ruin and the world's ending!"

The loser must 'back away' 1"/2cm from his opponent to represent he has lost the fight. The loser cannot move into touch with another enemy as it backs away but it can move within the 1"/2cm control zone of other enemies because models are assumed to back away as the combatants struggle. For the same reason, a model cannot back away over an obstacle, climb or attempt to mount up. If unable to comply the warrior is trapped – see the rules for trapped fighters (page 30).

The winner strikes at the loser and might hurt him by inflicting a wound. Where the winner has 1 Attack, roll one dice and refer to the Wound chart below. The Wound chart is the same as that used for shooting except that it is the warrior's own Strength that is compared to the enemy's Defence value rather than that of his weapon.

Most warriors have only 1 Wound on their characteristic profile. Where this is the case, the loser suffers a wound and is slain. The model is removed as a casualty. If the dice roll is insufficient to inflict a wound the loser is unharmed.

Once wounds have been worked out, the combat is complete and the side that has priority selects which combat to work out next. Once all combats have been worked out, the Fight phase is over.

Combats involving models lying on the ground are resolved with slightly different rules (see page 21).

The Orc rolls 3 and the Warrior of Minas Tirith rolls 4. The Warrior of Minas Tirith wins the fight.

The Orc is moved 1"/2cm back to show that he has lost the fight. Note that this means combatants will always separate once their fight is over.

Hatred for the Orcs burns deep in Gimli's eyes.

MULTIPLE ATTACKS

Some Heroes and large creatures have more than 1 Attack on their characteristic profile. If a model has 2 Attacks then roll two dice when working out fights instead of one and choose the best score. If a model has 3 Attacks, roll three dice and choose the best score, and so on. A model with multiple Attacks is therefore more likely to win a combat.

If a model with multiple Attacks wins a fight then it strikes the enemy once per Attack. So, a Hero with 2 Attacks rolls two dice to see if he inflicts a wound – both dice count so he either inflicts no wounds, 1 wound, or 2 wounds.

When working out who wins a fight, a Hero with 2 Attacks rolls two dice – an ordinary warrior with 1 Attack rolls one dice.

MULTIPLE WOUNDS

Some Heroes and larger creatures have more than 1 Wound on their characteristic profile. If a model has 2 Wounds it simply means it takes 2 wounds to kill it, 3 Wounds means it needs 3 wounds to kill, and so on. If such a warrior suffers a single wound make a note on your record sheet and carry on fighting. When the model loses its last wound it is slain.

Wound Chart

		1	2	3	4	5	6	7	8	9	10
	DEFENCE										
STRENGTH	**1**	4	5	5	6	6	6/4	6/5	6/6	–	–
	2	4	4	5	5	6	6	6/4	6/5	6/6	–
	3	3	4	4	5	5	6	6	6/4	6/5	6/6
	4	3	3	4	4	5	5	6	6	6/4	6/5
	5	3	3	3	4	4	5	5	6	6	6/5
	6	3	3	3	3	4	4	5	5	6	6
	7	3	3	3	3	3	4	4	5	5	6
	8	3	3	3	3	3	3	4	4	5	5
	9	3	3	3	3	3	3	3	4	4	5
	10+	3	3	3	3	3	3	3	3	4	4

Compare the Strength value of the attacker down the left hand side of the chart with the target's Defence value across the top of the chart.

The result indicates the minimum dice roll required to inflict one wound on your enemy. A score of 6/4 or 6/5 or 6/6 means you must roll a single dice and score a 6, followed by a further dice that must score either 4+, 5+ or another 6. A '–' indicates the target is impossible to hurt – it is just too tough!

For example, a Man defeats an Orc in a fight. The Man has a Strength of 3, the Orc a Defence of 5, and both have 1 Attack. The Man therefore requires a dice roll of 5 or more to inflict one wound on the Orc.

Rohan and Gondor stand together against the armies of the Dark Lord.

MULTIPLE COMBATS

If two, three or more warriors are fighting a single enemy roll one dice for each warrior as before. For example, where three Moria Goblins fight one Man of Gondor, the Goblins roll three dice and the Man rolls one. The player rolling multiple dice takes the highest scoring dice and ignores the rest. In this example, the highest scoring dice for the Goblin is compared to the Man's dice score and the highest score wins.

If any models involved in a multiple combat have 2 or more Attacks then just total up the number of attacks on both sides and roll the appropriate number of dice. Pick out the best scoring dice for each side. In the case of a draw, compare the single model's Fight value to the best Fight value from the multiple side. If they are equal, roll one dice – 1, 2, 3 the Evil side wins; 4, 5, 6 the Good side wins.

All the models on the losing side are beaten back from their enemy 1"/2cm. Where a single model is beaten back by two or more enemies the retreating player can retreat through any gap that is wide enough for the model to pass – if there is no gap the model is trapped as described overleaf. Where multiple models are backing away from a single model, each retreats exactly as in a one-on-one combat, which means none, some or all might be trapped. Once models have backed away work out strikes.

If the multiple side wins the fight, each model strikes against the loser. It doesn't matter whether individual models score higher or lower than their opponent – all models strike if their side wins.

If the single model wins the fight it can strike against one of the enemy if it has 1 Attack. If the model has more than 1 Attack, it strikes once per attack and can divide its strikes amongst its opponents as the player wishes. This is important as some enemies might have different Defence values or might be trapped. The player can roll for each strike before allocating the next if he prefers.

Top: Three Orcs each have 1 Attack so roll one dice for each – 3 Attacks against the Warrior of Minas Tirith's 1 Attack.

Bottom: Both sides compare their highest score – in this case the Orc's 6 wins the day.

TRAPPED FIGHTERS

Warriors who have been defeated must back away from their opponent as described earlier. Sometimes a model will be unable to back away because its path is blocked by an impassable feature, obstacle, the edge of the table, or by other models. This is always the case where a defeated warrior is surrounded by three equidistant enemies.

A model surrounded by three equidistant enemies – he has nowhere to back away to.

Note that a model is not allowed to back away by jumping an obstacle, climbing or mounting up – but it can back away by leaping over a sheer drop. This is up to the player. If the warrior leaps a drop of more than double the model's height, the player must roll to see if it is hurt as described in the Move Phase section (see page 20).

If a model can't back away, the defeated warrior is trapped. Any strikes made against a trapped model count as doubled. So, a model with 1 Attack will make two strikes, a model with 2 Attacks makes four strikes against a trapped model, and so on. The defeated model must be moved back as far as possible so that enemies are no longer touching – if necessary other models must be moved slightly to make sure there is a gap.

A model surrounded by two equidistant enemies and a terrain feature – he is trapped.

In a multiple combat where several models must move, the player whose models are backing away can move them in any order he wishes.

Making Way For Trapped Fighters

If a defeated warrior can't back away from his opponent because of friends blocking his path, then these friends can move up to 1"/2cm in order to make room. This is called 'making way for friends'. Models lying on the ground can make way for friends. Models don't have to make way – it is up to the player.

Models cannot make way if they are still engaged in combat with an opponent. Otherwise, the same rules apply as for backing away, so models can move into enemy control zones, but cannot move into a fight, for example.

The idea behind this rule is that it enables friends to move 1"/2cm to allow their comrades to avoid taking double strikes because they are trapped.

A friend backing away to make room.

Note that the rule for making way only allows a model to make way for a friendly model that has been defeated in a fight. A model cannot usually make way for another model that is making way. This means that in a dense mob, the models at the front will be pushed onto the enemy as those at the rear will be unable to make way (sounds like a fine Orc tactic to me!).

DEFENDING

In the Move Phase section we described how a model placed directly behind a barrier can defend it against an enemy – for example, a wall, hedgerow, or a pile of crates or barrels (see page 19). Models can also defend doorways, narrow corridors, and similar features, as explained in the Siege section of The Two Towers edition of the game. Here we shall only consider barriers.

Where a model is placed behind a barrier it will be impossible to place an enemy into base contact because the barrier will be in the way. To allow for this we introduce the following rule:

A model can charge an enemy that is defending a barrier by moving into the enemy's zone of control and contacting the barrier. The two models are assumed to be touching even though they are not actually in base contact.

Even though there is a wall between the two models, they are considered to be touching.

Because of the size of the zone of control it is possible to place up to three warriors on small bases or two warriors on large bases against a single defender. This is shown in the diagram below.

Three warriors fighting against a single defender.

It is also possible for up to three defenders to fight against a single charger because their control zones overlap. This is shown in the diagram below.

A single warrior is fighting against three defenders.

The procedure for defending is slightly different to the basic combat rules that we have already learned. In the case of ordinary combats, warriors who lose a fight are immediately moved back 1"/2cm before working out the effect of blows. In the case of defending combats, the defender does not move at all even if he is beaten. If the defender survives he repels the attack and the charger is automatically moved back 1"/2cm as if he had been beaten. Only if the defender is slain is the model removed and the charger is automatically moved over the barrier to occupy his space.

The Orc has won the fight but has failed to kill the defender. Therefore the Orc has to back away.

DEFENDING ONE-ON-ONE

To work out a one-on-one fight, roll to determine which side wins the fight as normal. If the charger wins, roll a dice to see if he strikes the barrier or his foe. On a roll of 1, 2 or 3, his blow strikes the barrier and has no effect, on a roll of a 4, 5 or 6, the blow strikes the defender and is worked out as normal. Roll for each strike separately when striking more than once.

If the defender wins the fight, his blows are struck as normal. It is not necessary to roll to see if he strikes the barrier. Because he is defending he has already thrust his weapon through or over the barrier in order to fight his opponent.

If neither model is slain at the end of the fight, the charger is moved back 1"/2cm, whilst the defender remains in place. If the defender has been slain, the charger is moved over the barrier to occupy the defender's space.

DEFENDING IN MULTIPLE FIGHTS

If two or three chargers attack a single defender then the chargers must fight the defender one at a time. The charging player can decide which of his models will fight first. This means that a defending model can potentially fight two or three times in the same combat round.

Once each charger has fought he is moved back 1"/2cm unless he has slain the defender or been slain himself. If the defender is slain then his opponent and any other chargers who have yet to fight will automatically cross the barrier. The charger who slew his foe moves into the space vacated by his enemy and remaining models are moved directly forward and over the barrier. If remaining models cannot be moved directly over the barrier for whatever reason, they can be moved next to the model that has already crossed or otherwise not at all.

If a single charger moves into the zones of control of two or three defenders (or more defenders move so that the attacker is now inside their control zone, joining in the defence to help the friendly model who has been attacked) then he must fight them all. All the defenders fight at once, rolling all their dice at the same time as they would for a normal multiple combat. This is because the defenders are all prepared to strike and don't have to struggle over the barrier to press their attack. If the charger wins the fight he must still roll to see whether his blows hit the barricade. If he should succeed in killing any of his opponents then he crosses the barrier automatically, immediately taking the place of a model he has slain.

The attacking Orc wins the fight against the two defenders and kills one of them.

As the defender has been killed by the first attacker, all three Orcs move across the barrier.

He can now immediately cross the barrier, replacing the model killed.

The Rohirrim smash into the Orcs' line.

MULTIPLE FIGHTS ON BOTH SIDES

Where there are several models on both sides of a barrier the combats are divided into as many separate one-on-one fights as possible by the player with priority. Remaining multiple fights are resolved as multiple combats with one model on one side as already described.

If attacked from both sides of the barrier, work out the fight on the defender's own side first.

The defender has been killed – all attackers can cross the barrier.

ATTACKED FROM BEHIND

If a defending model is also attacked from his side of a barrier, then the fight on his side of the barrier becomes a regular combat fought in the usual way. Work this out first.

If the defender is slain in this initial fight then enemies that would otherwise fight across the barrier can cross immediately as if they had killed him themselves.

The Orc who has just crossed the barrier moves into base contact with the defender and fights him along with the attacker still on the other side.

The defender has survived the initial attack and must now fight against the models attacking across the barrier.

If the defender is not slain, any chargers on the other side of the barrier can now fight. If the defender won the combat he can now defend the barrier exactly as described previously. If the defender was defeated in his first fight, he is unable to defend the barrier effectively – therefore he no longer counts as defending. The combat is fought as any other combat or multiple combat and the chargers do not have to roll to see if their strikes hit the barrier.

The ensuing combat is worked out between the defender and all the chargers that have yet to fight. As the defender was defeated during his last fight, he no longer counts as defending so the fight is straightforward to work out, even where chargers are separated by a barrier (see below).

The defender has backed away along the barrier and is now in the control zone of a new enemy. The two models may not fight in this Fight phase.

Backing away along a barrier might cause the defender to enter the zone of control of other enemy models. As the defender no longer counts as defending the barrier, no combat is fought between them. Ie, models not engaged in combat at the start of the Fight phase may not fight.

It's also possible, but unlikely, that a model attacking across a barrier is then charged by other enemies from his own side of the barrier. In this case, treat the fight as a normal multiple combat.

The defender has backed away, therefore his zone of control will not prevent one attacker on the other side of the barrier from crossing over.

Sometimes, a defender is obliged to move away from or along the barrier he is defending because he is beaten back 1"/2cm by an enemy on his side of the barrier. In this case it can happen that a charger on the other side of the barrier is no longer within his enemy's zone of control.

Should this occur, models no longer in the defender's zone of control can immediately cross the barrier and, if there is room, be placed into contact with the defender.

The Orc has charged the defender and has subsequently been charged by another Man from his own side of the barrier.

CAVALRY

Mounted Glorfindel

This section discusses all the rules for cavalry. We refer to all mounted models as cavalry. Cavalry are usually mounted on horses but Warg Riders are also cavalry.

Since all of the cavalry rules have been compiled into this section for ease of reference, you will find here a few Advanced rules. You may ignore them until you are more familiar with the game.

WHICH MODELS CAN RIDE?

Unless otherwise specified, only Men and Elves can ride horses, while only Orcs can ride Wargs. Other models can ride only the mounts included in their wargear options. Models with a Strength of 6 or more can neither ride nor be carried as passengers.

CHARACTERISTICS FOR MOUNTS

A cavalry model comprises a rider and his mount and therefore has two separate sets of characteristics:

	F	S	D	A	W	C
Rider of Rohan	3/4+	3	5	1	1	3
Horse	0	3	4	0	1	3

As you can see horses have no Attacks. When a Rider of Rohan fights an enemy, his horse takes no part in the combat – no dice is rolled on behalf of the horse and if the Rider of Rohan wins the fight, his horse does not strike blows. We'll explain more about how cavalry fight in combat later in this section.

MOVING CAVALRY

Cavalry models are moved in the same way as models that are on foot, with various additional rules and exceptions. You will find that most of these exceptions are obvious enough – such as horses not being allowed to climb ladders!

WHO SEES – RIDER OR MOUNT?

In the case of a mounted model, the 'model's eye view' is always taken from the perspective of the rider. As the rider is directing his mount it is his ability to see which counts, not that of the horse. This is important for establishing whether a warrior can see an enemy he is about to charge and when shooting (see page 16).

MOVING THROUGH DIFFICULT TERRAIN

Difficult terrain is either too dense or too dangerous for cavalry to move through at full speed. However, a rider can negotiate his way through difficult terrain moving very slowly and carefully. To represent this, all distance moved by cavalry models over difficult terrain counts as four times the actual distance (eg, a rider that moves 2"/4cm across difficult terrain counts as having moved 8"/20cm, see page 17). In addition, whilst in difficult terrain, cavalry never gain any of the combat bonuses they normally get when charging, including the bonuses for lances (see page 38 and page 52).

BARRIERS AND OBSTACLES

When it comes to moving over barriers, always consider the mount's height, not that of the rider. Note that because horses are often modelled in dramatic head-down positions you will have to estimate the horse's true height – easiest by measuring the height of a comparable horse with its head held high. It is the true size of the horse that affects its ability to cross a barrier – not the pose of its head!

Fortunately, most horses are more or less the same size so we might reasonably assume all to be the same for purposes of our game. The Riders of Rohan horse is a good 'mean' at 40mm tall. All barriers that are less than half this (less than 20mm high or wide) are crossed without penalty. Any barriers between half and double the horse's height are counted as obstacles (between 20mm and 80mm) and can be jumped. Any barriers taller or wider are impassable.

JUMPING

A mount cannot jump down a sheer drop more than double its own height.

Cavalry can jump over obstacles between half and double the height of the mount as described. Make a roll on the Jump chart (see page 19) in the same way as you would for a warrior on foot. Remember to reduce the dice result by -1 if the obstacle is taller or wider than the mount's height.

If a 1 is rolled when attempting a jump with a mounted model then a further attempt can be made. Roll again to see if it successful. However, if a further 1 is rolled then not only does the model fail to jump but the rider is thrown from his mount. See the Thrown Rider chart opposite.

OTHER EXCEPTIONS

Cavalry models cannot **climb**, **lie down** or **crawl**. Mounts cannot do so even if their riders dismount!

Cavalry models cannot climb ladders and steep or especially narrow stairs, but steps that are broad and shallow can be moved over at half the mount's usual pace. Eg, a broad flight of stone steps leading up to a building would probably be possible to move over, but a winding stairway in a tower would not. If in doubt about a feature, make sure that both sides are agreed whether steps are accessible to cavalry before the game begins.

MOUNTING AND DISMOUNTING

Rules are provided for riders to mount and dismount. To make full use of these rules we would ideally have separate models of warriors on foot and mounted, and separate models of horses (and Wargs) without riders. In practice, it is sufficient to have a mounted model and a foot version of the rider. Riderless mounts can be represented by using the mounted model with the addition of a suitable counter or marker, or by removing the rider figure if this is left loose. A small piece of paper placed on the model's base is enough to show that the rider has dismounted.

A model can mount a horse or similar mount whose height to the saddle is not more than twice the height of the rider. This is treated as a jump and a Jump test is made. If a 1 is rolled, the model fails to mount, a 2-5 is successful but the model cannot move any more this turn, and on a 6, the model's remaining move can be completed by the mount (eg, a Man moves 3" and gets in base contact with a loose horse, rolls a 6 for his Jump test to mount and can therefore finish his move by moving another 3").

Dismounting is automatic. The rider can dismount at the beginning of his move, in which case he can move on foot normally. Alternatively, he can dismount at any time during his mounted move, but will be unable to move further that turn and counts as having used up his full move regardless of the distance moved.

SPECIAL RULE – EXPERT RIDERS

Expert riders can re-roll the dice on the Jump chart when jumping an obstacle while mounted, and when trying to mount a horse (including as passengers). In addition, when mounted they benefit from the +1 Defence from their shield even while carrying a bow. If they dismount or are thrown, they must leave on the horse either their bow or their shield (in which case their Defence is reduced by 1 point). If they mount again, they immediately recover all their equipment, which was of course left on the horse.

ADVANCED RULE – CARRYING RAMS, LADDERS, ETC

Cavalry models cannot carry large or heavy burdens that would normally require two or more warriors to carry at a full pace move. For example, siege ladders, rams, and demolition charges. All these things require the full attention of warriors on foot and are impractical to carry whilst mounted. The same applies to any large, heavy or bulky burdens that are comparable.

ADVANCED RULE – PASSENGERS

Rules for carrying passengers allow for some very dynamic actions where riders pluck their friends from the midst of disaster or carry them towards their goal – just as Legolas carries Gimli and Arwen carries Frodo. Only models that can normally ride can be carried as passengers, with the exception of Dwarves and Hobbits, which do not normally ride horses, but can be carried as passengers.

The most convenient way of showing that a cavalry model is carrying a passenger is to place the passenger model on the cavalry model's base or as close as possible.

To mount up, either the passenger must move into contact with the cavalry model or vice versa. A standard Jump test is then taken by the passenger. On the roll of a 1, neither model can move further that turn and the passenger does not mount. On a 2-5, the passenger mounts but the cavalry model cannot move further that turn. On a 6 the passenger mounts and the cavalry model can complete its entire move that turn, assuming it's not already done so. Jumping down from a mount is done automatically, no test is required.

A passenger can jump down from a mount before the cavalry model moves, in which case both models can move normally. He can also jump down at any time during the cavalry model's move, but will be unable to move further that turn and counts as having used up his full move regardless of the distance moved.

A passenger cannot shoot with a bow or other missile weapons, cannot make use of magical powers, cannot make heroic actions, and cannot fight in combat. When shooting at a rider/passenger/mount, the shooter declares his target and shoots as normal. If the shot scores a hit then the shooter rolls a further dice to see who is hit: on a 1-3 the mount is hit, on a 4-5 the rider is hit, on a 6 the passenger is hit.

A passenger cannot fight in combat but he can be struck if the cavalry model is beaten. The enemy can choose to strike any or all of his blows against the passenger if he wishes.

If the rider is killed or dismounts, the passenger is automatically thrown (see the chart opposite).

SHOOTING & CAVALRY

When it comes to shooting at cavalry we must take into account the chance of a shot striking the mount rather than the rider. The following rules discuss this possibility and what to do when riders and their mounts fall casualty.

MOUNTED TARGETS

When shooting at a cavalry model, the horse is treated as if it were 'in the way' of the rider – a dice roll is made as for any other model partially obscuring the target. Therefore, on a 1-3 the mount is hit, while on a 4-6 the rider is hit. If there is also a passenger on the mount this situation is resolved differently (see opposite for details).

HITS ON MOUNTS

Hits on mounts are worked out in the same way as hits against warriors on foot. Should the mount be slain, its rider (and passenger) are thrown to the ground. The rider must be replaced with a foot version of the model. Roll a dice on the Thrown Rider chart to determine if the rider (and passenger) is hurt.

THROWN RIDER CHART

Dice	Result
1	**Knocked Flying** – The rider hits the dirt, suffering a Strength 3 hit. If he survives, he is placed lying down beside his mount and can do nothing else for that turn. If engaged in a combat, he fights lying down.
2-5	**Rises from the Dust** – The rider disentangles himself from his mount and dusts himself down. The rider can do nothing else for that turn – if engaged in a combat he cannot strike blows if he wins.
6	**Leaps into Action** – The rider bounds from the saddle of his plunging mount to confront his enemy. The model is replaced by a model on foot and suffers no further penalty.

"Now they sprang forward, formed, quickened to a gallop, and charged with a great shout."

FIGHTS & CAVALRY

The Riders of Rohan – horsemasters without peers.

For most purposes, cavalry fight exactly like warriors on foot – the rider fights against enemies in the same combat. Mounts do not attack – they are riding creatures not warriors – but their size and ferocity add to their rider's attacks as described below.

The following are the characteristics for a Warg Rider:

	F	S	D	A	W	C
Warg Rider	3/5+	3	4	1	1	2
Warg	0	4	4	0	1	2

CAVALRY CHARGE!

The greatest advantage of riding a horse is that a warrior on a charging horse is very difficult to stop – the sheer weight and impetus of the mounted attack will often bowl the enemy to the ground! We have two rules to represent this extra fighting ability.

If a mounted warrior charges a warrior on foot then he receives two special bonuses: '**extra attack**' and '**knock to the ground**'.

He receives these bonuses regardless of the number of enemy he charges, so long as all his opponents are warriors on foot. The bonuses apply even if the mounted warrior is subsequently charged by other enemy on foot.

These bonuses do not apply to mounted warriors fighting enemy cavalry.

Basically, in order to claim these bonuses, mounted warriors must have charged and be in base contact exclusively with warriors on foot when the fight is resolved.

Extra Attack

A mounted warrior with this bonus gains one extra Attack. So, a rider with 1 Attack would roll two dice in a fight, a warrior with 2 Attacks rolls three dice, and so on.

Knock to the Ground

If a mounted warrior with this bonus wins a fight, all his opponents are knocked to the ground, except for models with a Strength of 6 or more. These models cannot be knocked to the ground by cavalry unless the mount itself has a Strength of 6 or more.

A warrior that is knocked to the ground must back away 1"/2cm from his enemy as usual. The model is then placed on its side to show the warrior is lying on the ground. That means he will take double strikes from his enemies just like a model that has fought whilst lying down. If he is charged in the following turn before he has had a chance to stand up he will have to fight from the ground (see page 21).

A trapped warrior that is knocked down takes double strikes. Note the model does not take double double strikes because he is trapped and lying down – the penalty is for both.

STRIKES AGAINST MOUNTS

If a mounted warrior loses a fight, his foes can elect to strike either the rider or mount. This is the choice of the player making the attacks, and if he has several attacks to distribute he can strike against both the rider and mount. Note that a mount isn't considered to be 'in the way' as it is for hits from shooting – warriors are close enough to engage directly so we allow the attacker the choice.

If the mount is slain, the rider must roll to see if he is thrown. This is exactly the same as described for shooting. If a rider is slain the cavalry model is normally removed, unless the players have agreed to use the advanced rule for loose mounts, described on page 40.

FIGHTING ACROSS BARRIERS

Cavalry can defend barriers as normal, but they do not receive any of their charge bonuses when charging infantry that are defending a barrier against them.

SHIELDING

Mounted models cannot 'defend by shielding', but they still get the +1 bonus to their Defence value as normal if they're carrying shields (unless of course if they are also carrying a bow, in which case the shield is completely useless while they are mounted).

MONSTROUS MOUNTS

Some mounts are so large and powerful that they contribute to a fight far more than a horse or Warg would, often being far more dangerous than their rider. In gaming terms, if a mount's characteristic profile includes a Fighting and Attacks value different from 0, the beast is classed as a *monstrous mount*. Monstrous mounts count as cavalry and follow the same rules for normal cavalry, apart from the exceptions noted below.

SHOOTING

When shooting against a monstrous mount, the chance of hitting the mount rather than the rider is far higher. For each hit against the model, roll a further dice. On a result of 1-4 the mount is hit, on a result of 5-6 the rider is hit.

FIGHTS

When resolving a fight involving monstrous mounts, simply apply the rules for multiple combats, treating the mount as a separate model involved in the fight. As normal for multiple fights, add the dice for the mount's Attacks to the ones of the rider and other friends involved in the fight. Remember to roll separately the Attacks of models which have points of Might, two-handed weapons or other factors that can influence the result. In solving the fight, use the best Fighting value available (including that of the mount), as normal for multiple fights. If the fight is won, the mount will strike at the enemy using its own Strength value.

Monstrous mounts charge!

Monstrous mounts and their riders never get the *Extra Attack* bonus when charging, this being replaced by the mount being able to contribute its own attacks to the fight.

On the other hand, such is the mass, strength and ferocity of monstrous mounts, that they can *Knock to the Ground* even enemy cavalry if they win the fight when charging. This bonus is not lost if the monstrous mount is itself engaged by enemy cavalry, but it is lost if it is engaged by an enemy monstrous mount.

When a cavalry model is knocked to the ground, the mount is knocked to the ground and the rider is automatically thrown and knocked to the ground next to the mount, immediately suffering a Strength 3 hit as per Result 1 on the Thrown Rider chart. This represents the chance of the rider injuring himself in the fall or even being crushed under the weight of his own steed.

ADVANCED RULE – MAGICAL POWERS & CAVALRY

If a model employs a magical power (such as Immobilise for example) against a mounted model, the rider is always the target of the spell (unless otherwise stated in the spell's description), since we assume he is in control of his own steed's movement. If the rider is affected, then the steed is affected as well (the entire model is immobilised in the case of the above magical power). Of course, if the rider has any Will available and wishes to use it, he gets a chance to resist the spell normally. If the steed has any points of Will (a very rare occasion), or if a passenger has any points of Will, these can be used by the rider to resist the spell, even if the rider himself is not a Hero.

The Sorcerous Blast power works in a slightly different way. If such power is not resisted, both the steed and the rider are moved back by the blast, both suffer the hit from the blast, the rider is automatically thrown and both the rider and his steed are knocked to the ground.

Cavalry models in the path of a model that has been blasted away by a Sorcerous Blast (or are fighting it in close combat) suffer a similar fate. Both the steed and the rider are moved aside, both suffer a Strength 3 hit, the rider is automatically thrown and both the rider and his steed are knocked to the ground. The steed is not knocked to the ground if it has a Strength of 6 or more, unless the model that is being blasted has itself a Strength of 6 or more.

Isildur's heir has come home.

ADVANCED RULE – LOOSE MOUNTS

When a rider is killed, it is usually convenient to remove the entire model because in most situations we are not concerned with loose mounts that will otherwise get in the way of the action. However, there are occasions when it would be useful to be able to remount a loose horse. This can be quite important in some scenarios. Also, the rider can simply be thrown or dismount voluntarily, in which case he's very likely to want to mount his steed again at some point during the game. It is a good principle that Good models cannot ride the mounts of Evil models and vice versa.

If a mount happens to be a Hero as well (eg, Gwaihir), the model is never treated as a loose mount if the rider is killed or dismounts. The heroic mount continues to move and fight on its own like any other Hero.

To take into account situations where representing loose horses is important, we shall say that when a rider is slain, thrown or simply dismounts, the player can either remove the mount immediately or leave it in place. If the mount is removed we assume it runs away and takes no further part in the game. If the mount is left in place it remains where it is. Players should agree at the beginning of the game if they are using this advanced rule or not.

A loose mount can be represented by leaving the cavalry model on the tabletop and putting a suitable marker on or next to it. Alternatively, if you do not fix the riders permanently in place you can simply remove the rider. Another option is to have a few separate horse or Warg models to be used when the occasion demands.

Loose mounts do not move unless they have to retreat because of a failed Courage test. They also have no control zone, so other models can move past them easily. If a loose mount inhibits movement, then it will automatically move aside to allow other models to pass by. Whichever player is moving must reposition the loose mount, moving it the smallest distance to permit his warrior to pass.

Loose mounts can still block a warrior's line of sight and might be in the way of a shot. Good models cannot shoot at targets if friendly mounts are in the way – such a thing would be unthinkable! Evil models are under no such obligation, of course.

The enemy might conceivably wish to shoot or attack loose mounts. Loose mounts have no Attacks and so roll no dice in a fight and will therefore lose automatically.

CASUALTIES IN SCENARIOS

In a scenario, it is often important to know how many models have been slain. In the case of cavalry, the model is counted as slain once the rider is killed. The mount does not count towards the total of slain models.

COURAGE

In the case of cavalry models, only the rider need test his Courage. Mounts don't test if they have a rider. Loose mounts take tests as normal using their own Courage.

"Now for wrath!. Now for ruin! And for the Red Dawn!"

SCENARIO – THE AMBUSH

A scenario is an idea for a game that uses some models and some elements of scenery to recreate a scene taken from The Lord of The Rings, be it from the film, from the book, or even a completely made up one. The following scenario is very simple and gives you the opportunity to have a first go at the game using only the basic rules. Don't worry about using any of the advanced rules for now, just follow the instructions here on the right to set up your game and enjoy your first small battle!

Sauron's forces are on the move and none can stand against them. With the opening of the Black Gates, Sauron's assault on Middle-earth begins in earnest. All across the banks of the Anduin, bands of Orcs harass the defences of Gondor, which fall one by one. In the plains of eastern Anorien, a few Men attempt the long march back to Minas Tirith and the comparative safety of its walls. Little do they realise that they are shadowed by Orcs…

This scenario takes place in the fields of Anorien. The playing area is 24"/56cm by 24"/56cm and should have scattered ruins (use those from The Return of The King game box).

The Good side has 3 Warriors of Minas Tirith, 2 with shield and 1 with bow. The Evil side has 4 Mordor Orcs, 3 with shield and 1 with Orc bow.

The Good player deploys one of his models in the exact centre of the board and the other two within 2"/4cm of the first. The Evil player then deploys each of his Orcs anywhere along the table edge. No Orc may start within 12"/28cm of another.

The first side to kill all the models in the opposing force wins.

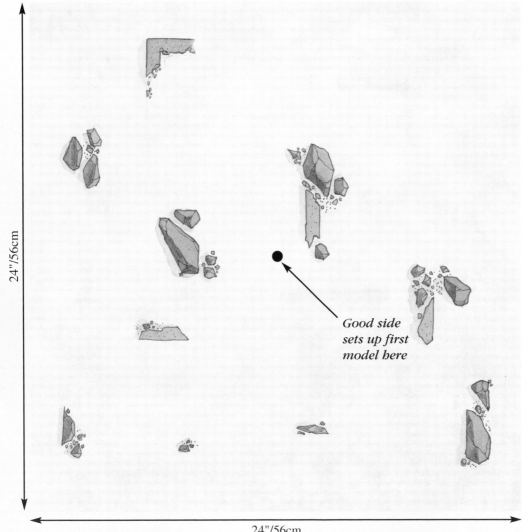

24"/56cm

Good side sets up first model here

24"/56cm

THE ELVES

The Elves are the eldest of all the races of Middle-earth, the Firstborn. Despising all evil things, the Elves have been the foremost protectors of Middle-earth in ages past. For many years their strength has held the fury of Sauron at bay, but the time of the Elves is now over, and the eternal war between light and dark must now be championed by Men.

Glorfindel, Elladan, Elrohir, Arwen and their Elvish brethren stand firm in the face of overwhelming odds.

Glorfindel

Elrond

"O Elbereth! Gilthoniel!
We still remember, we who dwell
In this far land beneath the trees,
Thy starlight on the Western Seas."
  - The Fellowship of The Ring

Matt Parkes' Mirror of Galadriel diorama.

"Noro lim, noro lim, Asfaloth!"

Another assault on Lothlorien is repelled through Elvish valour.

ADVANCED RULES

The pages that precede this section constitute the core rules of the game. The pages that follow deal with additional rules, profiles for different warriors, and scenarios. You don't need to use any of these extra rules to play a game, though they add further depth to the tactical options and some especially interesting and potent heroic characters. It is a good idea to make sure you are reasonably familiar with the way the core rules work before using the advanced rules.

COURAGE

Of course all of our warriors are courageous – it's just that some are more courageous than others! The rules that follow represent the fact that warriors will not always act as you, the player, might wish them to. There are times when even the bravest warrior would sooner retreat than fight. To take this into account we have the 'Courage test'.

If you're learning the game we recommend you ignore Courage until you're confident with the rules for moving, shooting and fighting. You can always introduce the Courage rules later. To begin with, it is reasonable to assume that any Courage test required by the following rules is passed.

To bear a ring of power is to be alone.

COURAGE TESTS

A Courage test is always taken in the same way. Two dice are rolled and added together, and the warrior's Courage value is added to the total. If the total score is 10 or more, the test is passed. If the score is less than 10, it is failed.

When a test is passed there is no effect.

When the test is failed the warrior retreats as described opposite.

In the case of mounted warriors only the rider need test – mounts do not need to test so long as they have a rider.

WHEN TO TEST

A warrior must take a Courage test for the following:

1. When attempting to charge a terrifying enemy.
2. At the start of a move once half its force is destroyed.
3. At the start of a move if the model is on its own.

Attempting to charge a terrifying enemy

If a warrior wishes to charge one or more terrifying enemies, a test must be taken as soon as the warrior comes to within 1"/2cm of the foes. If the test is passed, the model can complete its charge by moving into base contact. If it is failed, the model will not charge, losing heart at the last moment, immediately retreating as described opposite.

The ability to inspire terror is a special quality of some monstrous creatures as noted in the Forces section.

Note that a model armed with a spear/pike supporting a friend who is fighting a terrifying enemy does not need to take this test, since he is not going to charge the terrifying enemy.

At the start of each move
once half the model's force is destroyed

If half or more of the warriors on your side have been lost then every remaining warrior must test every turn before moving in the Move phase. Make the test for each model before it moves. Models that do not intend to move must still test as if they were about to do so unless already engaged in a fight. Models already fighting when it is their turn to move do not test for courage.

If the test is failed the warrior will retreat instead of making a normal move that turn. If the test is passed the warrior can be moved normally or not at all as the player wishes.

Once half the force is destroyed an army will quickly begin to disintegrate and this is often the moment when a battle is won or lost. Note that models that retreat from the table count as casualties, as well as models that have been slain.

At the start of a move if a model is on its own

Make this test if there are no visible friends within 6"/14cm, and at least two visible enemy within 6"/14cm for every Wound the model has remaining. So, a Hero with 3 Wounds need only test if faced by six enemies, but the same Hero with only 1 Wound remaining must test if faced by two enemies. As ordinary warriors usually have only 1 Wound they must test when they are on their own and outnumbered by two to one, or more.

Make the test for each model before it moves. Models that do not intend to move must still test as if they were about to do so, unless already engaged in a fight. Models already fighting when it is their turn to move do not have to test.

If the test is failed, the warrior retreats instead of making a normal move that turn. If the test is passed, the warrior can be moved normally or not at all as the player wishes.

Isolated warriors are less likely to act as you might wish and more likely to avoid combat.

Note that a test is not required if a model has already passed a Courage test for 'Once half the model's force is destroyed'. See Testing Twice below.

RETREATS

A retreat happens as soon as a Courage test is failed.

When a model retreats, it turns to face directly away from the nearest enemy model it can see and moves its maximum move distance in so far as it can. If no enemy are visible, the model moves toward the nearest table edge.

The retreating model suffers the usual movement penalties or tests for difficult terrain and obstacles. The retreating model can move round obstacles, terrain or other models to avoid them, so long as it finishes its move as far as possible from the enemy model it is retreating from.

Sometimes, a direct move away from the nearest enemy will take a model closer to other enemies as it runs in blind panic. A model may not move closer than 1"/2cm to an enemy as it retreats – it will always move round enemies in its path and cannot charge them.

If a model cannot retreat the required distance because its path is blocked by other models, impassable terrain, or for whatever reason, then the model retreats as far as it can. The model is still considered to have expended its full movement distance even if it is unable to move at all – so it won't be able to shoot a bow that turn, for example. However, it can still use any magical powers it has so long as it can normally use them whilst it is moving.

Models that have Retreated

Once a model has retreated, it suffers no further penalty. It is possible for a model to suffer a series of retreats one after the other – in which case it may find itself fleeing from the battle altogether – but a single failed Courage test only ever results in one retreat move.

Note that a model that fails its Courage test having already approached to within 1"/2cm of a terrifying enemy will effectively move twice that Move phase – once as it moves towards the enemy and once again as it moves away from the enemy. Terror can be a very motivating force on occasions!

Fleeing the Battle

If a retreating model's move is enough to reach the table edge it will move to the table edge and leave the battle. It will do this regardless of the direction, even if by doing so the retreating model moves closer to the closest enemy. The warrior flees the battle and the model is removed from the game just as if it had been slain.

STAND FAST!

The following rule applies only to Courage tests which are taken on account of half the army being destroyed. This is often the point where battles will be won or lost and where only the Heroes can force ordinary warriors to stand fast. Rules for Heroes, including Evil Heroes, are given in the next section of the rules manual.

Warriors do not have to test their courage at the start of their move if there is a visible Hero within 6"/14cm who has already tested his courage and passed. To benefit from this rule, players must test and move their Heroes before testing ordinary warriors. This is entirely up to the player – there is no obligation to do so – but it does save having to roll for every single model before moving.

TESTING TWICE

If half the force is already destroyed and a model is also on its own there is no need to test for courage twice. The first dice roll will stand for both tests. The same goes if a scenario calls for a test before moving – make one test and the result stands for all.

If the first test is a 'Stand Fast!' from a Hero, a successful result will also stand for both rolls.

HEROES

Heroes are extraordinary individuals – stern, mighty, and dangerous. A hero can fight and defeat several ordinary warriors with ease. In terms of our game, Heroes are not necessarily good or evil. The Forces of Darkness also have their own evil Heroes who are just as powerful as those of the Free Peoples. Aragorn, Gandalf and Boromir are obvious examples of Heroes, and opposing them are the Witch King, Saruman, and the monstrous Balrog.

MIGHT, WILL & FATE

Heroes have characteristic profiles just like ordinary warriors. In addition, they have three heroic characteristics, namely Might, Will, and Fate. Unlike other characteristics these are represented by a store of points that are used up during the game. Players must decide for themselves the best time to use their rare and precious Might, Will and Fate points.

MIGHT

This represents a Hero's ability to perform heroic feats. When a dice is rolled on behalf of a Hero to resolve the effect of something it has done, its score can be adjusted by expending Might. Might can also be used to perform heroic actions as described later.

Each point of Might that is expended can be used to adjust the dice score up or down by one to a maximum of 6 or minimum of 1. No dice can be augmented to more than 6 or reduced to less than 1. If a player rolls a 3, for example, he can expend two points of Might to turn the score into 5.

A player does not have to decide to use his Might until the dice has been rolled, or until both sides have rolled in the case of a roll to see who wins a fight. This means a player can always ensure the result he wants so long as he has enough Might points left.

If two opposing Heroes are fighting and both wish to use Might to win, both players must secretly indicate with hidden dice or written notes how much Might they are going to expend (minimum 1) and reveal simultaneously.

When rolling to determine the effect of a successful strike or missile hit, two rolls are sometimes required to inflict a wound (eg, 6/4+). In this case, the Might bonus is added to both rolls – 1 Might point expended on the first roll automatically adds to the second roll.

At the start of the game you must record the Might points available for each of your Heroes. As Might is used up you must keep a track of the remaining points. Once all a Hero's Might is gone he can no longer adjust dice rolls.

It is important to remember that a Hero can only use Might to affect his own dice rolls – not those of other characters whether friend of foe. In a multiple combat, it is therefore necessary to roll separately for a Hero's Attacks or use distinctly coloured dice to differentiate his rolls from those of other warriors. Might is never used to affect random 50/50 rolls, for example, deciding if a model can be seen if you are unsure, making a Spotting roll, rolling for objects in the way of a shot, or rolling for hitting a barrier when fighting a defending enemy. Also, Might cannot be used to affect the Priority roll made at the start of each turn.

Aragorn, Legolas and Gimli enter Fangorn in search of Merry and Pippin.

Can I use Might?

Might points can be used to add to or subtract from any dice roll made to resolve something the Hero has done – by far the most useful and usual occasions are:

When fighting – *To boost a dice roll to win a combat.*

When shooting – *To hit a target.*

Shooting and Combat – *To inflict a wound on an enemy the model has hit or struck.*

Courage – *To pass a Courage test.*

Making tests – *To affect Jumping, Climbing or Thrown Rider results.*

When using Will – *To cast a spell or pass a Magical Resistance test.*

When using Fate – *To pass a Fate roll.*

WILL

This represents the Hero's ability to employ or resist magical powers. Many Heroes have special magical powers. Each time a power is employed, the Hero's stock of Will is reduced. Each time a Hero attempts to resist a magical power, his stock of Will is reduced. Once a Hero's Will has been used up he may neither employ nor resist magical powers.

MAGICAL POWERS

If a Hero has magical powers he can attempt to use one power once in any turn. A Hero can resist any number of magical powers during a turn so long as he has Will points remaining.

A Hero can employ a magical power in the Move phase when it is the model's turn to move. The Hero must be able to see the target as we have already discussed. The Hero can target a visible model even if it is engaged in combat, unless specified differently in the magical power's description. In addition, a Hero must be free to move in order to use a magical power. A Hero already fighting an enemy when it is his turn to move cannot use a magical power.

A magical power can be used at any point during the model's movement – before moving, afterwards, or at any point between. A Hero might use a magical power against an enemy and then move into combat against the same enemy, for example.

When a Hero employs a magical power, the player states which power the Hero is using and nominates how many dice he will roll. The Hero's Will value is immediately reduced by 1 for each dice rolled. The player rolls all the dice together. If the highest scoring dice equals or beats the value required to use the power then the Hero has succeeded. If none of the dice score the minimum value needed, the Hero has failed to use the power – there is no effect. You will notice that the more dice a player uses the

Bravery often commands a steep price.

greater is his chance of scoring the value required and the greater his Hero's expenditure of Will.

If a Hero is the victim of a magical power he can resist it by rolling one or more dice. This is called 'magical resistance'. The player declares how many dice he will roll and the Hero's Will value is immediately reduced by 1 for each dice rolled. The player rolls all the dice together and picks out the highest score. If the highest scoring dice equals or beats the highest scoring dice of the attacker then the power is resisted and has no effect. If none of the dice equals or beats the highest scoring dice of the attacker then the Hero has failed to resist the spell's effects.

SPECIAL RULE

Resistant to Magic

Hobbits are naturally resistant to the influence of magic and the will of others. If a Hobbit attempts to resist a magical power with his Will and fails to roll the required score then he can re-roll the dice. This gives a second chance of success – but note that only one re-roll is allowed – you cannot re-roll a re-roll.

FATE

Fate represents a Hero's destiny and as such preserves him from harm, where ordinary warriors would otherwise die. If a Hero loses a wound then he would normally reduce his remaining Wounds value by 1. However, if the Hero has Fate points left he might be able to avoid harm by some heroic ruse.

If a Hero loses a wound then he can expend one or more of any Fate points he has to 'recover'. The player rolls a dice and simultaneously reduces the Hero's Fate store by 1. If the dice scores a 4, 5 or 6 then the roll is successful and the Hero recovers 1 wound. Any number of wounds can be recovered in this way but a Hero can never have more wounds than shown on his profile.

A player can use as many Fate points as he has available to try to recover a wound. The player can roll one dice at a time until he makes the score required, runs out of Fate, or decides to suffer the wound.

Fate points are most commonly expended in combat but a player can also use them if a Hero dies as a result of a fall or similar mischance. In this case, a successful result might mean that the Hero has not fallen to his death but landed on something soft placed in his path by fortune.

USING MIGHT, WILL & FATE TOGETHER

Might can be used to adjust Will or Fate dice rolls if the player wishes, so long as the Hero has sufficient Might points remaining. A very powerful Hero will be able to cheat death and resist the most potent of sorceries – for a while – but sooner or later even the greatest Hero will run out of one or other of Might, Will or Fate.

The sword and the King are reunited.

Most Heroes will have only a few points of Might, Will or Fate for an entire game, and will have to consider how to use them very carefully indeed. The more junior Heroes may have little more than a single Fate point or a couple of Might points to back their claim to fame. Others not only have a large store of points, but depend upon them utterly, such as the Ringwraiths.

HEROIC ACTIONS

As we have already described, priority is usually established at the start of each turn by rolling a dice. Whichever side has priority that turn takes all its moves and shots first, and decides the order in which combats are fought. This is the normal priority rule as described in the Turn Sequence (see page 13).

During the Move, Shoot, or Fight phase, any individual Hero can override the normal sequence by giving up one point of Might to make a 'heroic action'. The player must declare that he wishes to make a heroic action at the start of the phase.

If both players wish to make heroic actions in the same phase then the sides alternate picking a Hero to make a heroic action. Roll a dice to randomly determine which side has the first pick – 1, 2 or 3 the Evil side goes first; 4, 5 or 6 the Good side goes first.

Once all the Heroes who are making heroic actions have been indicated, work out their actions in the order they were picked. It is easier to remember the order if you place a dice beside each model as it is nominated – 1 is first, 2 is second, 3, 4, and so on. This sometimes allows Heroes to anticipate the enemy and cancel their heroic action, for example, by moving into base contact with a Hero who has declared a heroic move or by shooting before the Hero and his friends can do so and killing the Hero. If this happens, the points of Might used to declare the heroic action are spent and cannot be restored because the heroic action has not happened – the enemy has been quicker!

HEROIC MOVE

A Hero who makes a heroic action at the start of the Move phase will move before other models that are not making heroic actions. In addition, the Hero can shout "With me!" as he moves, and all friends within 6"/14cm will move at the same time. Friends moving in this way must begin and end their move within 6"/14cm of the Hero who is making the heroic action otherwise they cannot move with him. It is very important that players try and move the Hero before the other models that are going to join him in the heroic move. These models do not get to move at all if the heroic move is cancelled by the enemy getting to execute his own heroic move first and engaging the Hero calling the heroic move before he can move.

Gandalf marshals the defences of Minas Tirith.

HEROIC SHOOTING

A Hero can call a heroic action at the start of the Shoot phase by shouting "Fire!". This enables the Hero himself and all friends within 6"/14cm to shoot before other models that turn at whatever targets they wish, assuming they are able to. Note that a Hero does not need to be shooting himself to call a heroic shooting action, but he cannot do so if he is engaged in combat.

HEROIC COMBAT

If a Hero gives up one point of Might at the start of the Fight phase, the combat he is involved in is worked out before other combats that turn. In addition, if all enemy models in base contact with the Hero are slain, the Hero and any friends in the same multiple combat can move again before proceeding with the Fight phase. For example, the Hero and accompanying friends can charge other enemies or move to join other fights, although they don't have to, and can simply move away if they so wish.

When warriors fight heroic combats they will often move to join existing fights and in some cases this can change the way the fights are divided. Once the heroic combats have been worked out it may be necessary to rematch other

fights as a result. The player with priority decides how combatants are matched as normal.

A warrior who fights a heroic combat and then moves to join a further heroic combat cannot then move and fight again. A warrior can only benefit from one heroic combat during a single Fight phase.

Designer's Note. It's possible for a Hero's heroic action to affect another Hero – so two Heroes within 6"/14cm could benefit from either of them making a heroic move or shot. Similarly, two Heroes fighting together in a multiple combat would benefit if either used the heroic combat ability.

Once a model has moved or shot it has completed its movement and shooting for that phase. The heroic action enables the model to move or shoot first but does not enable it to move or shoot twice. A model that happens to be within 6"/14cm of a series of Heroes making a heroic move cannot move along with each – it only moves once!

Heroic combat is slightly different because a model gets the chance to move and fight a second time. However, a model can only benefit from a heroic combat action once per turn.

WEAPONS

So far in the game it makes no difference whether a warrior is armed with a sword, spear, or any other weapon – all warriors fight in the same way. Whilst this is perfectly good when it comes to learning the rules and making a start, there is clearly a good case for introducing unique rules to reflect the differences between one type of weapon and another.

MORE THAN ONE WEAPON

Warriors often carry several weapons; for example a bow, sword and a spear. If a warrior is armed with several different shooting weapons, eg, a throwing spear and a bow, he can use either one of them in the Shoot phase but he cannot use both in the same phase. If a warrior has several close combat weapons, eg, a sword and a two-handed axe, he can use either one of them in the Fight phase but he cannot use both in the same phase.

SWORDS & OTHER HAND WEAPONS

Most warriors carry a sword, axe, club or similar weapon in one hand – these are collectively called 'hand weapons' for that reason. All hand weapons are used more or less in the same way and how effective they are is more dependent upon a warrior's familiarity with his armament than any inherent difference between swords, axes, etc.

The rules already given assume a warrior is armed in this way so we need not burden ourselves with additional rules for hand weapons. They represent the standard or norm.

BLADED BOWS & CROSSBOWS

Evil warriors armed with Orc bows or crossbows can fight with them in close combat as well as shoot from a distance. These bladed weapons have sharp blades fitted into the bow stave itself. A warrior armed with this is considered to have a hand weapon – so he fights as if armed with a sword.

SPEARS

If a warrior on foot is armed with a spear held in either one hand or two hands, he can fight exactly as already described in the Fight Phase section of the book. In this respect a spear-armed man fights like a sword-armed man.

In addition, because of a spear's length, a spear-armed warrior can contribute one attack to a fight if he is in base contact with a friend who is touching an enemy. The extra length of the spear allows him to 'support' his own comrade against the foe. The spear-armed warrior does not need to be touching the foe to lend support in this way – he only has to be touching a friend who is himself touching the enemy. The friend must have a base of the same size as the spear-armed warrior, or smaller, for the spear-armed warrior to be able to support him. If the friend's base is bigger than the spearman's, the spearman cannot support his friend.

A spearman cannot offer support if he is or was himself engaged in combat during the same Fight phase.

The spear rule allows a warrior to support a friend – as the spear-armed Orc on the left is doing.

A spear-armed warrior who is supporting a friend as described is not part of the combat for all intents and purposes (ie, the Fight value, Strength and Might of the spearman do not come into the fight at all). The friend supported in this way by a spearman gets one extra attack for that combat. A model with 1 attack will have 2, a model with 2 will have 3, and so on. This extra attack represents the advantage offered to the friend by the support of the spearman, which allows the friend to be more effective in combat.

This fight is a multiple combat between two Men and one Orc, with a second Orc supporting with a spear.

Only one spear-armed warrior can support one friendly model at a time. If several spear-armed warriors are touching a single friend, only one of them can give an extra attack to the friend.

As noted opposite, spear-armed models cannot support warriors using two-handed weapons or defending themselves by shielding. See the rules for these weapons.

The spear rules allow warriors with spears to support their friends, and enables a huddle of spear-armed troops to bring their numbers to bear against the foe. This offers spear-armed warriors a different way of fighting that is especially valuable in larger battles where bringing as many men into a fight as possible can often carry the day.

Designer's Note. If you own a previous edition of the game you'll notice we've slightly changed the rules for spears (and pikes) – we found it is much simpler to say that the spearmen are not involved at all in the fight they are contributing to.

TWO-HANDED SWORDS & AXES

A two-handed sword or axe is a large, heavy weapon that needs two hands to wield it effectively (heavy glaives, halberds and similar weapons are considered to be in the same category). As with hand weapons, we won't worry unduly about the differences – they are fundamentally similar weapons that require a similar approach. Two-handed weapons are difficult to use because they are so heavy. Warriors pressed into combat for prolonged periods will tire easily as the strain of swinging their enormous blades takes its toll on their stamina. This is why only a minority of warriors favour them. The advantage though is that they are very dangerous – able to smash through armour and crush flesh and bone with horrific ease.

Models armed with two-handed weapons cannot carry bows, crossbows or shields as they need both hands to carry their weapons. It is also impossible to use a two-handed weapon whilst mounted.

If a model is fighting with a two-handed sword or axe, it automatically suffers a -1 penalty to its dice roll when working out which side wins the fight – a dice roll of 5 counts as 4, a roll of 6 as 5, etc. The minimum possible score is 1, so a roll of 1 still counts as 1 and not as 0. The score can still be enhanced to a maximum of 6 by the use of a Might point as described for Heroes. This penalty reflects that the weapon is heavy and difficult to use.

If fighting a multiple combat, it is necessary to distinguish models that are using two-handed weapons from others – so roll separately or use different coloured dice for them.

By way of compensation, a warrior fighting with a two-handed sword or axe adds +1 to his dice roll on the Wound chart – a roll of 1 counts as 2, 3 counts as 4, and so on. If two rolls are normally required to inflict a wound (eg, 6/4+) the bonus is added to both rolls. The maximum score on a dice is 6, so a roll of 6 still counts as 6. The bonus reflects the fact that the weapon is heavy and very destructive.

Orcs are brutal and cruel.

There is one further rule – because warriors armed with these weapons must swing them in great arcs it is inappropriate that friendly spearmen or pikemen should be able to support a warrior which is fighting with a two-handed weapon – their long weapons would instantly be knocked aside. So, a spear or pike-armed warrior cannot support a friendly warrior who is fighting with a two-handed weapon.

As you can see, a warrior armed with a two-handed weapon is less likely to win a combat but more likely to inflict a wound. To take full advantage of these weapons, it is a good idea to support warriors armed in this way with others carrying ordinary swords or other hand weapons, as these more nimble warriors are more likely to win fights than their unwieldy comrades.

ELVEN BLADES

The Elves fight with elegant curved blades of exceptional craftmanship. These weapons are so finely balanced that a skilled Elf warrior can swing their very long blades in a fluid series of cuts and thrusts. Elven blades are hand weapons, but a model wielding one can declare at the beginning of any Fight phase that he is going to use it with both hands. For the duration of that Fight phase, the Elven blade will count as a two-handed weapon. If the warrior also carries a shield or a spear then he cannot use his Elven blade as a two-handed weapon.

LANCES

Heavily armoured horsemen are sometimes equipped with long thrusting spears called lances. These are fixed in place underarm when the warrior is charging, thus allowing the warrior to bring the entire weight and impetus of his charging steed to bear against the enemy.

A cavalry model armed with a lance gets a special bonus when charging, even if it is subsequently charged in the same Move phase. A lance adds +1 to his dice roll on the Wound chart – a roll of 1 counts as 2, 3 counts as 4, and so on. If two rolls are normally required to inflict a wound (eg, 6/4+) the bonus is added to both rolls. The maximum score on a dice is 6, so a roll of 6 still counts as 6.

This bonus is in addition to any other cavalry bonuses for charging cavalry, but it also applies against enemy cavalry and is not lost if the warrior is engaged by enemy cavalry.

If fighting a multiple combat it is necessary to distinguish models that are charging with lances from others – so roll separately or use different coloured dice for them.

If the lance-armed warrior does not charge, he receives no bonus and instead the horseman will have to fight using the butt or shaft of his lance (counts as a dagger). If he also carries a hand weapon, he can use it instead at no penalty.

It is impossible to use a lance whilst on foot.

KNIVES & DAGGERS

Most models carry at least some kind of hand weapon, even if it is only a club. However, a few carry only a knife or no visible weapon at all, in which case we assume they have a knife tucked about their person somewhere.

A model armed only in this way is not well equipped for combat and therefore suffers a -1 dice penalty when working out who wins a fight – a roll of 4 counts as 3, a roll of 6 as 5, and so on. Rolls of 1 still count as 1 because it is the lowest score possible. Note that separate dice rolls will be required in multiple combats for models armed with knives and daggers.

Savage animals and monsters which would not normally need weapons to fight are not penalised just because they have no visible weaponry. They have claws, teeth, and whatever else nature has endowed them with.

SHIELDS

If a model has a shield, the warrior's ability to defend itself is taken into account by a suitable increase in the model's Defence value.

If a warrior has both a shield and a bow or crossbow it is assumed the warrior cannot carry both at the same time, so bow/crossbow-armed models receive no increase in their Defence value from carrying a shield but they do still benefit from the following rules for having a shield:

If a warrior is armed with a two-handed weapon or pike it cannot also carry a shield. It doesn't have enough hands!

A warrior armed with a shield is allowed to fight in a defensive manner by expending its entire effort fending off its foe's attacks. This is called 'defending by shielding' or just 'shielding'. If a player wants a warrior to defend by shielding, he must say it is doing so at the start of a fight.

Note that this cannot be done while mounted on a steed, only models on foot can defend by shielding.

If a warrior is shielding, then two dice are rolled for each single Attack characteristic he has when determining who wins the fight. So, a warrior that has an Attack value of 1 rolls two dice, an Attack value of 2 rolls four dice, an Attack value of 3 rolls six dice, etc. If the warrior wins the fight then he may not strike any blows against his enemy. His enemies are beaten back the usual distance but he cannot strike against them as they move back.

As you can see, the advantage of shielding is that it makes it more likely for the model to win the fight. The disadvantage is that should he win he strikes no blows. As such, shielding is only a practical response where it is more important for a warrior to survive the turn than it is for him to slay his enemy.

If a warrior is fighting a multiple combat, shielding is only effective if all the warriors on one side do so. In a combat with three models on the same side, for example, all three must decide to use the special shielding rule or none. In general, players will only want to shield when they are heavily outnumbered or facing vastly superior opponents – but it is left to the player to decide when shielding might be an effective option.

A model who is equipped with a spear or pike may not support a warrior who is shielding – the shield and the warrior's efforts to defend himself get in the way of the spear or pike shaft.

A warrior who is lying on the ground can defend himself by shielding if he has a shield. This is the best response to an enemy attack as a warrior who is on the ground cannot strike if he wins the fight in any case.

PIKES

A pike is a very long spear. Only a warrior on foot can carry a pike – the weapon is so long that it is impossible to use whilst mounted. Models armed with pikes cannot carry bows, crossbows or shields as they need both hands to carry their weapons.

In this situation, the Uruk-hai fighting against the Warrior of Minas Tirith is being supported by two friends and therefore has three Attacks.

The rules for pikes are the same as those for spears except:

A pike-armed warrior can support a friend engaged in combat by being in base contact with a spear- or pike-armed warrior who is already supporting the same friend, as shown below. This will give another attack to the friend engaged in combat, for a total of +2 attacks.

A pikeman and a spearman supporting a friend.

Otherwise – all the rules for spears apply and rather than repeat them we suggest you re-read the section on spears (see page 50).

THROWING WEAPONS

Throwing spears, javelins, and throwing axes are weapons designed specifically to be thrown rather than used in a fight like ordinary spears or axes. Though throwing weapons may appear superficially similar to weapons designed for fighting in close combat, they are generally smaller and heavier, and are balanced for flight rather than for use in combat. A model that has a throwing weapon can use it in a fight – in which case no special rules apply and it counts just like an ordinary sword or axe. A model armed with a throwing spear cannot fight through another model as can a regular spear-armed warrior.

A model can throw its weapon in the Shoot phase in the same way as a model armed with a bow or crossbow. Alternatively, a charging model can throw its weapon at the foe it is about to fight. This is an exception to the normal rules as it allows a warrior to 'shoot' as it moves.

An Orc battleline prepares to receive a charge.

A warrior can throw its throwing weapon as it charges. The player moves the model as if it were going to charge the enemy but instead of moving into touch it halts 1"/2cm away. It then throws its weapon at the enemy it is about to fight. The throw is then worked out exactly as if it had taken place in the Shoot phase, even though it is still the Move phase. Once the weapon has been thrown, the charger is moved into contact with the same enemy model or, if the enemy has been slain, the charger completes its move as the player wishes. You will notice that this potentially enables a warrior to slay an enemy as it charges and then charge a different enemy and fight. Note that models can only throw one of these weapons per game turn.

Designer's Note. *If you own a previous edition of the game you'll notice we've changed the throwing weapons rules – we found that the 'one use only' rule meant people either had to use too many models to represent a single warrior or be burdened with an awful lot of book-keeping. We have decided that the models will have an unlimited number of shots with their throwing weapons, representing the fact that they carry a number of them and/or they are picking up their weapons after throwing them as they move around the battlefield. To compensate, we have increased the cost of throwing weapons and reduced their range to 6"/14cm.*

Balin charges the Moria Goblin, stops to throw his axe and then, having failed to kill his enemy, completes his charge.

BOWS - VOLLEY FIRE

Groups of bowmen can coordinate their fire and loose volleys of arrows into the air in order to rain death on enemies very far away and even out of direct sight! This kind of fire greatly increases the range of the weapon, but it also considerably reduces its accuracy and is effective only against densely packed enemy formations.

Any group of six or more bow-armed models grouped together at the beginning of the Shoot phase (each warrior must be in base contact with at least one other of the group) can declare they are going to fire a volley. They can do this as long as they all have the same kind of bow (Elf bow, bow, Dwarf bow or Orc bow) and have all moved no more than half their Move distance in the previous Move phase, as normal for bow-armed models to be able to fire.

The range of bows firing a volley is doubled, but models that are closer than 18"/42cm cannot be targeted, being too close for indirect fire (for example, an Elf bow could hit targets between 18"/42cm and 48"/112cm).

The firing group can pick any enemy model within range and does not need to be able to see the target, as long as there is at least one friendly model on the battlefield that is able to see their target.

All models in the firing group that are within range of the target roll a dice. They score a hit only on the roll of a 6, regardless of their Shoot value.

The target model can be hit only once, regardless of the number of 6s rolled, but any excess hits can be spread among models within 6"/14cm of the target, following the following procedure.

Gandalf the White

The first hit is always on the target, then the player controlling the target picks a model within 6"/14cm of the target and allocates the second hit to it, then the player controlling the firing group can pick another model within 6"/14cm of the target and allocate the third hit on it, and the two players continue alternating like this until there are no hits left or all models within 6"/14cm of the target have been hit once.

If friendly models are within 6"/14cm of the target, Good models cannot shoot and must choose another target. Evil models can shoot as normal.

Barriers will count as 'in the way' only if they are between the firing group and the model hit, and the model hit is in base contact with the cover. Models inside a wooded area always benefit from an 'in the way' roll because of the trees and models inside buildings or with some other solid protection overhead cannot be hit at all by indirect fire.

Normally, models can be hit only once by volley fire, but extremely large creatures can be hit by more arrows. Models mounted on large bases (with bases of 40mm radius or more) can be hit once per Wound on their profile. This means that, for example, cavalry models can be hit twice (one on the rider and one on the mount), while a Balrog could be hit ten times!

PICKING UP WEAPONS

In general, we have not made provision for warriors picking up weapons from other warriors, from weapon stores or discarded weapons that might lie around the battlefield. Keeping track of which warriors have acquired which weapons would be impractical and would make little difference to the battle. However, for players who wish to add a further level of detail Heroes are allowed to take weapons in some situations.

If a Hero wins a fight and slays all of his opponents he can take one weapon or shield from any of them.

If a Hero does not have a shield and picks one up, he adds 1 to his Defence unless he also has a bow or crossbow. Models who carry pikes or two-handed swords/axe cannot pick up a shield. See the Shield rules.

If a Hero does not have a bow or crossbow and picks one up, he can shoot and is assumed to also pick up enough arrows to last for the rest of the battle. If unspecified his Shoot value will be the base Shoot value for his race.

If a Hero is already using a shield, then his Defence value is reduced by 1 if he subsequently picks up either a bow or crossbow. See the Shield rules.

Note that Heroes cannot pick up or use magical weapons or items from their enemy – Good and Evil magic is contradictory in nature and cannot be employed by the foe.

BANNERS

Most armies carry to battle banners, standards, icons, totems and other pieces of equipment showing the symbols of their people and leaders. Famous examples of such symbols are the White Tree of Gondor, the Red Eye of Sauron, the Horse of the Rohirrim and the White Hand of Saruman, but many more exist (see page 151 for more examples of banners).

EQUIPPING WARRIORS WITH BANNERS

At the additional cost shown in their entry in the Forces section, warriors can be given banners. A force can include a number of banners equal to or less than the number of Heroes it includes.

A model that is given a banner can wear armour and ride a steed, but it cannot use any other kind of weapons/equipment. Any weapons/equipment that the model is already carrying are lost if he is given a banner. Models carrying a banner count as armed with two-handed weapons, except that they do not get any bonus when rolling on the Wound chart. This represents the difficulty of defending oneself while holding up a heavy banner.

If a warrior carrying a banner is killed, a friendly warrior in base contact can drop all his equipment and pick up the banner (effectively, the player must remove the model and replace it with the one carrying the banner). Models cannot pick up a banner while they are engaged in combat. If the banner is not picked up, it is lost in the mayhem of battle.

Heroes can never carry and pick up banners, unless otherwise specified in their entry.

BANNER COMBAT BONUS

All models within 3"/8cm of one or more friendly banner bearers are in range of a banner. If at least one model in a fight is in range of a friendly banner, the entire fight is deemed to be in range of the banner. If a fight is in range of a banner, the side the banner belongs to can benefit from the banner's combat bonus.

The combat bonus of the banner allows the player to re-roll one of the dice rolled to determine who wins the fight. The player simply rolls the dice as normal, and can then decide to pick up **one** of the dice and re-roll it. As normal the second number rolled stands and cannot be re-rolled. Might can be used to modify the final result. Note that this effect **does not** apply to rolls on the Wound chart.

In a combat where both sides are in range of friendly banners, both players get to re-roll **one** dice, and they can decide to do so even after seeing the result of their opponent's re-roll. For example: in a fight the Good side's best roll is a 4 and the Evil side's is a 3. The Evil player decides to re-roll one of his dice, obtaining a 5 and taking the lead. At this point the Good player decides he will also re-roll one of his dice and scores a 6, winning the fight!

CAPTURING BANNERS

The victor of a scenario will always capture all the banners that the enemy has lost during the game. This does not normally have any effect on the game, other than offering the victor a splendid occasion to tease the loser. In some scenarios though, this might make a difference in the victory conditions, if specified in the scenario's objectives.

Warriors of Gondor and Rohan unflinchingly await their destiny.

THE DWARVES

Like the Elves, the Dwarves are an elder race whose days are fading as Men come into prominence. In most other ways, however, the Dwarves are quite dissimilar to Elves. Where Elves are tall and gracefully spoken, Dwarves are short and gruff. Where Elves prefer to dwell in the forests of Middle-earth, the Dwarves carve their halls deep within the roots of the mountains.

The Dwarves fall upon their foe with anger and determination.

"Baruk Khazâd! Khazâd ai-mênu!"

"Axes of the Dwarves! The Dwarves are upon you!"

The horde of Uruk-hai is no match for the skill and fury of Gimli son of Gloin.

Gimli takes his rest after a job well done!

Balin leads his kinsfolk into battle.

FORCES

Many people start off using whatever models they happen to have. That's a perfectly natural way to begin and there's nothing wrong with doing exactly that when you first play. Whilst you're learning the rules of the game it's not such a big deal who wins or whether the forces are exactly balanced.

Most players find that once their collection has grown and become more varied, it is more satisfying to fight battles where each side is as near equal as possible. This part of the rules manual explains how to select balanced forces for a game.

The section is divided into two separate force lists. The Good forces include Elves, Men, Hobbits, and Dwarves. The Evil forces include Orcs, Uruk-hai, Goblins and evil Men. Use the force list for the side you have elected to play.

POINT VALUES

The force list for each side gives characteristic profiles, weapons, special rules, and a points value for every type of model, including warriors and Heroes. The points value is a measure of the model's worth in the game.

It is usual for players to begin the game with an equal points value of warriors. As Good warriors are generally worth more than Evil warriors, this means the forces of Good will frequently find themselves outnumbered. Most Good warriors are of superior fighting quality compared to the majority of their opponents, so don't despair when you see hordes of Orcs on the other side of the table.

SCENARIOS

The different game scenarios employ forces of broadly different sizes. Some are small encounters and others larger battles. Inexperienced players are advised to play the smaller encounters before attempting a larger game. As players acquire more models and their collection expands, it will be possible to progress to larger, more demanding scenarios.

Though we have provided a number of scenarios based directly on the encounters portrayed in The Return of The King movie, many players enjoy making up their own scenarios too – taking the events portrayed in The Lord of The Rings as their inspiration.

HOW TO SELECT TROOPS

Begin by choosing which scenario to play. Each scenario can be played with any number of points worth of troops, but we have indicated what we feel is the ideal value for a points matched game.

Orcs on the march.

Having decided how many points to choose, each side secretly selects the models to take part in the game. Use the troop list for your own side to select your force and make a note of the points cost as you do so. You can choose models with a total value up to the points you have agreed, but no more. In most cases you will find you cannot match the points exactly but this doesn't matter so long as you do not spend more points than you are allowed.

In most cases, the scenario you are playing will limit the number or proportion of Heroes in your force or the number of bow-armed models. This is to ensure the scenario plays as it is intended even if you choose forces radically different to those in the actual event portrayed.

Oh – in case you were wondering – you can only have one of any named individual in your army. You can't have an army made up entirely of Aragorns, for example!

USING THE RECORD SHEETS

It is a good idea to work out your forces on a piece of scrap paper as you may wish to change your mind, or go back and revise details. Once you are satisfied with your final forces, make sure that you have added up their values correctly, you are then ready to transfer details to a record sheet.

You don't need to use a record sheet if you do not wish to but most players find it convenient to have a handy note of all the characteristics and relevant details for each game.

At the back of this book you will find a record sheet you can photocopy to use in your games.

Simply write down the details for each model onto the sheet. If your force includes several models of the same type, there is no need to make a separate entry for each model, a single entry will suffice in most cases. Once you have copied all the characteristics and made any notes you think will prove useful, your record sheet should be ready for use in your battles.

We have also repeated the Movement chart below for convenience.

Designer's note: You will notice that the force lists include Heroes from the Elder Age, as well as characters from the time of the Fellowship. The story of the Ring is a long one, spanning many generations of Men. We leave it to players to decide whether to restrict themselves to contemporary characters when they choose a force.

However, whether you choose contemporary or diverse characters, you will notice that the lists do not allow more than one character to carry the Ring.

MOVEMENT CHART

TYPE MAXIMUM MOVE OVER OPEN TERRAIN

	Inches	Cms
MAN/WOMAN/WIZARD	6"	14cm
HIGH ELF/WOOD ELF	6"	14cm
GWAIHIR	12"	28cm
ENT	6"	14cm
HOBBIT	4"	10cm
DWARF	5"	12cm
GOLLUM	5"	12cm
ORC	6"	14cm
MORIA GOBLIN	5"	12cm
URUK-HAI	6"	14cm
TROLL	6"	14cm
BALROG	6"	14cm
RINGWRAITH	6"	14cm
SAURON	6"	14cm
SHELOB	10"	24cm
FELL BEAST	12"	28cm
WARG RIDER	10"	24cm
HORSE RIDER	10"	24cm

As you can see distances are given in both inches and centimetres as they are throughout this rules manual. Either system can be used but stick to one or the other, don't mix them in the same game as the distances have been rounded for convenience. Note: The Move rate for Orcs has increased from 5" to 6" from the previous editions of the game.

THE FREE PEOPLES

Use this list to choose a Good force to the points value you have agreed with your opponent.

HEROES

Frodo Baggins (Hobbit)

Points value: 65

	F	S	D	A	W	C
Frodo	3/3+	2	3	1	2	6

Might: 3
Will: 3
Fate: 3

Frodo has undertaken the quest to carry the Ring to Mordor and cast it into the fires of Mount Doom, thus ending its power forever. Though Frodo is hardly as bold or fierce a warrior as many others in Middle-earth, he alone has the strength of character needed to succeed. For the Ring has a strong and evil will of its own. The Ring wants to be found!

Wargear

Frodo carries a sturdy blade (hand weapon). At an additional points cost, he can be given the following items of wargear. He can only carry Sting or wear his Mithril coat if Bilbo is not included in the force.

Sting	*15 pts*
Mithril coat	*25 pts*
Elven cloak	*10 pts*

Sting

Sting is a magical blade that shines with a blue light when Orcs are near. When Frodo carries Sting, he adds +1 to his Strength characteristic, giving him a Strength value of 3.

Mithril Coat

Mithril is a rare metal that is as light as a feather, and as hard as dragon scale. The wearer's Defence value is increased by +3, in Frodo's case from Defence 3 to 6.

Elven Cloak

If the wearer is partially concealed from view, he cannot be seen at all at distances of more than 6"/14cm – the wearer appears to melt into the background. This means that enemy archers can not shoot at ranges of greater than 6"/14cm unless they have a completely clear view of the target. If the model is riding a mount, the cloak has no effect.

Special Rules

Resistant to Magic. See page 47 for details.

Throw Stones. If a Hobbit does not move at all, he can declare he's 'stooping for a stone', and in the subsequent Shoot phase he can throw it, provided that he is not engaged in combat. This works exactly like a crossbow with a range of 8"/20cm and a Strength of 1.

The Ring. If Frodo is included in the force, he carries the Ring. Frodo can put on the Ring at any time during his own Move phase and becomes instantly invisible to all except the Ringwraiths. The model is deemed impossible to see. As the wearer is invisible, he automatically moves through other models and other models automatically move through him (they can't see him so pay no attention to him – we assume Frodo dodges out of the way).

Whilst Frodo is invisible he can neither charge or be charged by enemies who cannot see him – he is effectively ignored. It is best to avoid any potential for confusion by not placing other models in touch if possible. Frodo can even put the Ring on if he has already been charged, in which case he is immediately separated from all enemy that cannot see him.

If the Ring is already being worn then the Good player must roll a dice immediately before he moves Frodo in the Move phase. If the player does not wish to move Frodo he must still roll a dice – but can do so at any time during the Move phase. The roll is made on behalf of Frodo himself so we shall allow the Good player to use Frodo's Might points to modify this dice roll if he wishes to do so. On a score of a 1 or 2, the Evil player moves Frodo instead of the Good player. On a roll of 3, 4, 5 or 6, the Good player moves Frodo as usual. Regardless of which side moves Frodo, he is still part of the Good side and all other actions, such as shooting and fighting, remain under the control of the Good player. This means that when the Evil player moves Frodo, all he can do is move the model, including charging Frodo into any models that can see him (in this case, Frodo does not need to take Courage tests to charge terrifying enemies). He cannot perform heroic actions and cannot pick up or put down other items. He cannot be forced to perform any actions that would cause direct harm to the model (such as jumping down a cliff…) nor be moved off the table if the scenario allows. This represents the struggle between Frodo and the will of Sauron.

If the controlling player wishes Frodo to take the Ring off, he needs to pass a Courage test to be able to remove it. This test can be taken at any point during Frodo's move once it has been established which side has control of his movement. If the test is failed, Frodo must continue to wear the Ring until the next turn, when he will have another chance to remove it.

If Frodo is the only model left on the Good side and he's wearing the Ring, he counts as a casualty – his mind has been taken over by its power. As many scenarios depend on him surviving this is very important! If the Evil side's objective is to kill Frodo this is achieved if he is the only model remaining on the table from the Good side and he is wearing the Ring.

Sam Gamgee (Hobbit)

Points value: 35

	F	S	D	A	W	C
Sam	3/3+	2	3	1	2	5

Might: 2
Will: 2
Fate: 3

Sam is Frodo's stalwart companion and loyal friend – of all the Fellowship only Sam is unable to abandon Frodo to his lone journey to Mordor to destroy the Ring. Like his master, Sam comes to discover reserves of courage quite unexpected in a normally placid Hobbit. Faced with danger quite unknown in the Shire, Sam bravely confronts and defeats the dark forces that threaten his master.

Wargear

Sam carries a sturdy blade (hand weapon). At an additional points cost, Sam can be given the following item of wargear:

Elven cloak	*10 pts*

Special Rules
Resistant to Magic. See page 47 for details.

Throw stones. See Frodo entry for details.

Meriadoc Brandybuck (Hobbit)

Points value: 20

	F	S	D	A	W	C
Merry	3/3+	2	3	1	1	4

Might: 1
Will: 1
Fate: 2

Meriadoc Brandybuck, commonly called Merry, is a young hot-headed and meddlesome Hobbit, like his good friend Peregrin Took. It is by chance that Merry finds himself caught up in the greatest adventure of his life. Although he has lived a peaceful and happy life in the Shire, Merry shows a remarkable readiness to adapt to a life of excitement and discovery. Like all Hobbits he is less happy about the necessary culinary deprivations.

Wargear
Merry carries a sturdy blade (hand weapon). At an additional points cost Merry can have the following wargear:

Elven cloak	*10 pts*
Shield	*5 pts*
Armour	*5 pts*

Armour. If Merry wears armour, his Defence value is increased by +1.

Shield. If Merry carries a shield, his Defence value is increased by +1 and he can use the Shielding rule.

Special Rules
Resistant to Magic. See page 47 for details.

Throw stones. See Frodo entry for details.

Peregrin Took (Hobbit)

Points value: 20

	F	S	D	A	W	C
Pippin	3/3+	2	3	1	1	4

Might: 1
Will: 1
Fate: 2

Peregrin Took, commonly called Pippin, is the great friend and companion of the equally young and wild Meriadoc Brandybuck. By a chance encounter, they find themselves propelled from their rustic lives in the Shire into danger of the darkest and most terrible kind.

Together Merry and Pippin end up in a dark and dangerous adventure – one that is destined to change them from innocents to heroes.

Wargear
Pippin carries a sturdy blade (hand weapon). At an additional points cost Pippin can have the following wargear:

Elven cloak	*10 pts*
Shield	*5 pts*
Armour	*5 pts*

Armour. If Pippin wears armour, his Defence value is increased by +1.

Shield. If Pippin carries a shield, his Defence value is increased by +1 and he can use the Shielding rule.

Special Rules
Resistant to Magic. See page 47 for details.

Throw stones. See Frodo entry for details.

Gandalf the Grey (Wizard)

Points value: 150

Might: 3
Will: 6+1 free per turn
Fate: 3

	F	S	D	A	W	C
Gandalf	5/-	4	5	1	3	7

Of the Order of Wizards, Gandalf the Grey is second only to Saruman the White in power. It is Gandalf who leads the Fellowship until his loss in Moria at the hands of the fearsome Balrog. Gandalf's magical abilities are a great asset to the Fellowship though he is also able to hold his own in a fight.

Note. Your force can only include one Gandalf – Gandalf the Grey or Gandalf the White.

Wargear

Gandalf carries his staff and a sword (hand weapon). He can use either to fight with – his staff is a two-handed weapon.

Special Rules

Staff of Power. Gandalf's staff is not only a symbol of his authority but a potent talisman. To represent his staff's power he can expend 1 point of Will each turn without reducing his own Will store.

Magical Powers

Strengthen Will. Range 12"/28cm. Dice score to use: 4+. Gandalf can use this spell to restore the Will of one friendly Hero within range. The target's Will value is restored to its maximum. Gandalf cannot use this magical power to restore his own Will.

Sorcerous Blast. Range 12"/28cm. Dice score to use: 5+. This power can be used against a single enemy model. There must be no other models from either side obscuring his view of the target but partially obscuring cover is ignored. If the power is employed successfully the target is blasted directly away from Gandalf – roll a dice and move the target that number of inches or double that number of centimetres (1-6" or 2-12cm). Any models that lie within the path of the model as it moves back are automatically moved aside and knocked to the ground. If the model is fighting then all the models in the same conflict are knocked to the ground whether friends or foe. If models are blasted into obstacles they are also knocked to the ground. The target model counts as having been struck one blow at a Strength value of 5 and every model that is knocked to the ground is struck one blow at a Strength of 3.

Cast Light. Dice score to use: 2+. This power enables Gandalf to cause his staff to glow brilliantly. In darkness this illuminates an area 12"/28cm around him and anyone within this area can be seen as if it were daylight. Once cast this power lasts for the rest of the game so long as Gandalf has at least 1 point of Will remaining. If Gandalf's Will drops to zero the staff is extinguished. Because of the staff's brightness any enemy shooting at Gandalf or at a target that is partially obscured by Gandalf will require a roll of 6 to score a hit.

Immobilise. Range 12"/28cm. Dice score to use: 3+. The victim can do nothing further that turn. In combat his Fight value counts as 1 and he rolls one dice regardless of how many Attacks he normally has. If he wins a combat he will not strike. The victim can still use Might, Will and Fate but cannot make heroic actions. The effect lasts for the remainder of that turn.

Command. Range 12"/28cm Dice score to use: 4+. The victim can do nothing further that turn as described for Immobilise, except that the Good player can move the victim up to half a move as soon as the power takes effect. The player can do this even if the model has already moved that turn.

Terrifying Aura. Dice score to use: 2+. This power enables Gandalf to assume a terrifying aura. Once this power has been successfully cast Gandalf counts as terrifying to all Evil creatures so long as he has at least 1 point of Will remaining. If Gandalf's Will drops to zero the terrifying aura is extinguished. See the Courage section of the rules for more about terror.

"The Company of the Ring shall be Nine; and the Nine Walkers shall be set against the Nine Riders."

Bilbo Baggins (Hobbit)

Points value: 90

	F	S	D	A	W	C
Bilbo	3/3+	3	5	1	2	6

Might: 1
Will: 3
Fate: 3

Bilbo has lived a great many years and his days of adventure and travel seem far behind him. Though he has grown frail, his strong will and good heart have protected him from the terrible power of the Ring that he has guarded and protected for so long.

Wargear

Bilbo carries Sting and wears his Mithril coat. The rules for these are as described for Frodo – both bonuses have been added to Bilbo's profile (without them his Strength and Defence would be 2 each). Note that if Bilbo and Frodo are both included, Bilbo carries Sting and the Mithril coat, whilst Frodo carries the Ring.

Special Rules

The Ring. If Frodo is not in the force, Bilbo can carry the Ring, in which case the same rules apply as for Frodo.

Resistant to Magic. See page 47 for details.

Throw Stones. See Frodo entry for details.

Gimli (Dwarf)

Points value: 80

	F	S	D	A	W	C
Gimli	6/4+	4	8	2	2	6

Might: 3
Will: 2
Fate: 2

Like all Dwarf-kind Gimli, son of Gloin, is grim and plain-speaking but also a doughty warrior. His courage and his axe are equally valuable additions to the Fellowship on their journey. Gimli is heavily armoured in the fashion of Dwarf warriors and is well accustomed to the rigours of combat.

Gimli proves a stalwart warrior during the bitter fighting of the war against Sauron, slaying a multitude of Orcs with his fearsome axe.

Wargear

Gimli carries an assortment of fine Dwarf axes (hand weapon), some of which are balanced for throwing (count as throwing axes). He also carries an especially large axe that can be used with two hands (two-handed axe). He can use either an ordinary axe or his two-handed axe – though not both in the same Fight phase (not enough hands!).

At an additional points cost, Gimli can be given an Elven cloak – see Frodo for the rules for Elven cloaks.

Elven cloak	*10 pts*

Legolas (Wood Elf)

Points value: 85

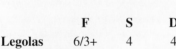

	F	S	D	A	W	C
Legolas	6/3+	4	4	2	2	6

Might: 3
Will: 2
Fate: 2

Legolas is the son of the King of the Wood Elves and like all his people he is a deadly accurate and keen sighted archer. Of the Free Peoples, he represents the Elves as part of the Fellowship.

Wargear

Legolas carries two short blades (he counts as being armed with a single hand weapon) and an Elf bow. At an additional points cost, Legolas can be given an Elven cloak (see Frodo for rules), armour, and/or a horse.

Elven cloak	*10 pts*
Armour	*5 pts*
Horse	*10 pts*

Armour. If Legolas wears armour, his Defence value is increased by +1 to 5.

Horse. Rules for horses and riders are given in the main rules section.

	F	S	D	A	W	C
Horse	0	3	4	0	1	3

Special Rule

Deadly Shot. Legolas is an expert archer even by the standards of his race. To reflect his prodigious skills, Legolas is allowed to shoot an Elf bow three times in the Shoot phase instead of once.

Aragorn – Strider (Man)

Points value: 175

Might: 3+1 free per turn
Will: 3
Fate: 3

	F	S	D	A	W	C
Aragorn	6/3+	4	5	3	3	6

Aragorn, also known as Strider, is a descendant of Elendil and the last heir to the throne of Gondor. His rough and weather-hewn appearance speaks of a hard life spent battling evil in wild places. Aragorn becomes the protector of the Hobbits and the greatest of the heroes of the Fellowship. His fate and that of the Ringbearer are inexorably bound together with the fate of Middle-earth itself.

Wargear

Aragorn carries a sword (hand weapon). At an additional points cost he can be given the following items of wargear:

Anduril, Flame of the West	*75 pts*
Elven cloak	*10 pts*
Armour	*5 pts*
Heavy armour	*10 pts*
Bow	*5 pts*
Horse	*10 pts*

Anduril, Flame of the West. This magical blade has been re-forged by the smiths of Rivendell using the fragments of Narsil, the sword of Elendil. When fighting with Anduril, Aragorn never needs to roll more than 4+ to score a wound, regardless of the opponent's Defence. His rolls to wound can be modified by using Might as normal.

Armour/Heavy Armour. Aragorn may have either armour or heavy armour – not both. Armour adds +1 to his Defence value, while heavy armour adds +2 to his Defence value.

Horse. Rules for horses and riders are given in the main rules section.

	F	S	D	A	W	C
Horse	0	3	4	0	1	3

Special Rule

Mighty Hero. Aragorn is a mighty hero – the heir of the Kings of Gondor. He may expend 1 point of Might per turn without reducing his Might store. Any additional points of Might expended during his turn will reduce his Might store as normal.

Boromir of Gondor (Man)

Points value: 105

Might: 6
Will: 1
Fate: 0

	F	S	D	A	W	C
Boromir	6/-	4	6	3	3	6

Boromir was a mighty warrior and the son of Denethor, Steward of Gondor. His forefathers ruled Gondor since the long past days of the Kings, protecting the lands of Middle-earth against the evil of Mordor. Boromir was the greatest warrior of the entire Fellowship yet his will was fatally weak and his doubts about their quest almost destroyed its chances of success.

Wargear

Boromir wears armour and carries a sword (hand weapon), a shield and the Horn of Gondor. At an additional points cost he can be given the following items of wargear:

Elven cloak	*10 pts*
Horse	*10 pts*

The Horn of Gondor. The blast of Boromir's fearsome horn is enough to drain the bravest foe of resolve. Boromir can blow the horn at the start of a fight if he is outnumbered by two to one or more. The enemy combatant with the highest Courage must take a Courage test. If this is passed the combat is fought as normal. If the test is failed Boromir automatically wins the fight and can strike blows against his enemies.

Horse. Rules for horses and riders are given in the main rules section.

	F	S	D	A	W	C
Horse	0	3	4	0	1	3

Elrond (High Elf)

Points value: 120

Might: 3
Will: 3
Fate: 3

	F	S	D	A	W	C
Elrond	6/-	4	7	3	3	7

Elrond is old even amongst the immortal Elves, having fought against Sauron in an earlier age and seen the Ring taken by Isildur before it was lost. He is the master of Rivendell and the greatest amongst the wise of Middle-earth. His judgement that the Ring should be destroyed starts the Fellowship on their perilous quest.

Wargear

Elrond wears heavy armour and carries an Elven blade.

Arwen Evenstar (High Elf)

Points value: 65

Might: 1
Will: 4
Fate: 1

	F	S	D	A	W	C
Arwen	6/-	3	3	1	2	6
Horse	0	3	4	0	1	3

Arwen is the daughter of Elrond and like her father an Elf of great power and courage. As an immortal she is destined to sail from Middle-earth into the West – yet her love for Aragorn holds her in the mortal realm and leads her towards an altogether different fate.

Wargear

Arwen carries an Elven blade. She can be given an Elven cloak and can ride Asfaloth at the following points cost:

Elven cloak	*10 pts*
Asfaloth	*10 pts*

Asfaloth. Asfaloth is a fast and loyal Elven horse. Rules for horses and riders are given in the main rules section.

Special Rule

Expert Rider. Arwen is an expert rider. See page 36.

Magical Power

Nature's Wrath. Range 6"/14cm radius. Dice score to use: 4+. Arwen can use this power to raise the forces of nature to send her enemies reeling. The spell affects all enemies within 6"/14cm of her – but only one affected foe can attempt to resist it. If resisted, all foes are unaffected, if the foe fails to resist then all are affected. All enemies within 6"/14cm of Arwen are knocked to the ground.

Gil-galad (High Elf)

Points value: 140

Might: 3
Will: 3
Fate: 1

	F	S	D	A	W	C
Gil-galad	8/-	4	7	3	3	7

Gil-galad was the High King of the Elves and mightiest warrior of his age. When Sauron assailed Gondor, Gil-galad swiftly led the Elves into war, fighting against Sauron. During this Last Alliance of Men and Elves Gil-galad fought on every battlefield, his bravery and leadership bringing inspiration and hope in those dark days.

Wargear

Gil-galad wears heavy armour and carries the mighty spear Aeglos. At additional cost he may carry a shield.

Shield	*5 pts*

Shield. If Gil-galad carries a shield, his Defence value is increased by +1 and he can use the Shielding rule.

Special Rules

Fearless. Gil-galad is completely unafraid of his foes, no matter how terrifying. He does not need to test his Courage when confronting a terrifying enemy.

High King of the Elves. Such is Gil-galad's awesome presence on the battlefield that the range of his 'Stand fast!' rolls is 12"/28cm rather than 6"/14cm.

Aeglos. Aeglos is a spear. In addition, due to the fell reputation of his skill with Aeglos, Gil-galad causes terror while he carries it.

Haldir (Wood Elf)

Points value: 55

Might: 3
Will: 1
Fate: 1

	F	S	D	A	W	C
Haldir	6/3+	4	4	2	2	5

One of the guardians of the forest realm of Lothlorien, Haldir's faith in the alliance between Men and Elves was so great that he willingly led his warriors to stand side-by-side with the defenders of Helm's Deep.

Wargear

Haldir carries an Elven blade. At an additional cost he can have any of the following items:

Elf bow	*5 pts*
Elven cloak	*10 pts*
Armour	*5 pts*

Armour. If Haldir wears armour, his Defence value is increased by +1 to 5.

Special Rule

Expert Shot. If Haldir carries an Elf bow, he is allowed to shoot twice in the Shoot phase instead of once.

Haldir leads the Elves into the battle of Lothlorien.

Elven Captain (Elf)

Points value: 50

Might: 2
Will: 1
Fate: 1

	F	S	D	A	W	C
Elf Captain	6/3+	4	4	2	2	5

The model shown is a conversion – see page 146.

We have included the option to have one or more Elven Captains as part of your force – note that you can include more than one if you wish. This represents the leaders amongst the Wood Elves or the High Elves of the Second Age who go unnamed in the story of The Lord of The Rings. If you choose Elven Captains invent suitable names for each.

Wargear

The Elven Captain represented by this profile has an Elven blade. He has been given a Fight value for shooting – if he does not carry a bow then copy this to your record sheet as 6/-. If he is given further armour make the necessary adjustment to his Defence.

At an additional cost he may have the following items:

Armour	*5 pts*
Heavy armour (High Elf Captain only)	*10 pts*
Shield	*5 pts*
Elf bow	*5 pts*

Armour/Heavy Armour. A model may have either armour or heavy armour – not both. The model must have some visible armour other than a helmet and, in the case of heavy armour, this must extend below the model's waist. An Elf Captain with armour adds +1 to its Defence value, a High Elf Captain with heavy armour adds +2 to its Defence value.

Shield. An Elf Captain that carries a shield adds +1 to its Defence value unless the model also carries a bow, in which case it adds nothing. See page 52 for details.

Theoden, King of Rohan (Man)

Points value: 60

Might: 2
Will: 0
Fate: 2

	F	S	D	A	W	C
Theoden	5/–	4	6	2	2	5

Though now old and apparently frail, Theoden is still a great warrior at heart. He is the King of Rohan and leader of the brave race of horsemen and doughty warriors that stands between the Tower of Orthanc and Gondor. Theoden and his people have fought alone against the growing might of Saruman – and Theoden himself is threatened by the enchantments of the evil wizard. The time approaches when Rohan must fight for survival against the gathering armies of Saruman's Uruk-hai: in that battle Theoden must lead his people wisely or all shall perish beneath the might of the White Hand.

Wargear

Theoden carries a sword and has heavy armour. At an additional cost he may have the following items:

Shield	*5 pts*
Horse	*10 pts*

	F	S	D	A	W	C
Horse	0	3	4	0	1	3

Expert Rider. Theoden is an expert rider. See page 36 for details.

Eomer, Captain of Rohan (Man)

Points value: 75

Might: 3
Will: 2
Fate: 2

	F	S	D	A	W	C
Eomer	5/4+	4	6	2	2	5

Eomer is the bravest and most gallant of all the Captains of Rohan – a realm under constant threat from the foul Orcs, Uruk-hai and Wild Men under the leadership of the evil Saruman.

Shield	*5 pts*
Horse	*10 pts*

Shield. If Eomer carries a shield, his Defence value is increased by +1 and he can use the Shielding rule.

	F	S	D	A	W	C
Horse	0	3	4	0	1	3

Expert Rider. Eomer is an expert rider. See page 36 for details.

Wargear

Eomer carries a sword and has heavy armour. At an additional cost he may have the following items:

Throwing spear	*5 pts*

Eowyn, Shield Maiden of Rohan (Woman)

Points value: 30

Might: 2
Will: 2
Fate: 2

	F	S	D	A	W	C
Eowyn	4/4+	3	3	1	1	5

Eowyn is the sister of Eomer and King Theoden's niece – and like her kin she is a born fighter. Unwilling to be left behind as her kin ride to battle in Gondor, she disguises herself as a man and joins the host of the Rohirrim.

Armour	*5 pts*
Shield	*5 pts*
Horse	*10 pts*

Armour. If Eowyn wears armour, her Defence value is increased by +1 to 4.

Shield. If Eowyn carries a shield, her Defence value is increased by +1 and she can use the Shielding rule.

	F	S	D	A	W	C
Horse	0	3	4	0	1	3

Wargear

Eowyn has a sword. At an additional cost, she may have the following items:

Throwing spear	*5 pts*

Expert Rider. Eowyn is an expert rider. See page 36 for details.

Captain of Men

Points value: 40

Might: 2
Will: 1
Fate: 1

	F	S	D	A	W	C
Captain of Men	4/4+	4	4	2	2	4

We have included the option for you to have one or more Captains of Gondor or Captains of Rohan. The rules for both are the same so we have just the one entry. Note that you can have more than one Captain of Men if you wish. This represents the leaders amongst the soldiery of Gondor and Rohan who go unnamed in The Lord of The Rings. If you choose Captains of Men invent suitable names for each.

Wargear

The Captain of Men represented by the profile has a sword and no defensive armament. He has been given a Fight value for shooting – if he does not carry a bow then copy this to your record sheet as 4/-. If he is given armour make the necessary adjustment to the model's Defence value.

At an additional cost he may have the following items:

Armour	5 pts
Heavy armour	10 pts
Shield	5 pts
Bow	5 pts

Throwing spear (Captain of Rohan only)	5 pts
Lance (Captain of Gondor only)	5 pts
Horse	10 pts

Armour/Heavy Armour. A model may have either armour or heavy armour – not both. The model must have some visible armour other than a helmet and, in the case of heavy armour, this must extend below the model's waist. A Captain with armour adds +1 to its Defence value, a Captain with heavy armour adds +2 to its Defence value.

Shield. A Captain of Men that carries a shield adds +1 to its Defence value unless the model also carries a bow, in which case it adds nothing. See page 52 for details.

Horse. The rules for horses and riders are given in the main rules section.

	F	S	D	A	W	C
Horse	0	3	4	0	1	3

Expert Rider. Captains of Rohan are expert riders. See page 36 for details.

Elendil (Man)

Points value: 165

Might: 3
Will: 3
Fate: 1

	F	S	D	A	W	C
Elendil	7/-	4	7	3	3	6

High King of the Dúnedain and of Gondor, Elendil led his people to Middle-earth where he met and befriended Gil-galad. One of the mightiest men that ever lived, Elendil's ultimate destiny was to fall before Sauron's might, perishing alongside his friend and ally, Gil-galad, on the slopes of Mount Doom.

Wargear

Elendil wears finely crafted heavy armour and carries the sword Narsil.

Special Rule

Narsil. Narsil is a potent blade. Its powers allow Elendil to fight a heroic combat in the Fight phase without expending Might to do so. See page 49 for rules for heroic combats.

Isildur (Man)

Points value: 100

Might: 3
Will: 1
Fate: 2

	F	S	D	A	W	C
Isildur	6/-	4	7	3	3	6

Isildur was the older son of High King Elendil, ruler of the north kingdom of Gondor. In the final moments of the Last Alliance, he snatched victory from Sauron's grasp and the Ring from his hand. By spurning the advice of the Elves and keeping the Ring, he set events in motion that would not truly conclude for thousands of years.

Wargear

Isildur wears finely crafted heavy armour and carries a sword.

Special Rule

The Ring. If neither Frodo or Bilbo are in the force, Isildur can carry the Ring, in which case the same rules apply as described for Frodo.

Gamling, Captain of Rohan (Man)

Points value: 50

	F	S	D	A	W	C
Gamling	4/–	4	6	2	2	4

Might: 2
Will: 1
Fate: 1

Gamling is a gallant Captain of Rohan, the bearer of the Royal Standard who fights valiantly beside his lord at Helm's Deep.

Wargear

Gamling carries a sword and wears heavy armour. At the additional points shown he can be given the following items of wargear:

Royal Standard of Rohan	*50 pts*
Horse	*10 pts*

Horse. The rules for horses and riders are given in the main rules section.

	F	S	D	A	W	C
Horse	0	3	4	0	1	3

Special Rules

Royal Standard of Rohan. This precious heirloom counts as a normal banner. In addition, any Hero of Rohan who has 0 Might points at the start of the turn automatically adds 1 point Might to his store if he starts the turn within 3"/8cm of the Royal Standard of Rohan. This does not include Gamling himself.

Expert Rider. Gamling is an expert rider. See page 36 for details.

Faramir, Captain of Gondor (Man)

Points value: 70

	F	S	D	A	W	C
Faramir	5/3+	4	5	2	2	5

Might: 3
Will: 2
Fate: 2

Faramir is the son of the Steward of Gondor and the younger brother of Boromir – he is also a brave warrior and the leader of the Rangers of Gondor in the disputed border city of Osgiliath. His men are expert forest fighters who are able to merge into and move amongst the undergrowth undetected, ambushing enemy columns and putting the foe to flight with clouds of well aimed arrows.

Wargear

He carries a sword and wears sturdy leather armour. At an additional cost he may have the following items:

Heavy armour	*5 pts*
Bow	*5 pts*
Lance	*5 pts*
Horse	*10 pts*

Armour/Heavy Armour. A model may have either armour or heavy armour – not both. If Faramir wears heavy armour he adds +1 to his Defence value, to a total of 6.

Horse. The rules for horses and riders are given in the main rules section.

	F	S	D	A	W	C
Horse	0	3	4	0	1	3

Damrod, Captain of the Rangers of Gondor (Human)

Points value: 50

	F	S	D	A	W	C
Damrod	4/3+	4	5	2	2	4

Might: 2
Will: 1
Fate: 1

Damrod is Faramir's Captain – a strong arm in a fight and deadly shot with a bow.

Wargear

Damrod carries a bow and sword, and wears sturdy leather armour.

Gandalf the White (Wizard)

Points value: 200

Might: 3

	F	S	D	A	W	C
Gandalf	5/-	5	6	1	3	7

Will: 6+1 free per turn

Fate: 3

After his cataclysmic battle with the Balrog, Gandalf returns to Middle-earth in the new guise of Gandalf the White. Now his powers are greater than ever before, surpassing even his old master Saruman.

Note. Your force can only include one Gandalf – Gandalf the Grey or Gandalf the White.

Wargear

Gandalf carries his staff and a sword (hand weapon). He can use either to fight with – his staff is a two-handed weapon. At an additional cost, he may have the following:

Elven cloak	*10 pts*
Shadowfax	*15 pts*

Shadowfax. The mightiest of the noble horses of Rohan, Shadowfax may only be ridden by Gandalf. He follows all the rules for horses, except his movement is 12"/28cm.

	F	S	D	A	W	C
Shadowfax	0	4	5	0	1	5

Special Rules

Staff of Power. Gandalf's staff is not only a symbol of his authority but a potent talisman. To represent his staff's power he can expend 1 point of Will each turn without reducing his own Will store.

Magical Powers

Terrifying Aura. Dice score to use: 2+. This power enables Gandalf to assume a terrifying aura. Once this has been successfully cast Gandalf counts as terrifying to all Evil creatures so long as he has at least 1 point of Will left. If Gandalf's Will drops to 0 the terrifying aura is extinguished. See the Courage section for details on terror.

Will of Iron. Range 12"/28cm. Dice score to use: 3+. Gandalf can use this spell to restore one point of Will to a friendly Hero within range. The target's Will is increased by 1, up to the starting amount shown on the model's profile. The Hero's Will can always be restored to a minimum of 1 even if the Hero had an original Will value of 0. Gandalf cannot use this magical power to restore his own Will.

Cast Blinding Light. Dice score to use: 2+. This power enables Gandalf to cause his staff to glow brilliantly. In darkness this illuminates an area 12"/28cm around him and anyone within this area can be seen as if it were daylight. Once cast this power lasts for the rest of the game so long as Gandalf has at least 1 point of Will remaining. If Gandalf's Will drops to 0 the staff is extinguished. Because of the staff's brightness any enemy shooting at Gandalf or at a target within 6"/14cm of Gandalf will require a roll of 6 to score a hit.

Effortlessly Immobilise. Range 12"/28cm. Dice score to use: 2+. The victim can do nothing further that turn. In combat his Fight value counts as 1 and he rolls one dice regardless of how many Attacks he normally has. If he wins a combat he will not strike. If he loses, he must back away as normal. The victim can still use Might, Will and Fate but cannot make heroic actions. The effect lasts for the remainder of that turn.

Instantly Command. Range 12"/28cm. Dice score to use 3+. The victim can do nothing further that turn as described for Effortlessly Immobilise, except that the Good player can move the victim up to half a move as soon as the power takes effect, even into base contact with an enemy (there is no need for a Courage test in order to charge a terrifying enemy). The player can do this even if the model has already moved that turn. The model cannot be moved out of a combat if it is already engaged. The model cannot be forced to perform any actions that would cause direct harm to the model (such as jumping down a cliff…).

Your Staff is Broken! Range 12"/28cm. Dice score to use: 3+. This power enables Gandalf to destroy the staff of Saruman, effectively relieving him from the position of master of their Order. Once this power has been successfully cast, Saruman loses all the advantages related with his staff (both the free point of Will and the possibility of using the staff as a two-handed weapon).

Ultimate Sorcerous Blast. Range 12"/28cm. Dice score to use: 4+. This power can be used against a single enemy model. There must be no other models from either side obscuring Gandalf's view of the target but partially obscuring cover is ignored. If the power is employed successfully the target is blasted directly away from Gandalf and knocked to the ground – roll a dice, add +2, and move the target that number of inches or double that number of centimeters (3-8" or 6-16cm). Except as noted below any other models that lie within the path of the blasted model are automatically moved aside and are also knocked to the ground. If the target or one of the models lying within the path of the target is fighting then all other models in the same fight are knocked to the ground whether friends or foe. The target model counts as having been struck one blow at a Strength value of 6, and every other model that is knocked to the ground is struck one blow at a Strength of 3 whether friend or foe. If a model with a Strength of 5 or less is blasted into a model which has a Strength of 6 or more, it stops immediately. The model with Strength 6 or more is not moved or knocked to the ground, but it is struck one blow from the impact as normal. If the model blasted away has a Strength of 6 or more, then it will affect any other model along its path.

"Stand firm!"

Treebeard (Ent)

Points value: 170

	F	S	D	A	W	C
Treebeard	8/4+	8	8	3	3	7

Might: 3
Will: 6
Fate: 3

Treebeard is the greatest of all the ancient race of Ents that roamed the forests of Middle-earth before even the Elves came and made their homes. Ents are giants that resemble nothing so much as trees, having lived for so many years in the forests and having become rather like the trees that they love. Ents care little for the world that is beyond the forest realm of Fangorn but the destruction of their beloved woodlands drives them into a raging fury of destruction.

Special Rules

Break Stone. Ents are powerful creatures with iron-hard limbs that can smash apart stone just as tree roots can crumble rock. When attacking fortifications, including doors, stone walls, towers and anything else that has Batter points, Treebeard counts his Strength as 10 and Attacks as 6.

Terror. In their fury the Ents are a truly terrifying sight. Treebeard evokes terror in the enemy, as described in the Courage section of the rules.

Throw Stone. Ents are creatures of great strength, able to tear rocks out of the ground and hurl them across the battlefield with crushing force. To represent this, if an Ent does not move at all he can rip a suitable rock from the ground (provided he's not engaged in combat) and in the subsequent Shoot phase he can throw it. This works exactly like a crossbow with a range of 18"/42cm and a Strength of 10. If the Good player wishes, this rock can be hurled at a castle wall or other building. If this is the case, the Good player nominates a target point and rolls to hit and to wound as normal. If the shot causes sufficient damage to create a breach, the breach occurs at the point the shot was aimed at.

"To Isengard with doom we come!"

The King of the Dead (Man)

Points value: 75

	F	S	D	A	W	C
King of the Dead	4/-	4	8	1	2	8

Might: 0
Will: 6
Fate: 3

A ghostly echo of the man that once was, this ancient king has sworn to lead his army into the fight against Sauron as penance for refusing to do so many centuries before.

Wargear

The King of the Dead carries a rusty sword and wears ancient armour.

Special Rules

Terror. The cursed King of the Army of the Dead evokes terror in the enemy, as described in the Courage section of the rules.

Blades of the Dead. The swords of the Dead have long lost their edge, and yet armour is of scarce use against them – the only defence is a brave heart. When determining what number the Dead need to wound their opponents, use the opponent's Courage rather than its Defence on the Wound chart. For example, when rolling to wound against an Orc archer, the King's Strength of 4 is cross-referenced on the Wound chart not with the Orc's Defence of 4, but with the Orc's Courage of 2 (so the King needs only a 3+ to wound the Orc).

Drain Soul. An enemy that suffers a wound from the King of the Dead is automatically slain regardless of the number of wounds on its profile. Heroes can use Fate to recover wounds suffered from the King but if even a single wound is not recovered, they are slain.

Denethor, Steward of Gondor (Man)

Points value: 15

	F	S	D	A	W	C
Denethor	5/-	4	5	2	2	5

Might: 0
Will: 3
Fate: 0

Once a great man, the Steward of Gondor is now weary with the responsibility of leading his people during such dark times. The loss of his favourite son Boromir, upon whom the old man had placed what little hope he had left, has proven an almost unbearable pain, seriously threatening the health of Denethor's mind.

Wargear

Denethor carries a sword and wears armour.

Special Rule

Broken Mind. Denethor is subject to dangerous fits of madness. At the start of every turn, before players roll for priority, the Good player must take a Courage test for Denethor. If the test is passed, all is fine. If the test is failed, Denethor is controlled by the Evil player as if he was one of his models. The only difference with other Evil models is that Good models cannot target Denethor with missile fire, magical powers that cause damage and cannot strike blows against him if they win a fight against him.

Gwaihir (Giant Eagle)

Points value: 75

	F	S	D	A	W	C
Gwaihir	8/-	5	8	2	3	6

Might: 1
Will: 1
Fate: 1

Whilst imprisoned in the Tower of Orthanc Gandalf sought Gwaihir's aid to make his escape. Riding upon the back of the huge eagle, Gandalf fled the clutches of Saruman.

Special Rules

Fly. Gwaihir moves by flying – his move is 12"/28cm. The Giant Eagle can fly over the top of any models or terrain without penalty. He cannot enter woods, buildings and other terrain that has been deemed impassable, but can land on top of any of these if the players so agree at the beginning of the game. Because it is not possible to fly underground, Gwaihir cannot take part in any scenarios that take place in Moria or other subterranean area.

Monstrous mount. Gwaihir can only be included in the army if Gandalf or Radagast is also included and can be ridden only by one of the two Wizards (though he will allow them to choose a passenger). Note that Gwaihir cannot pick up or use weapons or other objects.

Gwaihir and the Ring. Gwaihir will not carry the Ringbearer – we must assume that the whispering evil of the Ring is too powerful for his animal mind to conquer.

GOOD WARRIORS

High Elf Warrior

Points value: 9

	F	S	D	A	W	C
High Elf	6/3+	3	5	1	1	5

The High Elves are the deadliest warriors in all of Middle-earth, combining skill-at-arms with expertly fashioned wargear. They are proficient with swords, spears and bows, and are the bravest of all fighting troops.

Above is the base profile for a High Elf warrior. If the warrior does not carry a bow then miss out the 3+ value when you copy out the profile – ie, the Fight characteristic for a warrior without bow would be 6/-. The base profile might also change if the warrior carries a shield as noted opposite.

Wargear

The base profile for a High Elf warrior includes finely wrought Elven heavy armour. He can be given additional items at the following cost:

Elf blade	*1 pt*
Spear	*1 pt*
Elf bow	*2 pt*
Shield	*1 pt*
Banner	*35 pts**

*(max. one per Hero included in the same force)

Shield. A High Elf warrior that carries a shield adds +1 to its Defence value unless the model also carries a bow, in which case it adds nothing. See page 52 for details.

Banner. See the relevant rules on page 55.

Wood Elf Warrior

Points value: 7

	F	S	D	A	W	C
Wood Elf	6/3+	3	3	1	1	5

The Wood Elves are proficient with swords, spears and bows, and combine their skill-at-arms with great bravery.

Above is the base profile for a Wood Elf warrior. If the warrior does not carry a bow then miss out the 3+ value when you copy out the profile – ie, the Fight characteristic for a warrior without a bow would be 6/-. The Defence value might also change if the warrior wears armour or carries a shield as noted below.

Wargear

The base profile for a Wood Elf warrior does not include any equipment. He can be given additional items at the following cost:

Elf Blade	*1 pt*
Spear	*1 pt*
Elf bow	*2 pt*
Shield	*1 pt*
Armour	*1 pt*
Banner	*35 pts**

*(max. one per Hero included in the same force)

Armour. A Wood Elf warrior that wears armour adds +1 to its Defence value, giving a value of 4.

Shield. A Wood Elf warrior that carries a shield adds +1 to its Defence value unless the model also carries a bow, in which case it adds nothing. See page 52 for details.

Banner. See the relevant rules on page 55.

Warrior of Gondor (Man)

Points value: 6

	F	S	D	A	W	C
Warrior of Gondor	3/4+	3	4	1	1	3

The soldiery of Gondor have ever been embroiled in the struggle against the Dark Lord, meeting his armies with courageous hearts and blades of tempered steel.

This is the base profile for a warrior of Gondor. If the warrior does not carry a bow then miss out the 4+ when you copy out the profile – ie, the Fight value for a warrior without bow would be 3/-. The Defence value might also change if the warrior carries a shield as noted opposite.

Wargear

The base profile for a Gondor warrior includes armour and a sword (hand weapon). Any warrior can be given additional items at the following extra cost:

Spear	1 pt
Bow	1 pt
Shield	1 pt
Banner	25 pts*

(max. one per Hero included in the same force)

Shield. A warrior that carries a shield adds +1 to its Defence value unless the model also carries a bow, in which case it adds nothing. See page 52 for details.

Banner. See the relevant rules on page 55.

Warrior of Rohan (Man)

Points value: 6

	F	S	D	A	W	C
Warrior of Rohan	3/4+	3	4	1	1	3

The land of Rohan lies to the west of Minas Tirith and north of the White Mountains. Allies of Gondor since the earliest days of their realm, the men of Rohan have always been ready to go to their aid in time of war.

This is the base profile for a warrior of Rohan. If the warrior does not carry a bow or throwing spears, miss out the 4+ value when you copy out the profile – ie, the Fight characteristic for a warrior without bow would be 3/-. The Defence value might also change if the warrior carries a shield as noted opposite.

Wargear

The base profile for a Rohan warrior includes armour and a sword or axe (hand weapon). Any warrior can be given additional items at the following extra cost:

Throwing spears	1 pt
Bow	1 pt
Shield	1 pt
Banner	25 pts*

(max. one per Hero included in the same force)

Shield. A warrior that carries a shield adds +1 to its Defence value unless the model also carries a bow, in which case it adds nothing. See page 52 for details.

Banner. See the relevant rules on page 55.

No enemy has yet taken the Hornburg.

Rider of Rohan (Man)

Points value: 13

	F	S	D	A	W	C
Rider of Rohan	3/4+	3	5	1	1	3
Horse	0	3	4	0	1	3

The Riders of Rohan are horse-masters beyond compare, renowned for their great skill and bravery.

This is the base profile for a Rider of Rohan. Note that all Riders of Rohan carry a bow and a shield as well as a sword or axe (hand weapon).

Wargear

The base profile for a Rider of Rohan includes armour, shield, a bow, and either a sword or axe (hand weapon). Any warrior can be given the following:

Throwing spears	*1 pt*
Banner	*25 pts**

*(max. one per Hero included in the same force)

Special Rule

Expert Riders. The Riders of Rohan are expert riders. See page 36 for details.

Theoden leads his people to battle.

Rohan Royal Guard (Man)

Points value: 9

	F	S	D	A	W	C
Royal Guard	4/4+	3	6	1	1	3

Hand-picked from the very best warriors in all of Rohan, the Royal Guard are sworn to give their lives in the service of their king and to fight without fear. They wear intricately crafted heavy armour and carry the best weaponry that the armouries of Rohan have to offer.

This is the base profile for a Rohan Royal Guard. If the Guardsman does not carry a throwing spear, then miss out the 4+ Shoot value when you copy the profile to your record sheet.

Wargear

The base profile for a Royal Guard includes heavy armour, shield and a sword (hand weapon). He can be given the following:

Throwing spears	*1 pt*
Horse	*6 pts*
Banner	*25 pts**

*(max. one per Hero included in the same force)

	F	S	D	A	W	C
Horse	0	3	4	0	1	3

Banner. See the relevant rules on page 51.

Special Rules

Bodyguard. At the beginning of the game, choose one Hero of Rohan among those in your force for the Guard to protect. As long as this Hero is on the table, all Royal Guard models automatically pass all Courage tests they have to take. If the Hero is killed or leaves the table, the Royal Guard revert to the normal rules for Courage.

Expert Riders. The Royal Guard are expert riders. See page 36 for details.

Ranger of Gondor (Man)

Points value: 7

	F	S	D	A	W	C
Human	4/3+	3	4	1	1	3

The Rangers of Gondor are hand-picked from the inhabitants of Ithilien for their skill at woodcraft and archery. In the waning years of the Third Age, the Rangers constitute the first line of defence against the hordes of Mordor, holding the crossings of the Anduin against the servants of Sauron.

Wargear

The base profile for a Ranger of Gondor includes a sword (hand weapon), a bow and tough leather armour. Any warrior can be given additional items at the following extra cost:

Spear   *1 pt*

Warrior of Minas Tirith (Man)

Points value: 7

	F	S	D	A	W	C
Human	3/4+	3	5	1	1	3

The men of Minas Tirith have lived their whole lives under the shadow in the east, never faltering. It is through their valour that the lands beyond Gondor have been kept safe from Sauron's armies.

This is the base profile for a warrior of Minas Tirith – the best equipped soldiers in the whole of Gondor. If the warrior does not carry a bow then miss out the 4+ when you copy out the profile – ie, the Fight value for a warrior without bow would be 3/-. The Defence value might also change if the warrior carries a shield as noted opposite.

Wargear

The base profile for a Warrior includes heavy armour and a sword (hand weapon). Any warrior can be given additional items at the following extra cost:

Spear	*1 pt*
Bow	*1 pt*
Shield	*1 pt*
Banner	*25 pts**

*(maximum one per Hero included in the same force)

Shield. A warrior that carries a shield adds +1 to its Defence value unless the model also carries a bow, in which case it adds nothing. See page 52 for details.

Banner. See the relevant rules on page 55.

Guard of the Fountain Court (Man)

Points value: 10

	F	S	D	A	W	C
Guard of the Fountain Court	4/-	3	6	1	1	3

The Guard of the Fountain Court are selected from the very best warriors in all of Gondor, swearing to give their lives in the service of the lords of Minas Tirith and to be fearless in combat. They wear winged helmets made of mithril, intricately crafted heavy armour and carry the best weaponry that the armouries of the White City have to offer.

Wargear

The base profile for a Guard includes heavy armour and a spear. Any warrior can be given additional items at the following cost:

Shield   *1 pt*

Banner   *25 pts**

*(maximum one per Hero included in the same force)

Shield. A warrior that carries a shield adds +1 to its Defence. See page 52 for details.

Special Rules

Bodyguard. At the beginning of the game, choose one Hero of Gondor among those in your force for the Guard to protect. As long as this Hero is on the table, all Guard models automatically pass all Courage tests they have to take. If the Hero is killed or leaves the table, the Guard revert to the normal rules for Courage.

Banner. See the relevant rules on page 55.

"The out-companies with great cheer turned and smote their pursuers."

Knights of Minas Tirith (Man)

Points value: 13

	F	S	D	A	W	C
Knight of Minas Tirith	3/-	3	5	1	1	3
Horse	0	3	4	0	1	3

Tall, stern warriors mounted on swift steeds and bearing keen lances, the Knights of Minas Tirith are truly the pride of Gondor.

Wargear

The base profile for a Knight of Minas Tirith includes heavy armour, a lance and a sword (hand weapon). Any warrior can be given extra items at the following cost:

Banner   *25 pts**
*(maximum one per Hero included in the same force)

Banner. See the relevant rules on page 55.

The Army of the Dead (Man)

Points value: 15

	F	S	D	A	W	C
Warrior of the Dead	3/-	3	7	1	1	8

The oath-breakers of Erech now fight at Aragorn's side against Sauron. Only in doing this will the curse Isildur placed upon them many years ago be lifted.

Wargear

Being incorporeal creatures, the Warriors of the Dead count as armed only with hand weapons regardless of the actual equipment they are carrying, so the rules for their spears, two-handed axes and shields do not apply.

Special Rules

Blades of the Dead. The weapons of the Dead have long lost their edge, and yet armour is of scarce use against them – the only defence is a brave heart. When determining what number the Dead need to wound their opponents, use the opponent's Courage rather than its Defence on the Wound chart. For example, when rolling to wound against an Orc archer, a Warrior of the Dead's Strength of 3 is cross-referenced on the Wound chart not with the Orc's Defence of 4, but with the Orc's Courage of 2 (so the Warrior of the Dead needs only a 4+ to wound the Orc).

Terror. The ghastly warriors of the Army of the Dead evoke terror in the enemy, as described in the Courage section of the rules.

FANGORN & ISENGARD

At the southern end of the Misty Mountains are two strongholds of great power. Saruman's army musters in Isengard, a fortress of stone and iron. Not far away, the forest of Fangorn is where the Ents, the tree-shepherds of old, still walk the earth.

Treebeard, one of the oldest creatures in the whole Middle-earth.

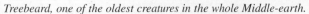

Radagast and Treebeard form an alliance against a common foe.

"And here you will stay, Gandalf the Grey, and rest from journeys. For I am Saruman the Wise, Saruman Ring-maker, Saruman of Many Colours!"

- Saruman to Gandalf, The Fellowship of The Ring

The captains of Isengard rally their troops.

Saruman the White.

You do not know pain, you do not know fear. You will taste man-flesh!

FORCES OF DARKNESS

Use this list to choose an Evil force to the points value you have agreed with your opponent.

HEROES

The Dark Lord Sauron

Points value: 400

	F	S	D	A	W	C
Sauron	9/-	8	10	3	5	7

Might: 3
Will: 3 per turn
Fate: Special (see below)

Sauron, the Dark Lord, the Enemy, the Lord of the Ring. He is driven by a consuming desire to dominate all of Middle-earth and by a burning hatred of Elves, Men and all who stand in his way. In distant times, when he still hadn't revealed his evil nature, he forged the Rings of Power and gave them as gifts to the rulers of the free races of Middle-earth. These kings didn't know that Sauron also forged the Ruling Ring for himself, imbuing into it a great portion of his own life force and powers. Through this mighty tool, Sauron could control the other Rings and enslave their bearers to his will. Only the Rings of the Elves he couldn't dominate, because he had no part in their making. His vast armies of Orcs and other fell creatures were about to subjugate all the Western realms of Middle-earth, but the Last Alliance of Men and Elves defeated his hordes and finally laid siege to his fortress of Barad-dûr in the land of Mordor. There, at a terrible price, the One Ring was taken from the hand of the Dark Lord and he was finally vanquished. But Sauron was not destroyed. As long as the Ring exists, Sauron's spirit endures.

Wargear

Sauron carries a mace (hand weapon) and is equipped with heavy armour. At an additional points cost, he can be given the One Ring (if only it was that easy!).

The One Ring   *100 pts*

The One Ring. As long as the One Ring is with him, the Dark Lord is all but invincible. Only by taking the Ring from him can he be defeated. This is represented by the fact that Sauron does not have points of Fate as such, but every time he is killed he can roll a dice. On a roll of 2 or more, the power of the Ring sustains him and he is left on the table with only one Wound remaining. Therefore, the only way to take down the Dark Lord is to cause him to lose all his wounds and then hope he rolls a 1 and does not recover his last one. This rare occurrence represents the last wounding strike actually separating the Ring from the Dark Lord (chopping his fingers off, for example).

Special Rules

Terror. Sauron is the living incarnation of all the fears of the free people of Middle-earth. He evokes terror in his enemies as described in the Courage section.

Master of Evil. All the servants of the Enemy fear the anger of their Lord far more than a simple death at the hands of their opponents. Similarly, the Good side's forces know that they are facing the ultimate Evil and are prepared to sell their lives to

defeat it once and for all. If Sauron is on the table, neither side needs to test for Courage if their forces are reduced to 50% of their original numbers.

Unstoppable! The power of the Ring is so great that to face the Dark Lord in combat is almost invariably to face one's death. Every time Sauron wins a fight against multiple opponents, he can choose to strike at the enemy three times as normal or to sweep his mace around in a deadly arc. If Sauron chooses this second option, all the enemies that have taken part in the fight (those in base contact and even those supporting friendly models with spears or pikes) suffer one strike from the Dark Lord.

Magical Powers

Sauron can use 3 points of Will per turn to cast magical powers and to resist the effect of magic. He has the following powers:

Transfix. Range 18"/42cm. Dice score to use: 2+. The victim can do nothing further that turn. In combat, his Fight value counts as 1 and he rolls one dice regardless of how many attacks he normally has. If he wins a combat he will not strike. The victim can still use Might, Will and Fate but cannot make heroic actions. The effect lasts for the remainder of that turn.

Compel. Range 18"/42cm. Dice score to use: 3+. The victim can do nothing further that turn as described for Transfix, except that the Evil player can move the victim up to half a move as soon as the power takes effect, even into base contact with an enemy (there is no need for a Courage test in order to charge a terrifying enemy). The player can do this even if the model has already moved that turn. The model cannot be moved out of a combat if it is already engaged. The model cannot be forced to do anything that would cause direct harm to it (like jumping down a cliff…).

Drain Courage. Range 18"/42cm. Dice score to use: 2+. The victim loses 1 point of Courage. This penalty applies for the rest of the battle. This ability can take effect several times on the same target, reducing the model's Courage value each time.

Sap Will. Range 18"/42cm. Dice score to use: 3+. The victim's Will value is reduced to 0. The effect lasts for the remainder of the battle – although it can be increased by the Strengthen Will or Will of Iron magical powers.

Chill Soul. Range 18"/42cm. Dice score to use: 5+. With a single gaze, the Dark Lord can drain all life force from his enemies. The victim suffers a wound, exactly as if wounded in close combat. If a cavalry model fails to resist this power, Sauron can choose whether the rider, the mount or a passenger will suffer the wound.

"It was no mere brigand or Orc-chieftain that ordered the assault upon the Lord of Mordor's greatest foe. A power and mind of malice guided it."

The Ringwraiths

Points value: 140 for the Witch King
120 each for the other Ringwraiths

	F	S	D	A	W	C
Witch King	5/-	4	8	1	1	6
Ringwraiths	5/-	4	8	1	1	6

Witch King/Ringwraith
Might: 3/2
Will: 20/14
Fate: 3/2

The nine Ringwraiths were once Kings of Men, the bearers of magical rings created by Sauron. Their rings granted endless life but gradually enslaved the Kings to Sauron's will. All that remains of them now are their twisted spirits – their bodies having faded into empty nothingness. They are the most deadly of all Sauron's captains and the most dangerous of the nine is the Witch King.

The Witch King is the leader of the Ringwraiths. Like the others, he is cloaked and armoured, and has no physical body but only a shadow-like existence held together by the force of his will.

Ringwraiths cannot be killed in the normal sense because they are not alive – but they can be banished. A Ringwraith that has been banished in this way will gradually reform as its embittered will shapes a new form for it to inhabit. This takes many days depending upon how far the Ringwraiths are from the influence of their master.

Wargear

The nine Ringwraiths carry wicked swords or maces (hand weapons). At an additional points cost, they can ride a horse or a Fell Beast, and the Witch King can also be armed with a Morgul blade.

Horse	*10 pts each Ringwraith*
Fell Beast	*60 pts each Ringwraith*
Morgul blade	*10 pts (Witch King only)*

Horse. The Ringwraiths ride huge black horses that carry them over Middle-earth as they search for their master's ring. Only a Ringwraith can ride these evil beasts – they will not permit any other creature to mount them. Rules for horses and riders are given in the main rules section.

	F	S	D	A	W	C
Horse	0	3	4	0	1	3

Fell Beast. Only a Ringwraith can ride these evil creatures – they will not permit anything else to mount them. Rules for cavalry are given in the main rules section. If the Ringwraith riding them is killed or dismounts, they will always take to the air and flee the field.

Special Rules for the Fell Beast

Fly. A Fell Beast moves by flying – its move is 12"/28cm. It can fly over the top of any models or terrain without penalty. It cannot enter woods, buildings and other terrain that has been deemed impassable, but can land on top of any of these if the players so agree at the beginning of the game. Fell beasts cannot be used in scenarios that take place in Moria or other subterranean area.

Monstrous Mount. A Fell Beast can carry a single rider. The usual rules for Monstrous Mounts apply.

Note that a Fell Beast cannot pick up or use weapons or other objects – it cannot shoot a bow, for example.

	F	S	D	A	W	C
Fell Beast	5	6	6	2	3	3

A Ringwraith prowls Osgiliath

Morgul Blade. Only the Witch King can carry a Morgul blade. This evil weapon is both magical and poisonous – a deep wound leaves a tainted shard from its blade in the foe's flesh. If the Witch King inflicts a wound on a model that has 2 or more Wounds, the player can use the Morgul blade. The blade can only be used once – afterwards its deadly tip is broken. The enemy who has suffered the wound now has a shard of the blade embedded in their body, and will lose a further wound at the start of each successive turn if they roll a 1 on a dice. Make this roll at the start of each turn before the Priority phase until the game is over or the victim is slain.

Might cannot be used to affect this roll, but Fate can be used to 'save' the wound, and Might can be used to boost the Fate roll as normal.

It is up to the Evil player to remind the opponent to test for the Morgul blade, if this is forgotten the shard simply had no effect that turn.

Note on choosing Ringwraiths. As there are eight ordinary Ringwraiths the Evil player can have up to eight ordinary Ringwraiths in his force. The Ringwraiths are not named – we suggest you paint a number under the base of each so that you can readily distinguish them on your record sheet. There is only one Witch King.

Special Rules

Will. Ringwraiths rely on Will far more than other Heroes. It is only by Will that they maintain corporeal form. The further they are from Sauron, the weaker is the bond between them and the lower their Will value. Therefore:

A Ringwraith must give up 1 point of Will at the end of the Fight phase if it has been in a fight. Note that Ringwraiths touching enemy must fight – as all models must – they cannot choose not to fight!

Once a Ringwraith suffers 1 Wound or has 0 Will remaining, it is banished. Ringwraiths cannot be destroyed completely in this way – their spirits slowly regenerate – but as this takes several days they are removed as casualties.

Terror. Ringwraiths are terrifying supernatural creatures. They evoke terror in their enemies as described in the Courage section.

Darkness. Ringwraiths do not see by the light of the world as we know it, but by the inner light of the life of living things. They are not affected by darkness and can see as well in pitch black as they can in daylight.

Ringwraiths and the Ring. If any Hero should put on the Ring then he becomes part of the twilight world of the Ringwraiths. He is both visible and vulnerable to them! A Hero wearing the Ring is not invisible to a Ringwraith as he is to other models. A Ringwraith does not have to give up Will if he is fighting against a model wearing the Ring – not even if other enemy are included as part of a multiple combat.

To represent this in a pleasing visual way, all Ringwraith models can be replaced by Twilight Ringwraith models as soon as the Ring is put on. The Twilight Ringwraiths are used whilst the Ring is worn. This is not necessary – but it certainly emphasises the point!

Magical Powers

Ringwraiths can also employ their Will to use magical powers and to resist the effect of magic just like other Heroes. They have the following powers:

Transfix. Range 12"/28cm. Dice score to use: 3+. The victim can do nothing further that turn. In combat, his Fight value counts as 1 and he rolls one dice regardless of how many Attacks he normally has. If he wins a combat he will not strike. The victim can still use Might, Will and Fate but cannot make heroic actions. The effect lasts for the remainder of that turn.

Compel. Range 12"/28cm. Dice score to use: 4+. The victim can do nothing further that turn as described for Transfix, except that the Evil player can move the victim up to half a move as soon as the power takes effect, even into base contact with an enemy (there is no need for a Courage test in order to charge a terrifying enemy). The player can do this even if the model has already moved that turn. The model cannot be moved out of a combat if it is already engaged. The model cannot be forced to perform any actions that would cause direct harm to it (such as jumping down a cliff…). If the victim has the Ring, he must put it on if the Evil player wishes.

Drain Courage. Range 12"/28cm. Dice score to use: 2+. The victim loses 1 point of Courage from his characteristic profile. This penalty applies for the rest of the battle. This ability can take effect several times on the same target – reducing a model's Courage value each time.

Sap Will. Range 12"/28cm. Dice score to use: 4+. The victim's Will value is reduced to 0. The effect lasts for the remainder of the battle – although it can be increased by the Strengthen Will or Will of Iron magical powers.

Black Dart. Range 12"/28cm. Dice score to use: 5+. The victim suffers a hit with a Strength of 9. If a cavalry model fails to resist this power, the Ringwraith can choose whether the Dart hits the rider, any passenger or the mount.

The Balrog

	F	S	D	A	W	C
Balrog	10/-	8	10	4	10	7

The Balrog is a mighty creature of great age and power – a monster of a rare and horrific kind. Of all the evil powers in the world it is amongst the most potent and formidable.

Special Rules

Lash. The Balrog has 4 Attacks, of which one is a special 'lash' attack with its long whip. When rolling for strikes use a different colour dice to represent the lash. If the Lash strike roll is sufficient to cause a wound the enemy is momentarily entangled in the whip. This allows the Balrog to make a further two strikes against the model with its fiery blade (hand weapon). That means a Balrog can sometimes make six strikes if it wins a fight – four strikes plus a further two strikes against an entangled enemy.

Terror. The Balrog is a huge terrifying monster! An enemy wishing to charge the Balrog must test its courage as described in the Courage rules.

Will. The Balrog is a magical creature and can shrug off the effects of all but the most potent sorcery. Instead of expending Will to resist magical attacks it always resists magic with the same number of dice as it has wounds left.

Goblin Mastery. Moria Goblins are far more frightened of the Balrog than of any enemy. If the Balrog is in the game Moria Goblins will automatically pass any Courage test they would normally be required to take. For example, this applies to the Courage test made because Boromir is blowing his horn – making Boromir's horn useless in this situation.

"From out of the shadow a red sword leapt gleaming."

Saruman (Wizard)

	F	S	D	A	W	C
Saruman	5/-	4	5	1	3	7

Saruman the White is the leader of the Order of Wizards and the most learned in the ways of Sauron the Enemy. But his studies have led him to dream of dominion, and by daring to look into the dread Palantir of Orthanc he has seen many dark and evil things that have stirred his greed and ambition. Now he would dare rise and take even Sauron's crown, but the truth is that his soul is already in thrall to the evil lord.

Wargear

Saruman carries his staff and a sword (hand weapon). He can use either his sword or staff to fight – his staff is a two-handed weapon.

Special Rules

Staff of Power. Saruman's staff is not only a symbol of his power but a potent talisman. Whilst he wields his staff Saruman can expend 1 point of Will each turn without reducing his own Will store.

Voice of Command. Such is the fear of failure that Saruman inspires in his followers that they will often fight to the last man if his eye is upon them. To represent this, the range of Saruman's 'Stand fast!' rolls is 12"/28cm rather than 6"/14cm.

Palantir. Saruman carries the Palantir, an ancient seeing stone that allows him to draw a line of sight to any point on the battlefield. Using the Palantir, Saruman can use his Effortlessly Immobilise and Instantly Command powers against any enemy on the battlefield. Saruman can only use the Palantir so long as he has at least 1 point of Will remaining in his store. If he has no Will left then he cannot use the Palantir even though his staff enables him to continue to use his magical powers.

Magical Powers

Terrifying Aura. Dice score to use: 2+. This power enables Saruman to assume a terrifying aura. Once this power has been successfully cast Saruman counts as terrifying to all enemies as long as he has at least 1 point of Will remaining. If his Will drops to 0 the terrifying aura is extinguished. See the Courage section of the rules for more about terror.

Sorcerous Blast. Range 12"/28cm. Dice score to use: 5+. This power can be used against a single enemy model. There must be no other models from either side obscuring Saruman's view of the target but partially obscuring cover is ignored. If the power is employed successfully the target is blasted directly away from Saruman and knocked to the ground – roll a dice and move the target that number of inches or double that number of centimetres (1"-6" or 2cm-12cm). Except as noted below any other models that lie within the path of the blasted model are automatically moved aside and knocked to the ground. If the target or one of the models lying within the path of the target is fighting, then all other models in the same fight are knocked to the ground whether friends or foe. The target model counts as having been struck one blow at a Strength value of 5 and every model knocked to the ground is struck one blow at a Strength value of 3. If a model with a Strength of 5 or less is blasted into a model which has a Strength of 6 or more, it stops immediately. The model with Strength 6 or more is not moved or knocked to the ground, but it is struck one blow from the impact as normal. If the model blasted away has a Strength of 6 or more, then it will affect any other model along its path. Eg, if the Balrog is blasted into a Goblin it will knock it to the ground but if a Goblin is blasted into the Balrog, the demon won't budge.

Effortlessly Immobilise. Range 12"/28cm. Dice score to use: 2+. The victim can do nothing further that turn. In combat his Fight value counts as 1 and he rolls one dice regardless of how many Attacks he normally has. If he wins a combat he will not strike. The victim can still use Might, Will and Fate but cannot make heroic actions. The effect lasts for the remainder of that turn.

Instantly Command. Range 12"/28cm. Dice score to use 3+. The victim can do nothing further that turn as described for Effortlessly Immobilise, except that the Evil player can move the victim up to half a move as soon as the power takes effect, even into base contact with an enemy (there is no need for a Courage test in order to charge a terrifying enemy). The player can do this even if the model has already moved that turn. The model cannot be moved out of a combat if it is already engaged. The model cannot be forced to perform any actions that would cause direct harm to the model (such as jumping down a cliff…).

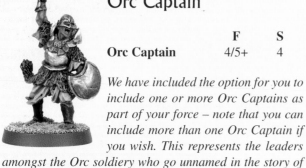

Orc Captain

Points value: 40
Might: 2
Will: 1
Fate: 1

	F	S	D	A	W	C
Orc Captain	4/5+	4	5	2	2	3

We have included the option for you to include one or more Orc Captains as part of your force – note that you can include more than one Orc Captain if you wish. This represents the leaders amongst the Orc soldiery who go unnamed in the story of The Lord of The Rings – the incidental warriors whose role on the battlefield is important in any war. If you choose Captains invent suitable names for each.

Wargear

The Orc Captain represented by the profile has a sword and wears crude Orcish armour. He has been given a Fight value for shooting – if he does not carry a bow then copy this to your record sheet as 4/-. If he is given further armour make the necessary adjustment to the model's Defence value. At an additional cost he may have the following items and ride a Warg:

Shield	*5 pts*
Orc Bow	*5 pts*
Warg	*10 pts*
Throwing spears	*5 pts (only if mounted on a Warg)*

Shield. An Orc Captain which carries a shield adds +1 to its Defence unless the model also carries a bow, in which case it adds nothing. See page 52 for details.

	F	S	D	A	W	C
Warg	0/-	4	4	0	1	2

Moria Goblin Captain

Points value: 35
Might: 2
Will: 1
Fate: 1

	F	S	D	A	W	C
Goblin Captain	3/5+	4	5	2	2	3

We have included the option for you to include one or more Moria Goblin Captains as part of your force – note that you can include more than one Captain if you wish. This represents the leaders amongst the Goblin soldiery who go unnamed in the story of The Lord of The Rings – the incidental warriors whose role on the battlefield is important in any war. If you choose Captains invent suitable names for each.

Wargear

The Moria Goblin Captain represented by the profile has a sword and wears spiny segmented armour. He has been given a Fight value for shooting – if he does not carry a bow then copy this to your record sheet as 3/-. If he is given further armour make the necessary adjustment to the model's Defence value. At an additional cost he may have the following items:

Shield	*5 pts*
Orc bow	*5 pts*

Shield. A Moria Goblin Captain that carries a shield adds +1 to its Defence unless the model also carries a bow, in which case the model adds nothing. See page 52 for details.

Lurtz, Uruk-hai Captain

Points value: 60
Might: 3
Will: 1
Fate: 1

	F	S	D	A	W	C
Lurtz	5/4+	4	6	2	2	4

Amongst a brutal race, Lurtz is a brutal leader, careless of the lives of his warriors, hungry for the blood of his foes. Untiring and determined, Lurtz is a foe to be feared.

Wargear

Lurtz is equipped with a sword (hand weapon), armour, shield and an Orc bow.

Uruk-hai Captain

Points value: 50
Might: 2
Will: 1
Fate: 1

	F	S	D	A	W	C
Uruk-hai Captain	5/4+	4	5	2	2	4

We have included the option for you to include one or more Uruk-hai Captains as part of your force – note that you can include more than one Uruk-hai Captain if you wish. This represents the leaders amongst the Uruk-hai soldiery who go unnamed in the story of The Lord of The Rings – the incidental warriors whose role on the battlefield is important in any war. If you choose Captains invent suitable names for each.

Wargear

The Uruk-hai Captain represented by the profile has a sword and armour. He has been given a Fight value for shooting – if he does not carry a bow then copy this to your record sheet as 5/-.

At an additional cost he may have the following items.

Shield	*5 pts*
Orc bow	*5 pts*
Crossbow (Uruk-hai of the White Hand only)	*5 pts*

Shield. An Uruk-hai Captain who carries a shield adds +1 to its Defence unless the model also carries a bow or crossbow, in which case it adds nothing. See page 52 for details.

Shagrat, Uruk-hai Captain

Points value: 55
Might: 3
Will: 1
Fate: 1

	F	S	D	A	W	C
Shagrat	5/-	4	5	2	2	4

The leader of the Uruk-hai garrison of the Tower of Cirith Ungol is as brutal and ferocious as any Uruk-hai captain, but he is also fanatically loyal to his Masters, obeying every order he receives from the Dark Tower to the letter.

Wargear

Shagrat has a sword and armour. At an additional cost he may carry a shield.

Shield	*5 pts*

Shield. If Shagrat carries a shield, his Defence is increased by +1 and he can use the Shielding rule.

Gorbag, Orc Captain

Points value: 45
Might: 3
Will: 1
Fate: 1

	F	S	D	A	W	C
Gorbag	4/-	4	5	2	2	3

A classic example of Orc selfishness and greed, Gorbag is prepared to order his warriors to attack the Uruk-hai guards of Cirith Ungol to steal from them the precious coat of mithril that belonged to Frodo and Bilbo Baggins before him.

Wargear

Gorbag wears crude armour and has a cruel Orc blade (hand weapon). At an extra cost he may carry a shield.

Shield	*5 pts*

Shield. If Gorbag carries a shield, his Defence value is increased by +1 and he can use the Shielding rule.

Wild Men Chieftain (Man)

Points value: 40
Might: 2
Will: 1
Fate: 1

	F	S	D	A	W	C
Wild Men Chieftain	4/-	4	4	2	2	4

The Wild Men of Dunland live upon the borders of Rohan. Like all their kind, the chieftains of the Dunlendings envy and hate the King of Rohan and all his subjects – and are all too ready to take up Saruman's cause to destroy Rohan!

A Wild Men Chieftain does not have any equipment. He can be given additional items as shown below:

Sword or similar hand weapon, or two-handed axe (choose one)	*Free*

Sharku, Warg Rider Captain (Orc)

Points value: 55
Might: 3
Will: 1
Fate: 1

	F	S	D	A	W	C
Sharku	4/–	4	5	2	2	3

Sharku is the chief amongst the Warg Riders, and the boldest of all that murderous horde.

Wargear

Sharku wears armour, has an orc blade (hand weapon) and rides a Warg. At an extra cost he may have a shield.

Shield						5 pts

Shield. If Sharku carries a shield, his Defence is increased by +1 and he can use the Shielding rule.

	F	S	D	A	W	C
Warg	0/–	4	4	0	1	2

Grishnakh, Orc Captain

Points value: 45
Might: 3
Will: 1
Fate: 1

	F	S	D	A	W	C
Grishnakh	4/–	4	5	2	2	3

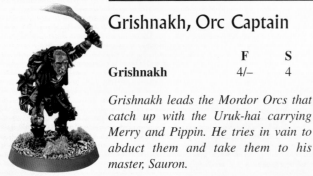

Grishnakh leads the Mordor Orcs that catch up with the Uruk-hai carrying Merry and Pippin. He tries in vain to abduct them and take them to his master, Sauron.

Wargear

Grishnakh has a sword and armour. At an additional cost he may carry a shield.

Shield						5 pts

Shield. If Grishnakh carries a shield, his Defence is increased by +1 and he can use the Shielding rule.

Gollum (Gollum... my preciousss...)

Points value: 0
Might: 1
Will: 0
Fate: 1

	F	S	D	A	W	C
Gollum	4/–	4	4	2	2	4

Many years ago, a small creature called Deagol discovered a ring in the Anduin river. This was, of course, the One Ring, and its evil power began to work at once, for he was murdered and the Ring taken by his companion Smeagol. In time Smeagol became Gollum – a twisted monster, obsessed with the Ring and consumed by his own remorse. But now Gollum has lost the Ring, 'stolen' from him by Bilbo and now borne by Frodo towards its destruction in the fires of Mount Doom. Gollum cannot bear to be separated from his 'precious' and would do anything, endure anything, to possess the Ring once more.

Special Rules

Gollum can be included in the Evil player's force if the Ringbearer is included on the opposing side. No points are paid for Gollum – he is 'free'.

Regardless of the scenario you are playing, Gollum is positioned on the table once both sides have placed all their other models. He must be placed within 6"/14cm of the Ringbearer.

So long as the Ringbearer is alive no Good model can shoot at or strike blows against Gollum. Good models are allowed to charge Gollum and fight, but will strike no blows if they win because they do not wish to kill Gollum. This applies to the Ringbearer himself as well as all other Good models. This restriction ceases to apply should the Ringbearer be slain. Once the Ringbearer is slain, Gollum becomes an enemy and can be shot and fought in the same way as any other enemy model.

Gollum is always controlled entirely by the player who has priority that turn. Whichever side has priority takes control of Gollum and moves him, fights with him, and so on. Regardless of which side controls him, Gollum must always move to within 6"/14cm of the Ringbearer in the Move phase if possible. If this is impossible, he must move as close to the Ringbearer as he can. Note that models can be moved in any order, so the Good player could quite reasonably move Gollum towards Frodo and then move Frodo away all in the same Move phase. When the Good player has priority he can always choose which of the pair to move first and this enables the Good player to keep Gollum at a safe distance from the Ringbearer.

If Gollum attacks and slays the Ringbearer, he automatically puts the Ring on when his opponent is killed. Once Gollum puts the Ring on he will run away and will never ever be heard of again. The model is removed and counts as a casualty.

Grima Wormtongue (Man)

Points value: 25
Might: 0
Will: 0
Fate: 0

	F	S	D	A	W	C
Grima	2/–	3	3	1	1	3

Grima is the treacherous councillor of King Theoden. Unknown to the King, Grima is secretly in league with Saruman and has been using every means at his disposal to turn Theoden's mind against his allies. Not only is Grima a cunning and persuasive advisor, he has poisons, potions and the sorcerous assistance of Saruman from afar to further his evil.

Wargear

Grima is armed with a dagger.

Special Rules

Grima can be included in the Evil player's force if Saruman is also included.

Regardless of the scenario you are playing, Grima is always placed on the table once both sides have placed all their other models. He can be placed in either the Evil side's deployment zone or the Good side's deployment zone.

So long as Saruman is alive no Good model can shoot at or strike blows against Grima. Good models are allowed to charge Grima and fight, but will strike no blows if they win because they do not wish to kill Grima but only to restrain him (being Good can be a pain sometimes you see!). This restriction ceases to apply should Saruman be slain. Once Saruman is slain, the depth of Grima's evil is revealed and Grima becomes an enemy who can be shot and fought in the same way as any other enemy model.

Grima is always controlled by the Evil player and is moved and fights when it is the Evil side's turn to do so as usual. Although he can fight he isn't very good at it (he's far too sneaky and grovelly) and his chief power is his ability to debilitate enemy Heroes by his endless whining, thereby spreading doubt and misery amongst his foes. This is represented by reducing the effect of Might. If a Good Hero is within 6"/14cm of Grima then 2 Might points must be expended to modify dice scores or use Heroic abilities instead of 1. As can be readily imagined this is a very powerful ability, and the Good player must try to occupy Grima and prevent him from using his power to sap the fighting power of the Good Heroes.

Note. For reasons impossible to fathom Grima is always more effective if the Evil player actually makes an effort to offer bad advice and make pessimistic forecasts of doom to his victims as he follows them about the battlefield.

Easterling Captain (Man)

Points value: 55
Might: 2
Will: 1
Fate: 1

	F	S	D	A	W	C
Easterling Captain	4/-	4	6	2	2	4

The Easterlings are the most disciplined and skilled warriors that are fighting for the Dark Lord. Their captains lead them with a martial prowess that Orcs will never be able to match.

Wargear

An Easterling Captain has an Easterling halberd (it counts as an Elven blade) and wears heavy armour.

"Dust rose smothering the air, as from nearby there marched up an army of Easterlings..."

Shelob (Giant Spider)

Points value: 90
Might: 0
Will: 6
Fate: 0

	F	S	D	A	W	C
Shelob	7/–	7	7	1	6	4

Shelob, the last child of Ungoliant, is an evil thing in spider-form, a horror that has haunted Middle-earth for countless years, preying on all living things.

Special Rules

Movement. Shelob moves 10"/24cm per turn. Like all spiders, Shelob can climb on any surface, regardless of its angle. Shelob therefore can move at full speed over any type of difficult terrain and ignores all obstacles except for water features and gaps such as chasms, ditches and other open spaces that she has to jump as normal.

Something evil lurks in the Mountains of Shadow.

Terror. Shelob is a repugnant, terrifying monster! She evokes terror in the enemy, as described in the Courage rules.

Venom. Models that suffer a wound from Shelob will lose a further wound at the start of each successive turn if they roll a 1 on a dice. Make this roll at the start of each turn before the Priority phase until the game is over or the victim is slain.

Might cannot be used to affect this roll, but Fate can be used to 'save' the wound, and Might can be used to boost the Fate roll as normal.

It is up to the Evil player to remind the opponent to test for the venom, and if this is forgotten, the poison simply had no effect that turn.

Pounce. A deadly hunting spider, Shelob often jumps on her prey using the huge weight of her bloated body to crush them. When charging, Shelob gets both bonuses that cavalry models get (ie, Extra Attack and Knock to the Ground). These bonuses are not lost if Shelob is engaged by enemy cavalry, but are lost if she is engaged by a Monstrous Mount. She can knock both enemy cavalry and infantry to the ground as if she herself were a Monstrous Mount.

Hunting instinct. Shelob is used to ambushing and dispatching her prey swiftly and effortlessly. If faced with a strong enemy, she is likely to retreat to safety. Every time Shelob suffers a wound, she must take a Courage test. If the test is failed she flees – the model is removed and counts as a casualty.

Troll Chieftain (Troll)

Points value: 140
Might: 2
Will: 1
Fate: 1

	F	S	D	A	W	C
Troll Chieftain	7/5+	7	8	3	3	4

A small number of the Trolls of Mordor are gifted with a form of primordial cunning and intellingence, which makes them the leaders of their race and a far more dangerous foe than the rest of their kin.

This is the basic profile for a Mordor Troll Chieftain.

Wargear

Troll Chieftains have some crude form of armour and carry brutal bludgeoning weapons (hand weapon).

Special Rules

Terror. Troll Chieftains are so huge and vicious that they evoke terror in the enemy, as described in the Courage rules.

Throw Stones. If a Troll Chieftain does not move at all, he can declare he's 'stooping for a stone', and in the subsequent Shoot phase he can throw it, provided that he is not engaged in combat. This works exactly like a crossbow with a range of 12"/28cm and a Strength of 8.

The Mouth of Sauron (Man)

Points value: 60

Might: 1
Will: 4
Fate: 1

	F	S	D	A	W	C
Mouth of Sauron	4/-	4	5	2	2	4

One of the race of those that are named Black Numenoreans, the Lieutenant of the Dark Tower has studied great sorcery under his Master and now carries Sauron's word to his servants and enemies alike.

Wargear

The Mouth of Sauron wears armour and carries a sword (hand weapon). At an additional points cost the Mouth of Sauron can ride a horse:

Horse   *10 pts*

Horse. The Mouth of Sauron rides a huge black horse to carry the word of his dark master to all the peoples of Middle-earth. Only the Mouth of Sauron can ride this evil beast – it will not permit any other creature to mount it. Rules for horses and riders are given in the main rules section.

	F	S	D	A	W	C
Horse	0	3	4	0	1	3

Magical Powers

Transfix. Range 12"/28cm. Dice score to use: 3+. The victim can do nothing further that turn. In combat, his Fight value counts as 1 and he rolls one dice regardless of how many Attacks he normally has. If he wins a combat, he will not strike. The victim can still use Might, Will and Fate but cannot make heroic actions. The effect lasts for the remainder of that turn.

Drain Courage. Range 12"/28cm. Dice score to use: 2+. The victim loses 1 point of Courage from his characteristic profile. This penalty applies for the rest of the battle. This ability can take effect several times on the same target – reducing a model's Courage value each time.

Sap Will. Range 12"/28cm. Dice score to use: 4+. The victim's Will value is reduced to 0. The effect lasts for the remainder of the battle – although it can be increased by the Strengthen Will or Will of Iron magical powers.

Terrifying Aura. Dice score to use: 2+. This power enables the model to assume a terrifying aura. Once this power has been successfully cast, the model counts as terrifying to all enemies as long as he has at least 1 point of Will remaining. If his Will drops to 0 the terrifying aura is extinguished. See the Courage section of the rules for more about terror.

One does not simply walk into Mordor.

EVIL WARRIORS
Moria Goblin Warrior

Points value: 4

	F	S	D	A	W	C
Moria Goblin	2/5+	3	4	1	1	2

These are small, mean-spirited creatures that live a troglodyte existence in the numerous delvings beneath the Misty Mountains. The ancient Dwarf tunnels of Moria have become home to these loathsome monsters. They scuttle through the tunnels with amazing dexterity, attacking, destroying and consuming intruders that venture into their dark realm. They are also known as Moria Orcs – for they are a low kind of degenerate Orc adapted to a life beyond the light.

This is the basic profile for a Goblin warrior. If the Goblin does not carry a bow then it is convenient to ignore the 5+ Shoot value when you copy the profile to your record sheet – ie, the Fight characteristic for a Goblin without a bow would be 2/-. The base profile can also change if the warrior carries a shield.

Wargear

The base profile for a Goblin warrior includes spiny Goblin armour. Though crudely made, this is quite extensive and often covers the entire Goblin from head to foot. Any warrior can be given additional items at the following cost:

Sword or similar hand weapon	*Free*
Spear	*1 pt*
Orc bow	*1 pt*
Shield	*1 pt*

Shield. A Moria Goblin warrior that carries a shield adds +1 to its Defence value unless the model also carries a bow, in which case it adds nothing. See page 52 for details.

Orc Warrior

Points value: 5

	F	S	D	A	W	C
Orc	3/5+	3	4	1	1	2

Orcs are the foulest creatures to walk Middle-earth. They are evil-hearted monsters that rejoice in slaughter and destruction. Orcs bear little loyalty even to their own kind and will readily fight amongst themselves over the spoils of their conquests. Inept workmen, their clothing is ill-made and ragged, their armour is crude, and their weapons as well-suited to butchery as to war. Yet they are numerous – untold thousands make up the armies of Saruman and Sauron and their natural cowardice makes them an ideal tool of evil intent.

This is the basic profile for an Orc warrior. If the Orc does not carry a bow then miss out the 5+ Shoot value when you copy the profile to your record sheet – ie, the Fight characteristic for an Orc without a bow would be 3/-. The base profile can also change if the warrior carries a shield.

Wargear

The base profile for an Orc warrior includes crude Orc armour. This is usually fairly meagre and often made of padded leather with reinforcing bands of metal. Any warrior can be given additional items at the following cost:

Sword or similar hand weapon, or two-handed sword/axe (choose one)	*Free*
Spear	*1 pt*
Orc bow	*1 pt*
Shield	*1 pt*
Banner	*25 pts**
	*(maximum one per Hero included in the same force)

Shield. An Orc warrior that carries a shield adds +1 to its Defence value unless the model also carries a bow, in which case it adds nothing. See page 52 for details.

Two-handed sword/axe. An Orc warrior equipped with a two-handed sword/axe cannot be given a bow or shield as well – he needs both hands to wield his weapon (see page 51).

Banner. See the relevant rules on page 55.

Uruk-hai Warrior

Points value: 10

Uruk-hai

	F	S	D	A	W	C
Uruk-hai	4/4+	4	5	1	1	3

If Orcs are the foulest creatures to walk Middle-earth then Uruk-hai are the most dangerous perversion of the breed. Where ordinary Orcs are crook limbed and timid, the Uruk-hai are strong, muscular, upright warriors of greater skill and courage. They are no less evil-hearted than their smaller cousins however. Their capacity for evil is greater still. Originally, they were created by Saruman and carried the White Hand of Isengard, but soon the Dark Lord Sauron too had in his service thousands of Uruk-hai bearing the Red Eye of Mordor.

This is the basic profile for an Uruk-hai warrior. If the warrior does not carry a bow miss out the 4+ Shoot value when you copy the profile to your record sheet – ie, the Fight value for a warrior without a bow would be 4/. The base profile can also change if the warrior carries a shield.

Wargear

The base profile for an Uruk-hai warrior includes armour. Any warrior can be given extra items for the following:

Sword or similar hand weapon, or two-handed sword/axe (Mordor Uruk-hai only)	**Free**
Orc bow	1 pt
Shield	1 pt
Pike (Uruk-hai of the White Hand only)	1 pt
Crossbow (Uruk-hai of the White Hand only)	2 pts
Banner	30 pts*

*(maximum one per Hero included in the same force)

Shield. An Uruk-hai warrior which carries a shield adds +1 to its Defence value unless the model also carries a bow or crossbow, in which case it adds nothing. See page 52 for details.

Pike. An Uruk-hai warrior which is equipped with a pike cannot be given a bow, crossbow or shield as well – he needs both hands to wield his weapon (see page 52 for more details).

Banner. See the relevant rules on page 55.

Uruk-hai Berserker

Points value: 15

	F	S	D	A	W	C
Berserker	4/–	4	6	2	1	8

Berserkers are the most dangerous of all Uruk-hai; fearless, caring nothing for their own lives, and armed with deadly swords almost as tall as themselves. As they approach the enemy they smear themselves with blood. The smell of which drives them into a screaming battle rage that makes them virtually unstoppable. A berserker can suffer a blow that would slay an ordinary Uruk-hai without even flinching – they feel no pain and have no desire other than the destruction of their enemies. For this reason they have a Defence value of 6 even though they wear no armour.

Wargear

The Berserker carries an extraordinarily long sword and no other weapons or armour. In any turn the Berserker can wield the long heavy sword either as an ordinary sword (hand weapon) or as a two-

handed sword – but he cannot change from one mode to the other during the same Fight phase.

A Berserker in all his gory glory!

Cave Troll

Points value: 70

	F	S	D	A	W	C
Cave Troll	6/5+	6	6	3	3	3

These are large and loathsome creatures that shun the light, preferring to hide away in dark caves and subterranean tunnels. They are both cumbersome and slow-witted but none-the-less dangerous creatures once roused to anger. Fortunately, there are only a few of these fearsome monsters compared to the vast hordes of Moria Goblins amongst whom they live and which, in all probability, form the bulk of their diet.

This is the basic profile for a Cave Troll of average size – being large creatures it is natural that they vary somewhat in dimensions.

Wargear

The Cave Troll has a crude club (hand weapon) and can also have a spear and/or a Troll chain at the following cost:

Spear	*1 pt*
Troll chain	*5 pts*

Troll chain. If the Troll wins a fight he can use his chain to lash out at one enemy as it moves back. This is worked out before rolling to see if the Troll's attacks score wounds. Roll a dice. If the score is greater than the target's Fight value or is a 6 (whether greater or not than the Fight value), the Troll has lashed his enemy as it moves back. All of the Troll's attacks are then worked out

and wounds determined – the lash is counted as one extra attack against the target.

Special Rules

Throw Stones. If a Troll does not move at all, he can declare he's 'stooping for a stone', and in the subsequent Shoot phase he can throw it, provided that he is not engaged in combat. This works exactly like a crossbow with a range of 12"/28cm and a Strength of 8.

"They have TWO Cave Trolls!"

Mordor Troll

Points value: 90

	F	S	D	A	W	C
Mordor Troll	7/5+	7	7	3	3	3

The Trolls of Mordor have been bred by Sauron so that they can withstand the light of the sun without turning to stone like normal Trolls do.

Even bigger and stronger than their subterranean kin, these monsters are amongst the most lethal troops of the armies of the Dark Lord.

This is the basic profile for a Mordor Troll of average size – being large creatures it is natural that they vary somewhat in dimensions.

Wargear

Mordor Trolls have some crude form of armour and carry brutal bludgeoning weapons (hand weapon).

Special Rules

Throw Stones. If a Troll does not move at all, he can declare he's 'stooping for a stone', and in the subsequent Shoot phase he can throw it, provided that he is not engaged in combat. This works exactly like a crossbow with a range of 12"/28cm and a Strength of 8.

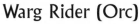

Warg Rider (Orc)

	F	S	D	A	W	C
Warg Rider	3/5+	3	4	1	1	2
Warg	0/-	4	4	0	1	2

Wargs are gigantic evil wolves – massive and dangerous creatures with a cunning and carnivorous intelligence. A Warg is so large and strong that an Orc can ride upon the creature's back much like a horse. These Warg riders scout far ahead of the main armies of Orcs and other evil creatures, spying out the land and picking off stragglers for interrogation or some far worse fate.

This is the base profile for an Orc warrior on a Warg. If the Orc does not carry a bow, miss out the 5+ Shoot value when you copy the profile – ie, the Fight characteristic for a Warg Rider without a bow would be 3/-. The base profile can also change if the warrior carries a shield.

Wargear

The base profile for a Warg Rider includes armour – this is often just crudely made from scraps of metal or leather. Any warrior can be given additional items as shown at the following extra cost.

Sword	*Free*
Throwing spears	*1 pt*
Orc bow	*1 pt*
Shield	*1 pt*
Banner	*25 pts**

*(maximum one per Hero included in the same force)

Shield. A Warg Rider that carries a shield adds +1 to its Defence value unless the model also carries a bow, in which case it adds nothing. See page 52 for details.

Banner. See the relevant rules on page 55.

Wild Man of Dunland (Man)

	F	S	D	A	W	C
Wild Man	3/–	3	3	1	1	3

The Dunlendings are savage tribesmen from the hills to the west of Rohan. For years they have envied the Rohirrim whose lands are so much more bountiful than the bleak uplands of Dunland. Now the Dunlendings have been driven to war by the poisoned council of Saruman. In company with Orcs and Wargs they rampage through Rohan, pillaging what they can and destroying what they cannot, murdering the people of the Westfold and driving them towards the refuge of Helm's Deep.

Wargear

The base profile for a Dunlending warrior does not include any equipment. Any warrior can be given additional items as shown below:

Sword or similar hand weapon, or two-handed axe (choose one)   *Free*

Easterling Warrior (Man)

	F	S	D	A	W	C
Easterling	3/–	3	5	1	1	3

Mysterious human warriors from the remote lands of the East, these are amongst the most well-equipped and disciplined troops available to the Dark Lord, whom they worship with fanatical loyalty.

This is the basic profile for an Easterling Warrior.

Wargear

The base profile for an Easterling Warrior includes sword and heavy armour. Any warrior can be given additional items at the following cost:

Spear	*1 pt*
Shield	*1 pt*
Banner	*25 pts**

*(maximum one per Hero included in the same force)

Shield. An Easterling Warrior which carries a shield adds +1 to its Defence. See page 52 for details.

Banner. See the relevant rules on page 55.

ARNOR

Arnor now lies in ruins, remembered only in tales and the memories of the very wise. Until the coming of the Witch King and the founding of his hateful realm of Angmar, it was once a proud and fair kingdom, able to rival the might of Gondor. All that now remains is a scattered people and crumbling ruins that conceal unquiet nightmares of an earlier age.

"... they seemed like black holes in the deep shade behind them."

"Cold be heart and hand and bone,
and cold be sleep under stone:
never more to wake on stony bed,
never, till the Sun fails and the Moon is dead."

- *The Fellowship of The Ring*

"Get out, you old Wight! Vanish in the sunlight!"

Aragorn defends Frodo from the Nazgûl.

Twilight Ringwraiths

SCENARIOS

A scenario sets the scene for a battle – it describes the circumstances of the encounter, who is involved, and what each side is trying to achieve. Most importantly the scenario describes what the battlefield looks like. Most of the scenarios also include special game rules that apply only for that scenario. Special rules are not a necessary feature of a scenario but they often help to make the game a unique challenge.

SCENARIO FORMAT

Each scenario is divided into a number of sections namely: Description, Participants, Points Match, Layout, Starting Positions, Objectives and Special Rules.

Description describes the incident in The Return of The King movie depicted in the scenario. All the scenarios are based upon or inspired by incidents portrayed in the movie and can be fought as accurate re-enactments should you wish.

Participants explains which characters took part in the incident in the film itself. In most cases, it's impossible to be sure exactly how many Orcs or Uruk-hai fight on the Evil side – there are so very many! – so we've estimated a number that gives a balanced game. Where troops have wargear options in the Force lists these are specified – otherwise troops always have their mandatory wargear as given in the lists.

Heroes can take any options given in the list unless indicated otherwise in the Special Rules.

Points Match provides you with a way of playing the same scenario with any Evil forces versus any Good forces.

Use the **Force Lists** to select your own warriors to take part in the scenario by choosing models as described in the Points Match section. All the scenarios can be fought with any forces. Note that an equal points match won't necessarily enable you to play with the actual participants – which is why we've devised two ways to play each scenario – use either the participants or points match for your game.

The **Layout** section explains how to set up the table for the battle using whatever scenery is required.

Starting Positions describes where the models are placed at the start of the game.

The **Objectives** explains what each side has to do to win the scenario. Every scenario has different objectives and requires you to develop an appropriate tactical approach – what works in one game may not work in another!

Special Rules are just that – rules that apply uniquely to that scenario. Most scenarios have special rules of one kind or another to represent the circumstances of the battle.

MAKING UP YOUR OWN SCENARIOS

Once you have played a few of our scenarios you will probably want to make up your own. The events in The Lord of The Rings provide plenty of inspiration for you to create your own scenarios – and even the same incident can be portrayed in different ways in a tabletop game.

When creating your own scenarios, it's a good idea for the player who has invented the scenario to act as a referee whilst other players take part in the game. The referee foregoes the chance to play – but he is available to adjudicate and interpret the rules as necessary. When you make up new rules for a scenario you'll often find you have to change things a little as you go along the first time you play. If playing a scenario that someone has made up always be prepared to defer to the referee (even the minions of evil aren't allowed to argue with the referee!).

EXPERIENCED PLAYERS

As players gain experience we find that they become quite adept at using the special abilities of the Good Heroes. As there are so many Good Heroes, and because they are so impressively heroic, this tends to disadvantage the Evil side. Although there are Evil Heroes, their abilities are rather more limited or specialised than the Good Heroes' abilities. The scenarios have been designed so that most players will find them reasonably well balanced when played – but as players become more adept the Evil side will find it harder and harder to win. There are two ways to make up for this.

A good way of ensuring balance is to play twice and swap sides – so that each player gets to represent the Good side as well as the Evil side. This is rather a good thing to do anyway – no one likes to play the bad guy all the time!

Another way of rebalancing the game is to make things tougher for the Good guys. Either make the objective tougher for the Good side or make the Evil side more potent by providing it with additional troops. An experienced Good player can take on at least twice the number of Evil troops given in the scenarios – there's a challenge for you!

SCENARIO ONE – SKIRMISH IN OSGILIATH

Description

This scenario is a minor Orc incursion on the western half of Osgiliath, to test the defences in preparation for Sauron's all-out assault across the Anduin river.

We have arranged the details so that this makes a suitable introductory game for new players. If you have never played before we would suggest you first make sure you are familiar with the basic rules by playing through the encounter Getting Started on page 174.

Participants

On the Good side there are 24 Warriors of Minas Tirith, of which 8 are armed with sword & shield, 8 with spear & shield and 8 with bow.

On the Evil side there are 24 Orcs, of which 8 are armed with hand weapon & shield, 8 with spear, 4 with Orc bow and 4 with two-handed weapons.

Points Match

If you want to play this game with other warriors, choose a points value of troops for the Good side and then give the Evil side a points value equal to three quarters (75%) of the Good one (for example, 200 Good against 150 Evil). Each side can choose warriors up to the total agreed value, but neither side can have Heroes and no more than a third (33%) of the number of models can carry bows or crossbows. All models must be on foot. Don't worry if you can't spend all the points available – a few points short won't make any difference.

Layout

In order to represent the ruined city of Osgiliath, place on the playing surface all the plastic pieces of scenery included in the game box. Feel free to add more ruined walls and other debris if you have more in your collection – the more the merrier! The river Anduin is assumed to run along one of the long table edges, as shown on the map.

Starting Positions

The Good player places his models first, eight of them (representing sentinels) no further away than 12"/28cm from the Anduin river and the remaining models no further away than 12"/28cm from the opposite long table edge (representing the reinforcements called up by the sentinels).

The Evil models are placed once the Good models are in position. They can be placed no further away than 24"/56cm from the river Anduin and more than 6"/14cm away from any Good model.

Objectives

Both forces are trying to eliminate the enemy quickly, before more reinforcements arrive. The first force to reduce its enemy to half (50%) of its original numbers at the end of any turn wins the game.

Should both forces be reduced to half of their original numbers at the end of the same turn, the result is a draw.

Special Rules

None.

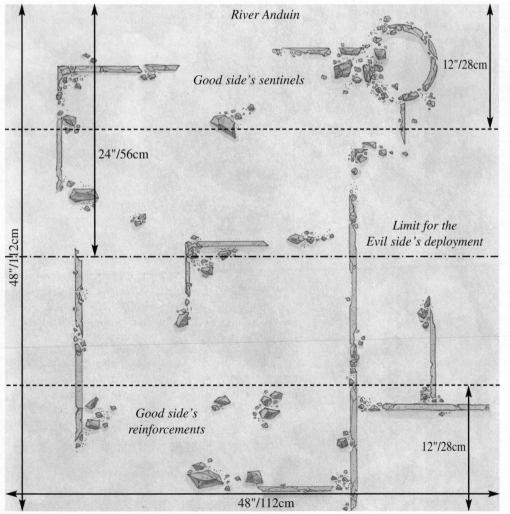

River Anduin

Good side's sentinels

12"/28cm

24"/56cm

Limit for the Evil side's deployment

48"/112cm

Good side's reinforcements

12"/28cm

48"/112cm

SCENARIO TWO – REARGUARD

Description

Finally Sauron strikes. Innumerable Orcs under the command of the Black Captain swarm across the Anduin on barges and improvised rafts and the defenders, outnumbered hundreds to one, are overwhelmed. Soon their officers decide to order the retreat and abandon the western side of Osgiliath to the Enemy. The only thing that can stop an orderly retreat from turning into a complete rout and a massacre is the sacrifice of a few groups of gallant warriors. These heroes prepare to dig in and sell their lives dearly in order to keep the enemy busy near the river and buy time for the rest of the Men to fall back to Minas Tirith.

Participants

On the Good side there are 24 Warriors of Minas Tirith, of which 8 are armed with sword & shield, 8 with spear & shield and 8 with bow.

On the Evil side there are 24 Orcs, of which 8 are armed with hand weapon & shield, 8 with spear, 4 with Orc bow and 4 with two-handed weapons.

Points Match

If you want to play this game with other warriors, choose a points value of troops for the Good side and then give the Evil side a points value equal to three quarters (75%) of the Good one (for example 200 Good against 150 Evil). Each side can choose warriors up to the total agreed value, but neither side can have Heroes and no more than a third (33%) of the number of models can carry bows or crossbows. All models must be on foot. Don't worry if you can't spend all the points available – a few points short won't make any difference.

Layout

In order to represent the ruined city of Osgiliath, place on the playing surface all the plastic pieces of scenery included in the game box. Feel free to add more ruined walls and debris if you have more in your collection – the more the merrier!

Starting Positions

The Good player places his models first, no closer than 6"/14cm to any table edge.

The Evil models are not deployed at the start of the game, but can move onto the table as per the Special Rules below.

Objectives

The Good force is trying to buy time for their retreating comrades, so you must count the number of turns played until all Good models have been removed from the table (have been killed or have retreated off a table edge). Once this happens, compare the number of turns with the chart below:

12 turns or less – Evil major victory.
13-18 turns – Evil minor victory.
19-24 turns – Good minor victory.
25 or more turns – Good major victory.

Special Rules

Countless Orcs! In the first Evil Move phase, all Evil models can move onto the table from any point along any of the table edges. Every turn, after the Evil player has finished moving his models, all the Evil models that have been killed in the previous turn can move onto the table from a point along any of the table edges. Newly arrived models can act normally but may not charge. The numbers of the Evil forces are so great they automatically pass all Courage tests they have to take.

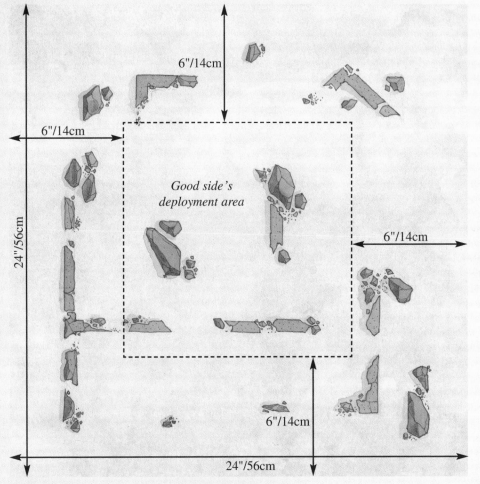

Good side's deployment area

6"/14cm

6"/14cm

6"/14cm

6"/14cm

24"/56cm

24"/56cm

SCENARIO THREE – IN THE CLUTCHES OF SHELOB

Description

As a terrified Frodo runs up the path to Cirith Ungol after having survived his first encounter with the monstrous spider, he does not realise that the creature has come out and is after him. At the same time, the brave Sam emerges from the dark tunnels, just in time to see his beloved master about to be attacked by the monster.

Participants

On the Good side is Frodo and Sam.

On the Evil side there is Shelob.

Points Match

If you want to play this game with other warriors, choose around 100 points of Good Heroes to fight against Shelob. Don't worry if you can't spend all the points available – a few points short won't make any difference.

Layout

The board should be littered with boulders and areas of rocky difficult terrain.

Starting Positions

Shelob is placed in base contact with the centre of the north or south table edge.

The Good player then places a Hero (Sam) in base contact with the centre of the west table edge and a second Hero (Frodo) in the centre of the table. If the Good side has a third Hero, then it can be placed in base contact with the centre of the table edge opposite to Shelob.

Objectives

To win, Shelob must kill both of the Hobbits. Differently from the normal rules, if she kills the Ring bearer, the Good side does not lose the game, because, as we know, Frodo is not really dead and Sam can continue the quest.

The Hobbits must either kill Shelob or, more likely, cause her enough pain to convince her to flee back to her lair (see Shelob's Special Rules). Alternatively, the Good side wins if the Ring bearer exits the table from the east table edge.

Special Rules

Samwise the Brave! Such is Sam's determination to save Frodo or to avenge him if the worst should come to pass, that he will automatically pass any Courage test he has to take.

The Phial of Galadriel. Sam carries the glass phial that Galadriel gave Frodo as the Fellowship departed from Lorien. The pure light of this Elven artefact is the bane of all evil and its bearer causes terror in Shelob, as described in the Courage section.

Not here, not so close to the Eye! Frodo would not dare to put on the Ring so close to the ever-watchful Enemy, so in this scenario he cannot use it.

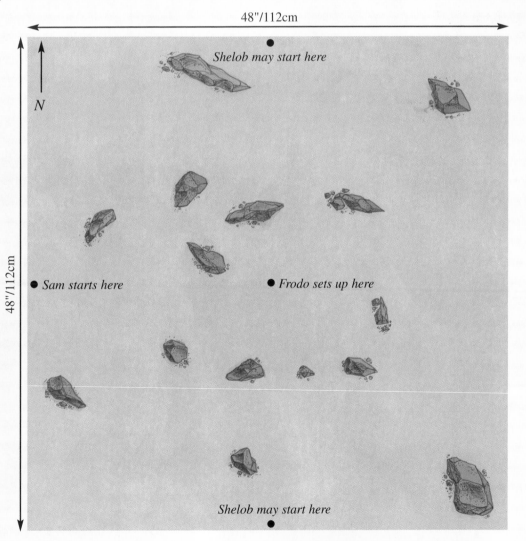

48"/112cm

48"/112cm

N

Shelob may start here

Sam starts here

Frodo sets up here

Shelob may start here

SCENARIO FOUR – THE PRIDE OF GONDOR

Description
Under strict orders from his father Denethor, Faramir leads the heavy cavalry of Gondor in a desperate charge against the Orc horde that has occupied Osgiliath. The brave Men are met by a rain of black darts, as a sinister figure soars high in the East sky.

Participants
On the Good side there are Faramir (mounted on a horse) and 15 Knights of Minas Tirith. One Knight can be given a banner.

On the Evil side there is a Ringwraith mounted on a Fell Beast and 20 Orcs armed with Orc bow. One Orc can be given a banner.

Points Match
If you want to play this game with other warriors, choose an equal points value for each side of at least 250 points per side. No more than a third (33%) of the models on the Good side can carry bows or crossbows. Don't worry if you can't spend all the points available – a few points short won't make any difference.

Layout
The Evil side's table edge represents what's left of the western outskirts of Osgiliath and should therefore have some scattered ruined walls and other debris for the Orcs to entrench themselves in. The rest of the table is an open grassy field with just the odd bush or tree.

Starting Positions
The Good player places his models first, no further away than 12"/28cm from his table edge.

The Evil player then places his Orcs, no further away than 12"/28cm from his table edge. The Ringwraith (or the most expensive Evil Hero in a Points Match) is not deployed at the beginning of the game.

Objectives
The first force to reduce the opposition to a quarter (25%) of its original numbers at the end of any turn wins the game.

Should both forces be reduced to a quarter of their original numbers at the end of the same turn, the result is a draw.

Special Rules
Nazgûl! At the end of each Evil side's Move phase except the first, after finishing to move their models, the player must roll a D6. If he rolls a 4, 5 or 6, the Nazgûl has arrived on the field and can move in from the Evil side's table edge (Might cannot be used to influence this dice roll). The newly arrived model can act normally but may not charge in the turn it arrives.

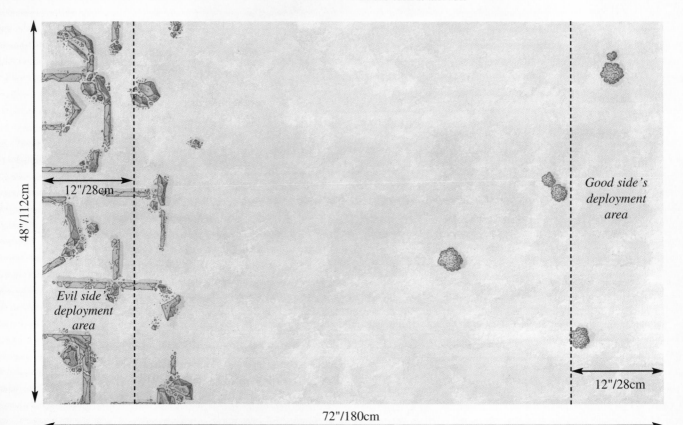

48"/112cm

12"/28cm

Evil side's deployment area

Good side's deployment area

12"/28cm

72"/180cm

SCENARIO FIVE – THE WHITE RIDER

Description

After the disastrous sally attack against the Orcs occupying Osgiliath, Faramir retreats back towards Minas Tirith. Wounded and exhausted, the son of the Steward of Gondor tries to lead to safety the few of his men that survived the onslaught. The Black Captain has other plans though and is determined to wipe them out to a man, dispatching some of his fellow Ringwraiths to hunt them down.

The people of Minas Tirith on the walls watch in dismay as the winged monsters close in for the kill, but when everything seems lost out of the city gates a white figure speeds to help the beleaguered knights. Will Gandalf the White and the noble Shadowfax reach Faramir and his men in time?

Participants

On the Good side is Gandalf the White on Shadowfax, Faramir (mounted on a horse) and 4 Knights of Minas Tirith.

On the Evil side are two Ringwraiths mounted on Fell Beasts.

Points Match

If you want to play this with other warriors, choose an equal points value of at least 300 points per side. The Evil side can take only Heroes and the Good side must take two Heroes and can spend the rest of its points on warriors. No more than a third (33%) of the models on either side can carry bows or crossbows. Don't worry if you can't spend all the points available – a few points short won't make any difference.

Layout

The game area represents the esplanade in front of the walls of Minas Tirith and is therefore an open grassy field with just the odd bush or tree. The first gate of Minas Tirith is at the centre of the Good side's table edge (see map).

Starting Positions

First, the Good player places all his models, except Gandalf, no further away than 12"/28cm from the Evil side's table edge. Gandalf (or the most expensive Good Hero in a Points Match) is placed in base contact with the gate of Minas Tirith.

The Evil player then places his models, no further away than 6"/14cm from his table edge.

Objectives

The Good player wins if both Good Heroes reach safety by moving off the table through the gate of Minas Tirith.

If only one of the Heroes makes it, the result is a draw.

If both Good Heroes are killed, the Evil player wins.

Special Rules

Captain Faramir is wounded! Faramir (or the cheapest of the two Good Heroes in a Points Match) has been wounded during his charge against the Orcs in Osgiliath, so starts the game having already lost a point of Might, Will, Fate and a Wound.

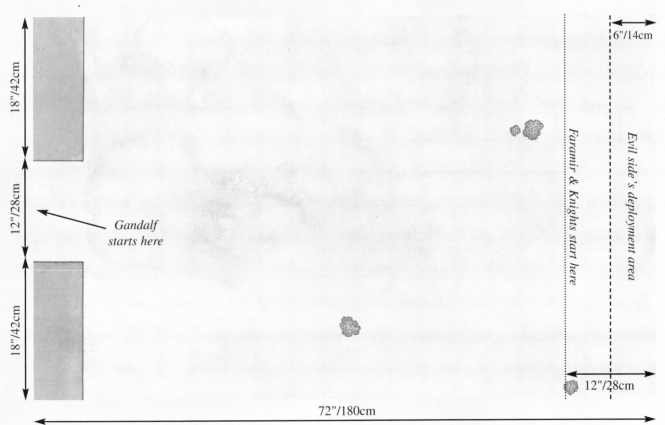

SCENARIO SIX – MINAS TIRITH

Description

After the destruction of the first gate of Minas Tirith, the Orcs pour into the streets and bitter street fighting erupts among the blazing buildings as the defenders try to repel the enemies. In the thick of the fray, the leaders of the two forces, the Witch King and Gandalf the White, finally meet in a titanic clash.

Participants

On the Good side there is Gandalf the White, Pippin (in armour), a Captain of Gondor on foot, 8 Guards of the Fountain Court and 24 Warriors of Minas Tirith, of which 8 are armed with sword & shield, 8 with spear & shield and 8 with bow. Two Good Warriors can be given a banner.

On the Evil side there is the Witch King mounted on a Fell Beast, 1 Orc Captain, 1 Mordor Troll, 5 Easterlings with shields & spear, 5 Easterlings with shields & sword, and 24 Orcs (of which 8 are armed with hand weapon & shield, 8 with spear, 4 with Orc bow and 4 with two-handed weapons). Two Orcs can be given a banner.

For both sides, all models must be on foot, with the exception of their most expensive Hero.

Points Match

If you want to play this game with other warriors, choose an equal points value for each side of at least 500 points per side. No more than a third (33%) of the models on either side can carry bows or crossbows. Don't worry if you can't spend all the points available – a few short won't make any difference.

Layout

This battle takes place in the streets of Minas Tirith, among ruined and burning buildings, the table should be covered in as many buildings as possible, with the exception of a wide central square (see map).

Starting Positions

The Evil player places his models first, no further away than 12"/28cm from his table edge. The Good player then places his models, no further than 12"/28cm from his table edge.

Objectives

The first force to reduce the opposition to a quarter (25%) of its original numbers at the end of any turn wins the game. Should both forces be reduced to a quarter of their original numbers at the end of the same turn, the result is a draw.

Special Rules

Burning buildings. To represent that all the houses and palaces in the first ring of the White City are ablaze or seriously damaged, models cannot enter buildings.

Horns in the distance! When the horns marking the arrival of the Riders of Rohan on the fields outside Minas Tirith are heard, the Witch King decides to abandon the fight in the streets to deal with this new threat. If the Good side is reduced to half their starting numbers, the Good player can roll a dice at the end of each turn. If a result of 6 is rolled, the Riders have arrived and are charging the Orcs outside the city, forcing the Witch King to abandon the game. Remove his model from the battle (he effectively counts as a casualty).

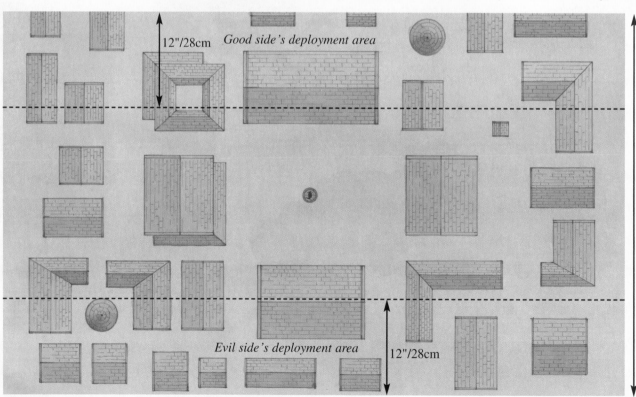

SCENARIO SEVEN – THE CHARGE OF THE ROHIRRIM

Description

The sound of the horns announces to the beleaguered defenders of Minas Tirith that Rohan has responded to their plea and has come to honour the old alliance with Gondor.

As the defenders renew their efforts in the streets of the White City, thousands of Rohirrim charge the Orcs on the field outside, trying to break the siege.

Participants

On the Good side there is Eomer, Theoden, Gamling, Eowyn and Merry (starts as a passenger on Eowyn's horse), a Captain of Rohan, 6 mounted Rohan Royal Guard armed with throwing spears and 18 Riders of Rohan (of which 6 are armed with throwing spears). Two Riders can be given a banner.

On the Evil side there is 4 Orc Captains, 2 Mordor Trolls and 36 Orcs, of which 12 are armed with hand weapon & shield, 12 with spear, 6 with Orc bow and 6 with two-handed weapons. Three Orcs can be given a banner. All Evil models are on foot.

Points Match

If you want to play this game with other warriors, choose an equal points value for each side of at least 500 points per side. No more than a third (33%) of the models on either side can carry bows or crossbows. Don't worry if you can't spend all the points available – a few points short won't make any difference.

Layout

This battle takes place on the fields of Pelennor, and is therefore a rather featureless grassy field, with just the odd tree, bush or short section of dry stone wall.

Starting Positions

The Evil player places his models first, no further than 12"/28cm from his table edge. The Good player then places his models, no further than 12"/28cm from his edge.

Objectives

The Good side must attempt to break through by reaching the opposite side of the board, and move off the table with as many models as possible, including at least one Hero. The Evil side must try to slay as many of their enemy as possible before they can break through their lines.

The game is played until the end of the turn in which all of the Good force has been destroyed/has broken through, or **ten turns** have been played. At this point, count the number of Good models that have broken through. Remember that models that retreat off the table because of a failed Courage test, count as slain.

If more than half of the Good force (including a Hero) has moved off the Evil side's table edge, the Good side wins. If less than a third (33%) of the Good force has moved off the Evil side's table edge, or if all the Good Heroes are slain, the Evil side wins. In any other case, it is a draw.

Special Rules

None.

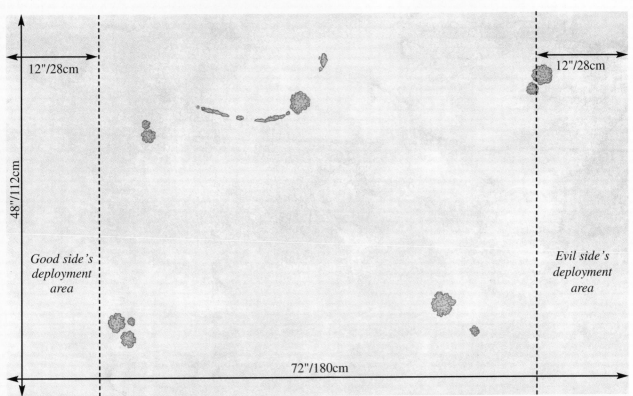

SCENARIO EIGHT – THE FATE OF THEODEN

Description

The King of Rohan stands alone after many deeds of great valour on the battlefield. With all his bodyguards lying dead around him, Theoden prepares to face the Black Captain himself. Meanwhile, Eowyn and Merry ride desperately to his aid, fearing they are too late to save him.

Participants

On the Good side there is Theoden, Eowyn and Merry (starts as a passenger on Eowyn's horse).

On the Evil side there is the Witch King (must be mounted on a Fell Beast).

Points Match

If you want to play this game with other warriors, choose an equal points value for each side of at least 150 points per side. All points must be spent on Heroes. Don't worry if you can't spend all the points available – a few points short won't make any difference.

Layout

This battle takes place on the fields of Pelennor, and is therefore a rather featureless grassy field, with just the odd tree, bush or short section of dry stone wall.

Starting Positions

The Good player first places Theoden (or his most expensive Hero in a Points Match), no further away than 12"/28cm from the Evil side's table edge.

The Evil player places his models, no further away than 6"/14cm from his table edge and more than 10"/24cm away from the Good Hero.

The Good player finally places the rest of his models, no further away than 6"/14cm from his own table edge.

Objectives

The first force to completely wipe out the opposition wins the game. If twenty turns are played without achieving the above condition, the Good side wins.

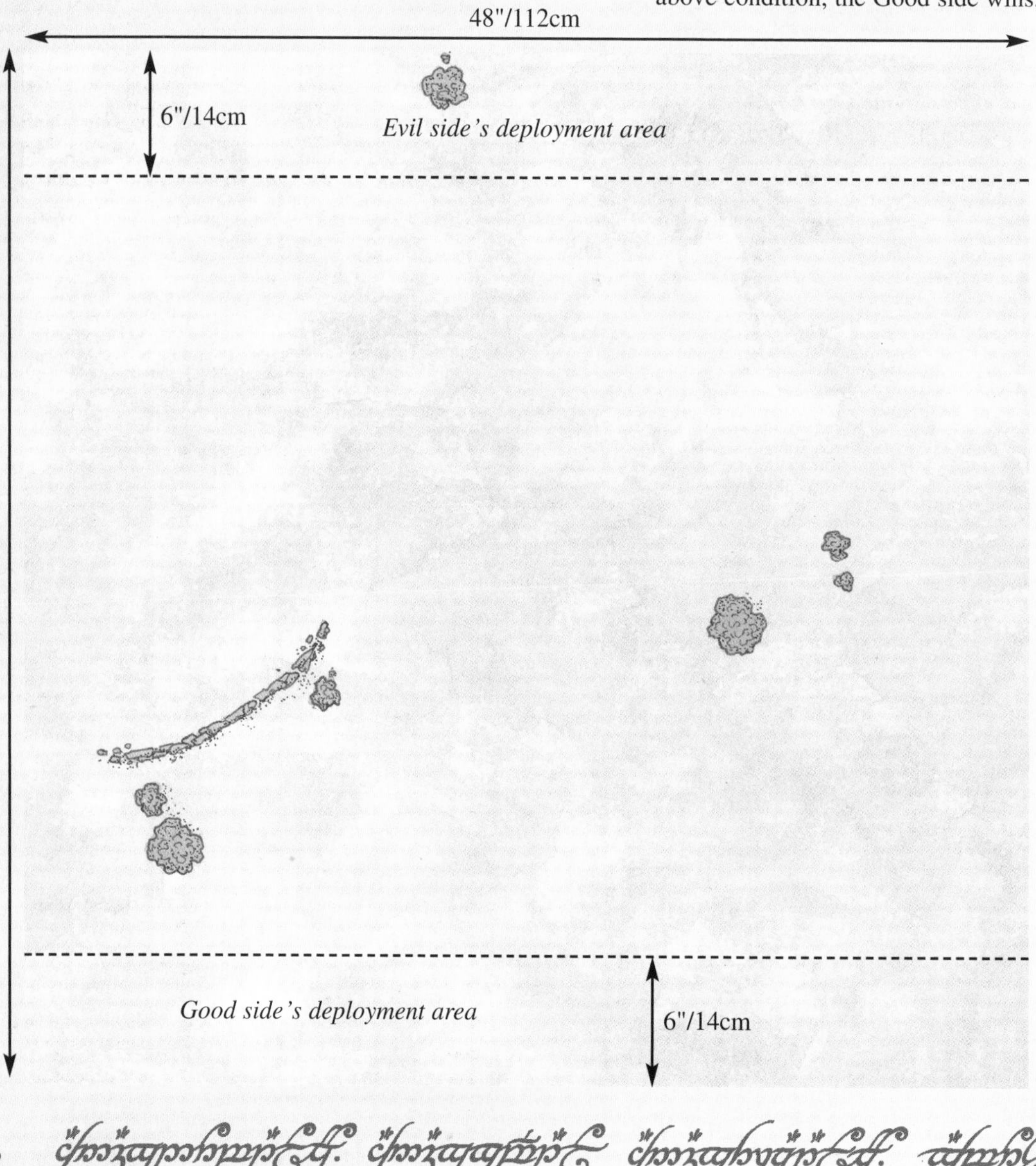

Special Rules

The King is attacked! Eowyn and Merry are so devoted to King Theoden that they would gladly give their lives for him. As a result of this, they automatically pass any Courage test they have to take during this game. In a Points Match, this applies to all Good Heroes except the most expensive one.

48"/112cm

6"/14cm

Evil side's deployment area

48"/112cm

Good side's deployment area

6"/14cm

SCENARIO NINE – THE ARMY OF THE DEAD

Description
The arrival on the Anduin of the black-sailed ships of the Corsairs of Umbar seems to spell doom for Minas Tirith. Great is the surprise of the servants of the Enemy when instead of their allies from Umbar, an army of the living dead pours from the ships and attacks them, led by both their ghostly king and by the Heir of Isildur wielding the newly re-forged Anduril, Flame of the West.

Participants
On the Good side there is Aragorn (he cannot wear heavy armour… yet!), Legolas, Gimli, the King of the Dead and 15 Warriors of the Dead.

On the Evil side there are 2 Orc Captains, 2 Mordor Trolls and 36 Orcs, of which 12 are armed with hand weapon & shield, 12 with spear, 6 with Orc bow and 6 with two-handed weapons. Two Orcs can be given a banner.

All models on both sides are on foot.

Points Match
If you want to play this game with other warriors, choose an equal points value of at least 500 points per side. No more than a third (33%) of the models on either side can carry bows or crossbows. Don't worry if you can't spend all the points – a few short won't make any difference.

Layout
This battle takes place on the fields of Pelennor, and is therefore a rather featureless grassy field, with just the odd tree, bush or short section of dry stone wall. The river Anduin lies behind the Good side's deployment area.

Starting Positions
The Evil player places his models, no further away than 12"/28cm from his table edge. The Good player then places his models, no further away than 12"/28cm from his own table edge.

Objectives
The Good side must attempt to break through by reaching the opposite side of the board, and move off the table with as many models as possible, including Aragorn (or the most expensive Good Hero in the case of a Points Match). The Evil side must try to slay as many of its enemy as possible before they can break through their lines.

The game is played until the end of the turn in which all of the Good force has been destroyed/has broken through. At this point, count the number of Good models that have broken through. Remember that models that retreat off the table because of a failed Courage test, count as slain.

If more than half of the Good force (including Aragorn) has moved off the Evil side's table edge, the Good side wins. If less than a third (33%) of the Good force has moved off the Evil side's table edge, or if Aragorn is slain, the Evil side wins. In any other case, the game is a draw.

Special Rules
None.

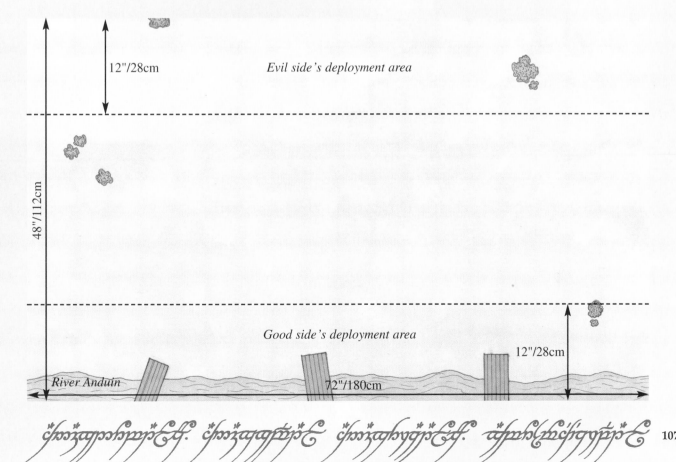

12"/28cm   *Evil side's deployment area*

48"/112cm

Good side's deployment area

12"/28cm

River Anduin   72"/180cm

SCENARIO TEN – THE BATTLE OF THE PELENNOR FIELDS

Description

The attack of the army of the Dead has tilted the balance of the battle in favour of the Free Peoples, and the Orcs have been caught between the Riders of Rohan, the Dead led by the returned King and the sallying defenders under Gandalf. But alas, the army of the Enemy is vast and it has not been defeated yet, much bitter fighting will still be needed to decide the day. Will the armies of Sauron rally and eventually make their numeric superiority count, or will the counter-attack of the forces of Good break their spirit and destroy them?

Participants

On the Good side there is Aragorn, Legolas and Gimli (all three are on foot), the King of the Dead, Eomer, Gamling, Gandalf the White, Pippin, 9 Warriors of the Dead, 12 Riders of Rohan (four of which are armed with throwing spears), 4 mounted Rohan Royal Guard armed with throwing spears, 24 Warriors of Minas Tirith (of which 8 are armed with sword & shield, 8 with spear & shield and 8 with bow). One Rider of Rohan and two Warriors of Minas Tirith can be given a banner.

On the Evil side there are 2 Ringwraiths mounted on Fell Beasts, 2 Orc Captains on foot, 1 Easterling Captain, 2 Mordor Trolls, 5 Easterling Warriors armed with shield & sword, 10 Easterling Warriors armed with shield & spear, and 36 Orcs (of which 12 are armed with hand weapon & shield, 12 with spear, 6 with Orc bow and 6 with two-handed weapons). One Easterling and two Orcs can be given a banner.

Points Match

If you want to play this game with other warriors, choose an equal points value for each side of at least 500 points per side. No more than a third (33%) of the models on either side can carry bows or crossbows. Don't worry if you can't spend all the points available – a few points short won't make any difference.

Layout

This battle takes place on the fields of Pelennor, and is therefore a rather featureless grassy field, with just the odd tree, bush or short section of dry stone wall.

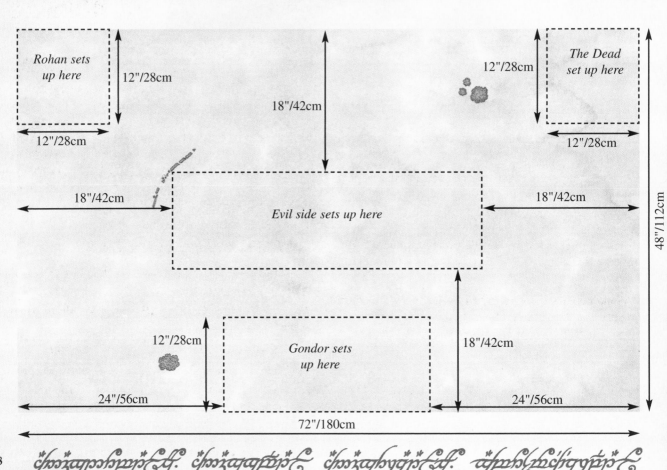

"Down from the either side of the Morannon poured Orcs innumerable."

Starting Positions

The Good player places his models first as shown on the map. One group (Rohan) includes Eomer, Gamling, the Riders of Rohan and the Royal Guards. The second group (the Dead) includes the King of the Dead, the Warriors of the Dead, Aragorn, Legolas and Gimli. The third group includes all remaining Good models.

The Evil player then places his models as shown on the map.

Objectives

The first force to reduce the opposition to a quarter (25%) of its original numbers at the end of any turn wins the game.

Should both forces be reduced to a quarter of the original numbers at the end of the same turn, the result is a draw.

In addition, if Aragorn is slain, the Evil side wins.

Special Rules

Linking scenarios together. Players may agree not to use the Heroes listed in the Participants section of this scenario and instead play it as a final showdown, pitching all named Heroes that have been used in the scenarios leading to The Battle of Pelennor Fields (as listed below). Players will need to play these scenarios first and then use the Heroes that have survived in the previous scenarios as participants in The Battle of Pelennor Fields. Such Heroes will begin the battle exactly as they had finished the previous game (ie, Might, Will, Fate and Wounds lost are not restored), with the exception that they can always replace any steed they had in a previous scenario if it was killed.

These Heroes and Scenarios are:

Faramir and a Ringwraith from Scenario 4.

Gandalf the White, Pippin and the Witch King from Scenario 6.

Theoden, Eomer, Gamling, Eowyn and Merry from Scenario 7.

Aragorn, Legolas, Gimli and the King of the Dead from Scenario 9.

Note that the Warriors listed in the Participants of this scenario do not change, only the Heroes will be different.

SCENARIO ELEVEN – THE TOWER OF CIRITH UNGOL

Description

The situation of the Hobbits is desperate. Frodo has barely recovered from Shelob's poison and is now held prisoner by Orcs and Uruk-hai in the sinister watch tower of Cirith Ungol. Sam has just realised his dear master is still alive, and is determined to try to rescue Frodo, come what may! Hope is suddenly rekindled in the brave Hobbit when he realises that the Orcs from Morgul, commanded by Gorbag, have attacked Shagrat's garrison of Uruk-hai in an attempt to steal the precious Mithril coat. The confusion of the fight offers to the new Ring bearer an occasion to get to Frodo and save him, but will he make it in time?

Participants

On the Good side there is Frodo, Sam, Shagrat and 15 Mordor Uruk-hai (of which 10 are armed with sword & shield and 5 with two-handed weapons).

Shagrat and his Uruk-hai are on the Good side for this game because they have orders from Barad-dûr to keep the prisoner (Frodo) alive and must therefore protect him from the Orcs.

On the Evil side there is Gorbag and 24 Orcs (of which 8 are armed with hand weapon & shield, 8 with spear, 4 with Orc bow and 4 with two-handed weapons).

Points Match

If you want to play this game with other warriors, choose an equal points value for each side of at least 200 points per side. No more than a third (33%) of the models on either side can carry bows or crossbows. Don't worry if you can't spend all the points available – a few points short won't make any difference. The Good side must spend at least half of his points on models from the Evil forces.

Layout

This battle takes place in the courtyard of Cirith Ungol, see map for details.

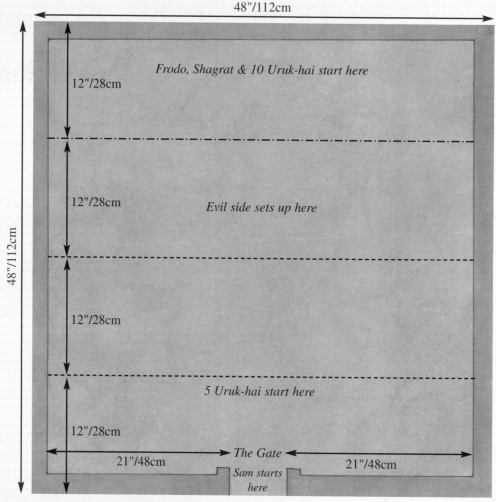

48"/112cm

12"/28cm — *Frodo, Shagrat & 10 Uruk-hai start here*

12"/28cm — *Evil side sets up here*

12"/28cm

12"/28cm — *5 Uruk-hai start here*

48"/112cm

21"/48cm — *The Gate* — 21"/48cm

Sam starts here

Sam hides from the desperate searching of the Uruk-hai.

Starting Positions

The Good player places his models first, as shown on the map.

The Evil player then places his models, as shown on the map.

Objectives

If an Evil model takes Frodo's Mithril coat and leaves the table by moving off through the gate, or if both Hobbits are slain, the Evil side wins.

If both Sam and Frodo leave the table by moving off through the gate, the Good side wins.

When one side achieves its objective, the game ends instantly and that side wins.

Special Rules

The Mithril Coat. Shagrat is carrying the coat at the start of the game. To take the coat from a model, it must be killed in close combat. If this happens, any of the models that fought it that turn can be given the coat. Note that the coat cannot be worn by anyone during this scenario. If the model carrying the coat is killed by missile fire, place a marker to indicate where the Mithril coat is. Models can pick it up by moving into contact with the marker.

Samwise the Brave! Frodo starts the game in very poor condition after his encounter with Shelob and his captivity in Cirith Ungol. He has no wargear whatsoever (counts as armed with a knife) and no points of Might, Will and Fate left. Sam on the other hand has the Ring, Sting and the Phial of Galadriel. Such is the Hobbits' determination, that they will always pass any Courage test they have to take.

The Phial of Galadriel. Sam carries the glass phial that Galadriel gave Frodo as the Fellowship departed from Lorien. The pure light of this Elven artefact is the bane of all evil and its bearer causes terror in all Evil models, as described in the Courage section (note that this only applies to Orcs in this scenario).

SCENARIO TWELVE – THE BLACK GATE OPENS

Description

The Captains of the West have decided that the best course of action is to distract the Eye of Sauron from the Ring bearer by putting more pressure on the Dark Lord. For this reason they lead a group of volunteers to the very doors of Mordor, challenging Sauron to come forward. This desperate sacrifice could buy the Ring bearer just enough time to complete his quest, but there is another one that hunts the Ring…

Participants

On the Good side there is Aragorn, Gandalf the White, Legolas, Gimli, Eomer, Gamling, Pippin, Merry, 12 Riders of Rohan (four of which are armed with throwing spears), 4 Rohan Royal Guards (two of which are armed with throwing spears), 4 Knights of Minas Tirith, 12 Warriors of Minas Tirith (of which 4 are armed with sword & shield, 4 with spear & shield and 4 with bow). One Rider of Rohan and one Warrior of Minas Tirith can be given a banner.

You will also need Sam and Frodo. Frodo has no wargear except for the Ring (he counts as armed with a dagger) and Sam has no wargear except for Sting.

On the Evil side there is the Mouth of Sauron, 2 Ringwraiths mounted on Fell Beasts, 1 Troll Chieftain, 1 Orc Captain on foot, 1 Easterling Captain, 1 Mordor Troll, 12 Easterling Warriors armed with shield & spear and 36 Orcs (of which 12 are armed with hand weapon & shield, 12 with spear, 6 with Orc bow and 6 with two-handed weapons). One Easterling and two Orcs can be given a banner.

You will also need Gollum.

Points Match

If you want to play this game with other warriors, choose an equal points value for each side of at least 500 points per side. No more than a third (33%) of the models on either side can carry bows or crossbows. Don't worry if you can't spend all the points available – a few points short won't make any difference.

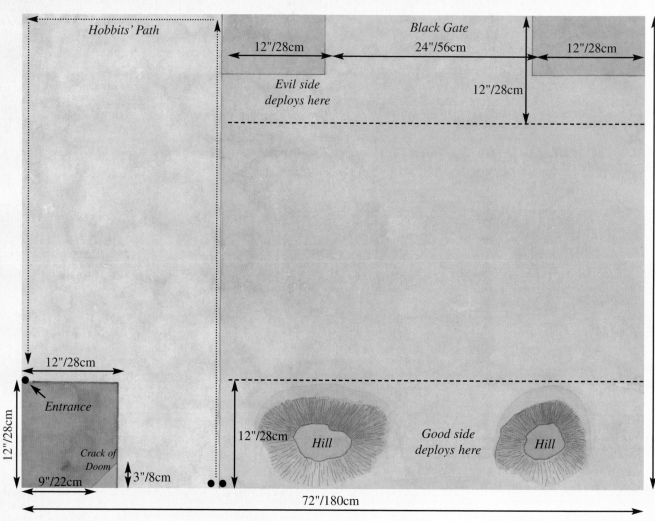

Samwise the Brave.

Layout

This battle takes place on a 4'x4' board, representing the esplanade in front of the Black Gate of Mordor. You will also need a small 1'x1' surface, representing the Chambers of Fire within Mount Doom. See map for details.

Starting Positions

The Good player places his models first, within 12"/28cm of his edge of the table.

Sam and Frodo are not deployed.

The Evil player then places his models within 12"/28cm of his edge of the table.

Gollum is placed within 3"/8cm of the Crack of Doom on the smaller gaming area (see map opposite).

Objectives

The Evil side wins if Gollum captures the Ring. The Good side wins if Frodo moves to the very edge of the Crack of Doom (the Ring is then cast into the fire and destroyed).

If all Good Heroes fighting in front of the Black Gate are slain, the Good side cannot win – even if the Ring is destroyed, the game counts as a draw.

Special Rules

The End of a Long Journey. Both Sam and Frodo start the game in very poor conditions after their nightmarish march through Gorgoroth. They have limited wargear (see Participants) and no points of Might, Will and Fate left. Frodo cannot use the Ring so close to the power of its maker. Such is the Hobbits' grim determination in this direst of circumstances that they will always pass any Courage test they have to take.

Initially, they are placed next to the main gaming area, in base contact with the Good side's table edge (see map). To represent the last part of their journey, the ascent of Mount Doom, they have to follow the dotted line marked on the map as Hobbits' Path. Every turn, during the Good side's Move phase, they can move normally along this path as they make their way up the barren mountainside.

The two Hobbits have obviously nothing to do with the battle taking place in front of the Black Gate and their ascent is essentially used as a turn track for the scenario.

Stinker. Gollum is laying in wait for the weary Hobbits and cannot move until the turn following the one when the Hobbits enter the Chambers of Fire.

Gollum's evil personality is now dominant and as a result of that his special rules do not apply and he is controlled by the Evil player normally, just like any other Evil model.

The Final Battle. The army of the Dark Lord pouring out of the Black Gate is immense. To represent this, when an Evil model is slain it will come back in the following turn by moving onto the table through the Black Gate. This does not apply to the Mouth of Sauron and the Ringwraiths.

In addition, both sides do not need to take Courage tests if their force is reduced to half its initial numbers – this is a fight to the death!

THE LAST ALLIANCE

At the end of the Second Age, Sauron's might was so great that no nation could stand before it. Against this power the Free Peoples of Middle-earth stood united. At the head of this great alliance strode the High Kings of both Elves and Men, Gil-galad and Elendil. Bound by friendship and common cause, they faced the armies of Sauron, sacrificing themselves to defeat him.

"Never again shall there be any such league of Elves and Men; for Men multiply and the Firstborn decrease, and the two kindreds are estranged."

- The Fellowship of The Ring

The Orcs are trapped between the onslaught of Elves and Men.

Led by Elrond, the Elves stand firm in the face of the Orc assault.

The men of Numenor prepare another volley.

Elendil

Gil-galad

**"Gil-galad was an Elven-king.
Of him the harpers sadly sing:
the last whose realm was fair and free
between the Mountains and the sea"**

- *The Fellowship of The Ring*

Isildur takes up his father's sword and the destiny of the free world is changed.

THE WAR OF THE RING

This section of the book contains rules and scenarios that will allow you to recreate a few of the innumerable battles that took place in other parts of Middle-earth at the same time as the events narrated in The Return of The King.

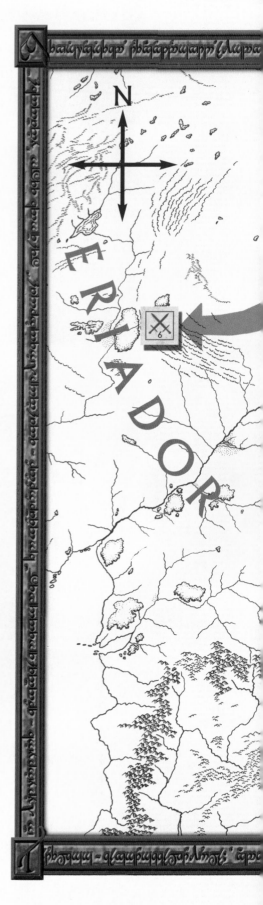

"Now is a time of war and strife, not in the land of Gondor alone, but in every corner of the West. Sauron's power has grown, his confidence fed by the unbridled might that is his to command, his brooding malice once more given free reign. The Black Gates of the Land of Shadow have opened, issuing forth Trolls, Orcs, Southrons, and Easterlings, the hosts of Mordor in all her dark glory. From Lindon to the Iron Hills the earth shakes beneath the marching feet of this endless swell of troops, the soldiery of the Eye. Inexorably, through a process as deliberate as it is destructive, are the bastions of the Free Peoples brought unto siege.

In Mirkwood, Thranduil finds his borders become embroiled in war once more, and his people hard pressed against the foul creatures that seek to lay low their sylvan realm. Far to the north, in Erebor and in Dale, it is only through the combined strength of Men and Dwarves fighting as one that Sauron's hand is denied. The Dark Lord is doubtless enraged by their continued resistance yet still they stand firm, a defiance that causes the forces of the Eye to break upon the Lonely Mountain like a dark forbidding sea. To the west, Orcs prowl all along the borders of Lorien and Fangorn, seeking to humble the two woodland realms of old, for Sauron hates and fears the power concealed by the trees. Yet even now his own might is not sufficient to swiftly overcome the opposition in these places. Once more he is halted by the will of they that have opposed him through all the long years of his power.

Each of these battles has a part to play in these, the closing days of the Third Age. For though it is true that this conflict will ultimately be decided as a result of a more subtle gambit than war, the smaller battles that are fought across the face of the world are all but unimportant. For even should Sauron fall, even should he be brought so low that he cannot rise once more, if all that is good and great in the world is crushed in his death throes, then this will be a hollow victory indeed."

"Now why did we not wish for some of our own kinsfolk, Legolas?"
"I do not think any would come. They have no need to ride to war; war already marches on their own lands."

Gimli to Legolas, The Return of The King

Key to Battles
1. The plains of the Anduin and the crossings of the Carrock are all but overrun by Goblins.
2. Esgaroth and Erebor are embattled by Goblins from the Grey Mountains and the armies of Mordor.
3. Sauron's forces move west from the Sea of Rhûn and invade Thranduil's Halls and eastern communities of Men.
4. The forces of Dol Guldur and Moria assault Lorien three times. Broken by their losses in the third attack, the Orcs flee into the Wold.
5. Goblins and Trolls sweep out of the Misty Mountains. Reinforced with fell creatures from Angmar, they lay siege to Rivendell.
6. With the Rangers no longer present, the denizens of Angmar terrorise Bree and the local villages.
7. Orcs fleeing the abortive attacks on Lorien are crushed by Treebeard and a host of Ents. Many of the surviving Orcs drown in their desparation to cross the river.
8. Reinforced by the survivors of Saruman's forces, Sauron's army pillages Rohan, but does little damage to the population which has taken refuge in strongholds.

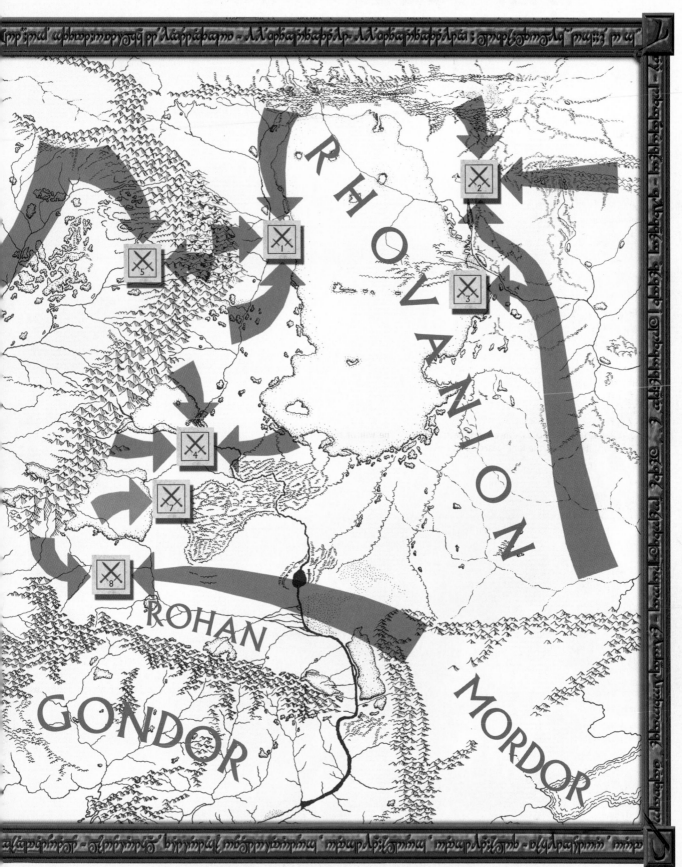

GOOD HEROES

Galadriel (High Elf)

Points value: 120

	F	S	D	A	W	C
Galadriel	6/-	3	3	1	3	7

Might: 3
Will: 6+1 per turn
Fate: 3

Galadriel is a great sorceress, both mighty and terrifying. Wise beyond mortal measure, her powers are held in awe by lesser folk and her domain is closed to them. By the magics she wields through Nenya – the Mithril ring of adamant – Lothlorien is kept safe from the ravages of time and the assaults of the forces of evil. So mindful is she of the threats to her realm that it is only due to their exceptional circumstance that the Fellowship are permitted to enter Lothlorien.

Wargear

When necessary, Galadriel wields a dagger. At an additional cost she may be given her mirror, an enchanted item of great power.

> *Mirror of Galadriel*   25 pts

Mirror of Galadriel. The visions the mirror shows change with each person, but are always relevant and heavy with much portent. The mirror is deployed within 6" of her at the start of the game – it may not subsequently be moved. Once per turn, one Good Hero within 6"/14cm of the mirror may recover their Fate to its starting value. A Hero may not use the mirror to increase their Fate beyond its starting level.

Special Rule

Lineage of the Firstborn. Galadriel is descended from the mightiest of Elvenkind, her power almost beyond reckoning. Galadriel may expend a single point of Will each turn without depleting her own store. In addition, her aura of power is so great that her appearance induces terror in all Evil creatures.

Magical Powers

Effortlessly Immobilise. Range 12"/28cm. Dice score to use: 2+. The victim can do nothing further that turn. In combat his Fight value counts as 1 and he rolls one dice regardless of how many Attacks he normally has. If he wins a combat he will not strike. The victim can still use Might, Will and Fate but cannot make heroic actions. The effect lasts for the remainder of that turn.

Command. Range 12"/28cm. Dice score to use 4+. The victim can do nothing further that turn as described for Immobilise, except that the Good player can move it up to half a move as soon as the power takes effect, even into base contact with an enemy. The player can do this even if the model has already moved this turn. The model cannot be moved out of a combat if it is already engaged. The model cannot be forced to perform any actions that would cause direct harm to it (such as jumping down a cliff…).

Blinding Aura. Dice score to use: 2+. This power enables Galadriel to reveal a portion of her power as a corona of white light. In darkness, this illuminates an area 12"/28cm around her and anyone within this area can be seen as if it were daylight. Once cast, this power lasts for the rest of the game so long as Galadriel has at least 1 point of Will remaining. If Galadriel's Will drops to 0 the aura fades away. Because of the brightness of the aura, any enemy that are shooting at Galadriel or at a target within 6"/14cm of Galadriel will require a roll of 6 to score a hit.

Celeborn (High Elf)

Points value: 100

	F	S	D	A	W	C
Celeborn	6/-	4	4	1	3	7

Might: 3
Will: 3+1 per turn
Fate: 3

Celeborn is one of eldest of the Elves of Middle-earth, wise and powerful almost beyond comparison. His advice has often proved crucial in the councils of the Wise since the Last Alliance of Men and Elves.

Wargear

Celeborn carries a finely crafted dagger. He may also have the following:

Elven Blade	5 pts
Heavy Armour	10 pts
Shield	5 pts

Special Rule

Lineage of the Firstborn. Celeborn is descended from the mightiest of Elvenkind, to the first kings of the Elves. He may expend a single point of Will each turn without depleting his own store. Also, his aura of power is so great that his appearance causes terror in all Evil creatures.

Magical Powers

Immobilise. Range 12"/28cm. Dice score to use: 3+. The victim can do nothing further that turn. In combat his Fight value counts as 1 and he rolls one dice regardless of how many Attacks he normally has. If he wins a combat he will not strike. The victim can still use Might, Will and Fate but cannot make heroic actions. The effect lasts for the remainder of that turn.

Aura of Command. Dice score to use: 2+. This power enables Celeborn to reveal a portion of his power, steadying the resolve of the forces around him. While this spell is in effect, all Good models within 6"/14cm of Celeborn will automatically pass any Courage tests they are compelled to take. Once cast, this power lasts for the rest of the game so long as Celeborn has at least one point of Will remaining. If Celeborn's Will drops to zero, the aura fades away.

Radagast the Brown (Wizard)

Might: 3
Will: 6+1
Fate: 3

	F	S	D	A	W	C
Radagast	5/-	4	5	1	3	7

Living on the borders of Mirkwood, Radagast is a member of the Order of Wizards to which both Gandalf and Saruman belong. Less given to displays of power than his fellows, Radagast is a master of hues and shapes and his skill with the birds and beasts of Middle-earth is without equal. Although Saruman derides Radagast's abilities and has never held him in anything other than contempt, Radagast is a dedicated member of the White Council and Gandalf considers him a valuable ally.

Wargear

Radagast carries his staff and a sword (hand weapon). He can use either to fight with – his staff is a two-handed weapon. At an additional cost Radagast may ride a horse.

Horse		*10 pts*

Horse. Rules for horses and riders are given in the main rules section.

	F	S	D	A	W	C
Horse	0	3	4	0	1	3

Special Rules

Staff of Power. Radagast's staff is not only a symbol of his authority but a potent talisman. To represent his staff's power, he can expend 1 point of Will each turn without reducing his own Will store.

Gwaihir. If Radagast is included in the army you may also include Gwaihir at the points cost indicated. This is an exception to the usual rule that Gwaihir may not be included in any force that does not also include Gandalf.

Master of Birds. Radagast is frequently accompanied by a raven that acts as his eyes and ears. To represent the raven scouting the battlefield on his behalf, Radagast is always assumed to have line of sight to any point on the battlefield.

One with Nature. Radagast has a strong connection with nature and through his skills is able to blend with his surroundings and is used to travelling through all manner of terrain. To represent this, whilst on foot he may move through areas of difficult terrain without penalty and always counts as wearing an Elven cloak.

Magical Powers

Terrifying Aura. Dice score to use: 2+. This power enables Radagast to assume a terrifying aura. Once this power has been successfully cast, Radagast counts as terrifying to all Evil creatures so long as he has at least 1 point of Will remaining.

In addition, due to Radagast's mastery of beasts, mounted models must always pass two Courage tests to charge Radagast; one with the mount **and** one with the rider (with their respective Courage value). If Radagast's Will drops to zero, the terrifying aura is extinguished. See the Courage section of The Two Towers rules manual for more about terror.

Immobilise. Range 12"/28cm. Dice score to use: 3+. The victim can do nothing further that turn. In combat his Fight value counts as 1 and he rolls one dice regardless of how many Attacks he normally has. If he wins a combat he will not strike. The victim can still use Might, Will, and Fate but cannot make any Heroic actions. The effect lasts for the remainder of that turn.

Renew. Range 12"/28cm. Dice score to use: 3+. Radagast can use this spell to restore one Wound to one friendly model.

Panic Steed. Range 12"/28cm. Dice score to use: 2+. This power may only be directed against a mounted model. The target is immediately thrown as the steed rears and throws him from the saddle. Remove the steed from play and roll on the Thrown Rider chart to determine the effect of the fall.

Aura of Dismay. Dice score to use: 5+. Radagast casts an intricate web of deception that causes his foes to see that which they most fear in place of their enemies. This power can only be cast at the end of Radagast's move. If successfully cast, any friendly models that end their move within 6"/14cm of Radagast (including Radagast himself) count as causing terror for the remainder of that Move phase.

King of Men

Might: 2
Will: 2
Fate: 1

	F	S	D	A	W	C
King of Men	5/4+	4	4	2	2	5

There are many Kings of Men, some ruling great nations such as Rohan or Gondor. Other Kings rule smaller realms, such as that of Dale. We have included this option should you wish to include Kings of Men in your force.

Wargear

Kings of Men carry swords. At additional cost they may be given the following equipment:

Armour	*5 pts*
Heavy armour	*10 pts*
Shield	*5 pts*
Throwing spear	*5 pts*
Horse	*10 pts*

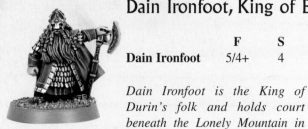

Dain Ironfoot, King of Erebor (Dwarf)

Points value: 125

Might: 3
Will: 3
Fate: 2

	F	S	D	A	W	C
Dain Ironfoot	5/4+	4	9	3	3	7

Dain Ironfoot is the King of Durin's folk and holds court beneath the Lonely Mountain in Erebor. Though stricken in years, Dain is a mighty king descended in direct line from Durin, the sire of his race. He has fought many battles across the face of Middle-earth, and grown wise in the arts of leadership and battle. As a result, Dain commands incredible loyalty from his followers so much so that they will never surrender while he lives.

Wargear

Dain wears Mithril armour and carries the great axe Barazantathûl, both heirlooms of his family.

Special Rules

Voice of Command. The Dwarves hold Dain in supreme regard, and will do his bidding without question. While Dain is still alive and on the table, all Dwarves will automatically pass any Courage tests that they are required to make.

Old. At the time of the War of the Ring, Dain is more than 250 years old, and is not as agile as he once was. To represent this, whenever Dain has to make a Jump or Climb test the Good player rolls two dice and must choose the lowest. This roll can be influenced by Might in the usual way.

Barazantathûl. Although not innately magical, this two-handed axe is of great craftsmanship and possessed of exceptional balance. When Dain fights with this axe, he adds +1 to his dice roll on the Wound chart, as normal with two-handed weapons, but he does not suffer the usual -1 penalty to the dice for deciding which side wins the fight.

Dwarf King

Points value: 75

Might: 2
Will: 2
Fate: 1

	F	S	D	A	W	C
Dwarf King	6/4+	4	8	2	2	6

Dwarf Kings rule the realms of the Dwarves across Middle-earth, from Ered Luin to beyond the Iron Hills. Gruff and uncompromising, they are firm allies to their friends and death to their foes. We have included this option should you wish to include Dwarf Kings in your force.

Wargear

Dwarf Kings carry hand axes (hand weapons) and wear Dwarf heavy armour. At an additional cost they may have the following:

Two-handed axe	5 pts
Throwing axes	5 pts

Dwarf Captains

Points value: 60

Might: 2
Will: 1
Fate: 1

	F	S	D	A	W	C
Dwarf Captain	5/4+	4	7	2	2	5

We have included the option to have one or more Dwarf Captains as part of your force – note that you can include more than one if you wish. You can use this profile for famous heroes such as Óin and Ori. Other Dwarves that are named in the fragments of the book of Mazarbul, such as Flói, Frár, Lóni and Náli, can be represented by this profile, as well as all the leaders amongst the Dwarves who go unnamed in the story of The Lord of The Rings.

Wargear

Dwarf Captains have Dwarf armour and axes (hand weapon).

At an additional cost they may have the following:

Two-handed axe	5 pts
Shield	5 pts
Throwing axes	5 pts

Shield. A Dwarf Captain who carries a shield adds +1 to his Defence value and can use the 'shielding' rule in a fight.

Two-handed axe. A Dwarf Captain who carries a two-handed axe cannot also carry a shield. He can use either his ordinary axe or his two-handed axe, though not both in the same Fight phase.

GOOD WARRIORS

Dwarf Warrior

Points value: 8

	F	S	D	A	W	C
Dwarf Warrior	4/4+	3	6	1	1	4

The sharp axes of the Dwarves and their stubborn courage are rightly feared among the servants of Evil.

Above is the base profile for a Dwarf Warrior. If the warrior does not carry a bow then miss out the 4+ value when you copy out the profile – ie, the Fight characteristic for a warrior without a bow would be 4/-. The base profile might also change if the warrior carries a shield as noted below.

Wargear

The base profile for a Dwarf warrior includes Dwarf armour. He can be given additional items at the following cost:

Axe or two-handed axe (choose one)	*Free*
Dwarf Bow	*1 pt*
Shield	*1 pt*
Banner	*30 pts**

*(max. one per Hero included in the same force)

Two-handed axe. A Dwarf Warrior who carries a two-handed axe cannot also carry a bow or shield – he needs both hands to wield his weapon.

Dwarf Bow. Dwarf bows are powerful shortbows of exceptional craftmanship. They have a Strength of 3 and a Range of 18"/42cm.

Shield. A Dwarf Warrior model which carries a shield adds +1 to its Defence value unless the model also carries a bow, in which case it adds nothing. Models that are primarily bow-armed don't increase their Defence value if they carry shields, as they need their hands free to use or carry their bow. They can still use the 'shielding' rule in a fight though, so there is some benefit to carrying both a shield and a bow.

Banner. See the relevant rules on page 55.

Khazâd Guard

Points value: 11

	F	S	D	A	W	C
Khazâd Guard	4/-	4	7	1	1	4

The veterans of the Khazâd Guard, hand-picked from among the strongest Dwarf warriors, are sworn to defend their Lord with their lives. They wear terrifying war-masks and are equipped with the best weapons and armour.

Wargear

The Khazâd Guards wear Dwarf heavy armour and carry axes (hand weapons) and two-handed axes. They can use either their ordinary axe or their two-handed axe – though not both in the same Fight phase.

Special Rules

Bodyguard. At the beginning of the game, choose one Dwarf Hero among those in your force for the Khazâd Guard to protect. As long as this Hero is on the table, all Khazâd Guard models automatically pass all Courage tests they have to take. If the Hero is killed or leaves the table, the Khazâd Guard revert to the normal rules for Courage.

The Dwarves fall upon the Goblins with unrestrained fury.

SCENARIO ONE – THE LONG NIGHT

DESCRIPTION

There are many villages around the lake town of Esgaroth and the Dwarves of Erebor have a strong friendship with them. Many Dwarven traders, heavily guarded against attack, travel back and forth between the villages and the Lonely Mountain, and it is one such trade caravan that is present in a small human village when a force of Sauron's Uruk-hai attack! It is deep in the night and with the Orcs roaming across the land there is little chance of receiving aid from another village until it is light. Faced with a common foe, the Dwarves choose to stand beside their allies. As the women and children barricade themselves within the houses, the Men and Dwarves stand side by side, with spear and axe ready to meet the attacking Uruk-hai. Their only hope is to hold the village until sunrise, the soonest that help can arrive.

Participants

The Good side consists of 1 Dwarf Captain, 2 Khazad Guard, 4 Dwarves with shields, 6 Dwarves with Dwarf bows, 2 Captains of Men on foot, 4 Men of Rhovanion (use Men of Rohan) with shields, 4 Men of Rhovanion with throwing spears & shield, and 4 Men of Rhovanion with bows.

The Evil side has 1 Uruk-hai Captain, 10 Uruk-hai with swords and shields, and 5 Uruk-hai with Orc bows.

POINTS MATCH

If you want to fight this battle with alternative forces, choose at least 250 points for the Good side and 200 points for the Evil side. No more than a third (33%) of the Evil force may be armed with bows or crossbows.

LAYOUT

The scenario is played on a board 48"/112cm by 48"/112cm. The village covers most of the board, with the perimeter dotted with trees and rocky outcrops. In the centre of the village there should be an open area about 6"/14cm square with barricades placed around it (see map). Ideally, the village should be fortified (the result of hasty preparations), so the Uruk-hai must cross at least one ring of obstacles to reach the defenders.

STARTING POSITIONS

The Good player deploys his force within the open area in the village. The Evil player then deploys four models within 6"/14cm of the centre of each table edge.

OBJECTIVES

The Good side wins if at least four models can survive within the boundaries of the village for more than 20 turns. Help from other villages arrives and the attackers are driven off.

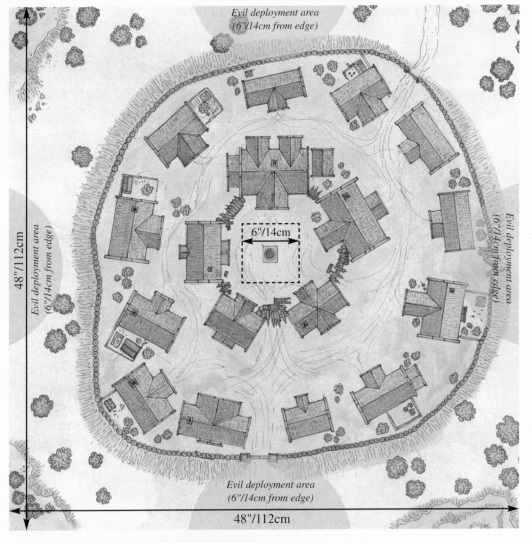

Evil deployment area (6"/14cm from edge)

48"/112cm

Evil deployment area (6"/14cm from edge)

6"/14cm

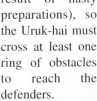

Evil deployment area (6"/14cm from edge)

Evil deployment area (6"/14cm from edge)

48"/112cm

Desperate fighting erupts at the barricades.

The Evil side wins if all the Good models are killed before twenty turns have passed. The would-be rescuers arrive only to find burnt out buildings and half-eaten corpses.

If less than four Good models survive within the boundaries of the village beyond twenty turns, then the game is a draw. The defenders manage to buy enough time for the women and children to be rescued but the village is abandoned.

SPECIAL RULES

Unrelenting Assault. The Uruk-hai attack is fragmented but unceasing. When an Evil model is slain, the Evil player may move it on from a board edge of his choice at the start of his next Move phase. The Evil player may not bring on more than two models from the same board edge each turn. If more than two models are available to the Evil player, he must bring them on from several edges or keep them in reserve for future turns.

NOTES

Faced with superior unlimited foes and only a token defence force, the defender must try to make the most of his defensible position. The barricades can make the Good

player's position a strong one, but he is unlikely to be able to defend every inch of them. The Good player shouldn't be afraid to move his models around to maximise coverage to where the Uruk-hai threaten to break through – every dead Uruk-hai will need at least three turns to get back into the fight. In this way it is a good idea to fire at the nearest enemy models – they will have further to walk when they come back on. It's also a good idea to pair a Man with each Dwarf if you can, the higher Fight value of the Dwarf will tie the fight if the dice scores are a draw – every little helps.

The Evil player needs to find weaknesses in the defender's position and exploit them as quickly as possible – twenty turns is not as much as it looks. Try to avoid engaging the enemy across the barricades, but instead loop around their defences and break through into the courtyard if you can. Another key thing to remember is not to be worried about getting your archers into combat, they are more than a match for the humans and can go toe-to-toe with the Dwarves. Your main obstacles to victory will be the Khazâd Guard and the Captains, try to take them out as quickly as possible, this will leave you free to mop up the survivors.

SCENARIO TWO – A ROCK & A HARD PLACE

DESCRIPTION

Murin, a Dwarven King from the Blue Mountains, has travelled east with an army intending to assist his kin in Erebor. Shunning the dark forest of Mirkwood, Murin's group skirts the northern border of the wood. In the depths of night, a large band of Goblins streams down from the Grey Mountains. They take the Dwarves by surprise and many on both sides are slain. Murin himself is gravely wounded. With the battle appearing hopeless, Murin's personal guard hurry him from the field and attempt to reach the possible safety of the forest. Unfortunately, Murin's wounds slows the group and they are encircled by bloodthirsty Goblins. Murin's fate looks grim, but help is at hand. Keen-eyed Elves from Mirkwood have spotted his plight and now attempt to save him from his pursuers. Will they get there in time?

PARTICIPANTS

The Good side consists of Murin (a Dwarf King), 1 Dwarf Captain, 4 Khazâd Guard, 8 Dwarf Warriors with shields, 2 Dwarf Warriors with two-handed axes, and 4 Dwarf Warriors with Dwarf bows. Also on the Good side are 10 Wood Elf warriors armed with Elf bows. Two Dwarves can be given a banner.

The Evil side has 3 Moria Goblin Captains, 12 Moria Goblins with spears, 12 Moria Goblins with swords and shields, and 12 Moria Goblins with Orc bows.

POINTS MATCH

If you want to play this game with other forces, choose at least 300 points for each side. The Good side should include at least 1 Hero.

LAYOUT

The scenario is played on a board 48"/112cm by 72"/180cm. There is a large hill strewn with rocky debris roughly 12"/28cm from one of the short board edges (see map). The remainder of the board should be covered with trees and plenty of rocky outcrops.

STARTING POSITIONS

The Good player deploys the Dwarves anywhere on the hill. The Evil player then deploys the Goblins anywhere in that half of the board, but no closer than 6"/14cm to the Dwarves. Finally, the Good player deploys the Elves within 12"/28cm of the Mirkwood board edge (see map).

OBJECTIVES

The Good side wins if Murin escapes the board from the Mirkwood board edge.

The Evil side wins if Murin is slain.

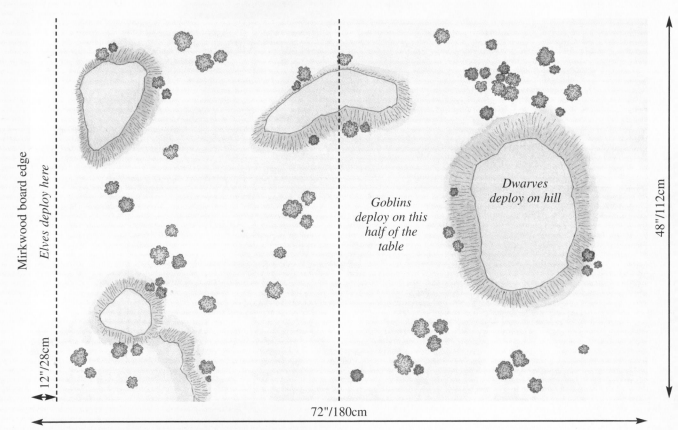

Mirkwood board edge

Elves deploy here

12"/28cm

Goblins deploy on this half of the table

Dwarves deploy on hill

48"/112cm

72"/180cm

The Dwarves fight to the death in defence of their king.

SPECIAL RULES

Strong Winds. Due to the high winds, from the start of the game all missile shots are considered to have an extra obstacle 'in the way' as soon as they are fired. From the fourth turn onwards, at the end of each turn, the player with priority must roll a D6. On a roll of a 4, 5 or 6, the winds abate for the rest of the game and shooting returns to normal.

Murin. To represent the severe wound already taken by Murin, he starts the game with no Fate and only a single Wound. However, due to the loyalty that his presence inspires, none of the Dwarves will ever take a Courage test while he lives. Note that this does not apply to the Elves.

NOTES

Strategy for the Goblins in this case is very straightforward – Attack! The Evil player has an overwhelming advantage in numbers in the initial turns of the game and should attempt to capitalise on this as much as he can. There are two main options open: wear down the numbers of the Dwarves, or go straight for Murin. Killing the Dwarves has an added bonus because if enough of them are killed, the Elves will begin to take Courage tests – even one failed test will buy a little more time.

The Dwarf player needs to think carefully about protecting Murin – nothing else matters! With the Wood Elves slowly gaining on the embattled Dwarves and the possibility that the wind will drop, the later game is very much in the favour of the Good side – but it does mean the Dwarves have to hold out until fortune swings their way. If the Good player is lucky he may even be able to sneak Murin past the Goblins and make a break for the table edge. If not, the Good player will probably have to think about killing or driving off all the Goblins.

SCENARIO THREE – BARUK KHÂZAD!

DESCRIPTION

With the power of Sauron once more on the rise, roads that once were safe are now full of danger. Once such road is the one linking the Lonely Mountain and the Dwarven holds in the Iron Hills. The Dwarves still travel between the two kingdoms, but are wary of the possibility of ambush. One party is not alert enough, and in the dead of night a force of Orcs attacks from the south. The Dwarves muster a desperate defence, but the sheer numbers of their foes are their undoing and they are all slain. As the Dwarves of Erebor look to the east for the arrival of their folk, the birds bring news of the massacre to Radagast the Brown, who in turn carries the sad tidings to the Lonely Mountain. Enraged by the attack, Dain leads a force of Dwarves to avenge their fallen. Given new stamina by their anger, the Dwarves swiftly overtake the fleeing Orcs and bring them to battle in the bright light of day…

PARTICIPANTS

The Good side consists of Dain Ironfoot, Radagast the Brown, 2 Dwarf Captains, 6 Khazâd Guard, 8 Dwarf Warriors with shields, 4 Dwarf Warriors with two-handed axes, and 6 Dwarf Warriors with Dwarf bows. Two Dwarves can be given a banner.

The Evil side consists of 2 Orc Captains (on foot), 2 Orc Captains (riding Wargs), 12 Orcs with swords and shields, 6 Orcs with Orc bows, 6 Orcs with spear, 6 Orcs with two-handed weapons, 5 Warg Riders with throwing spear and shield, and 5 Warg Riders with Orc bows. Two Orcs can be given a banner.

POINTS MATCH

If you want to play this scenario with different forces, choose 400 points of troops for each side. The Evil force must include at least one Hero.

LAYOUT

This scenario is played on a board 48"/112cm by 48"/112cm and takes place in the Wilderland surrounding Erebor. The board should be covered with trees and several hills with severe cliff faces. The Orc deployment area should be scattered with debris and fallen trees to represent the desolation they have caused.

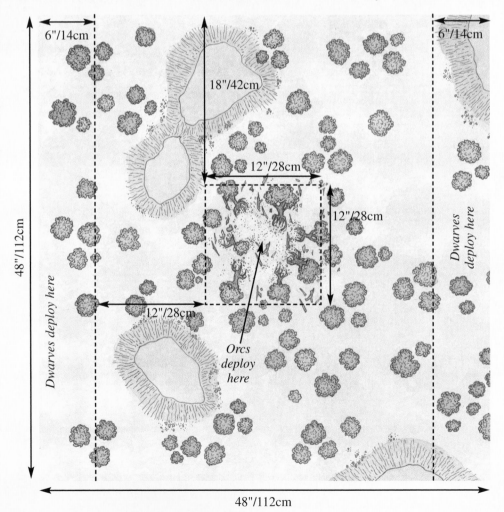

"The axes of the Dwarves are upon you!"

STARTING POSITIONS
The Evil player deploys the Orcs in the Evil deployment zone. The Good player then splits his forces into two equal sized groups and deploys one in each of the Dwarf deployment areas.

OBJECTIVES
The Good side wins if the Orcs are reduced to 25% or less of their starting numbers before the Dwarves are.

The Evil side wins if the Dwarves are reduced to 25% or less of their starting numbers before the Orcs are.

SPECIAL RULES
Cowardly. Surrounded, and with the sun shining bright above them, the Orcs are desperate to escape the fury of the Dwarf attack and only their Captains keep them in order. To represent this, in a turn following one where an Orc Captain has been killed, every Orc must test its Courage in the same way as if the Evil force had been reduced to below half strength. In subsequent turns, the Orcs may move as normal (unless another Captain has been slain).

Dwarven Fury. The Dwarves have come to avenge those slain by the Orcs. All Dwarves must always charge an enemy model if able to do so.

NOTES
The forces of Evil are very much on the back foot here with two dozen angry Dwarves and Radagast the Brown bearing down on them from two sides at once. It is easy for the Dwarf player to get lured into a sense of complacency by this, but a word of caution should be issued. The Dwarven Fury rule can prove to be a huge disadvantage for the Dwarf player and one that the Evil player should look to exploit, pulling the Dwarves apart prior to leaping on the tattered formation and tearing them apart. Another thing the Evil player should take advantage of is the fact that the Dwarves are slower than the Orcs, allowing the Evil player to pounce on one Dwarven force while the other catches up. The best tactic for the Dwarf player is to keep all this under consideration and try to keep the advantage on his side – all things being equal, one Dwarf is worth as much as two Orcs and it is in this advantage that your best chance lies.

SCENARIO FOUR – DAIN'S LAST STAND

DESCRIPTION

Even as Aragorn leads the armies of the Free Peoples to the Black Gate, the Lonely Mountain falls under siege. In recent years, Sauron had offered the Dwarves friendship in exchange for news of 'Baggins' and the 'trinket' that he carried. Dwarves do not break friendships lightly, and the Dwarves of Erebor owed Bilbo much. Dain refused Sauron's offer, spurning both his promises and threats, though he knew that in doing so he earned the wrath of the Lord of the Rings. As the Third Age draws to a close, Sauron has remembered the defiance of the Dwarves and has despatched a portion of his forces northwards. The kingdom of Dale falls swiftly and King Brand fights a rearguard action northwards. Soon the Lonely Mountain is a refuge for the survivors. As Sauron's force marches to the gates of Erebor, Dain and Brand draw their plans of battle – Dwarves and Men will fight alongside each other once again!

PARTICIPANTS

The Good side consists of Dain Ironfoot, 2 Dwarf Captains, 8 Khazâd Guard, 10 Dwarves with shields, 10 Dwarves with Dwarf bows, and 5 Dwarves with two-handed axes. In addition, the Good player has King Brand (use a King of Men to represent Brand), 8 Warriors of Rhovanion with shields and throwing spear (use Warriors of Rohan), 8 Warriors of Rhovanion with shield and 8 Warriors of Rhovanion with bows. Two Dwarves and two Men can be given a banner.

The Evil side has 2 Orc Captains, 1 Uruk-hai Captain, 1 Easterling Captain, 8 Orcs with sword and shields, 8 Orcs with spear, 4 Orcs with Orc bows, 4 Orcs with two-handed weapons, 10 Uruk-hai with swords and shields, 5 Uruk-hai with Orc bows, 4 Uruk-hai with two-handed weapons, 12 Warg Riders with throwing spear and shield, 8 Warg Riders with Orc bows, 10 Easterlings with shields, 5 Easterlings with shields and spears, and 2 Mordor Trolls. Two Orcs and one Uruk-hai can be given a banner.

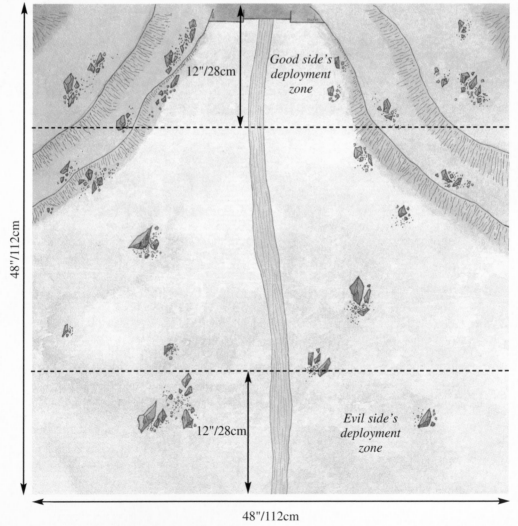

The Dwarves muster to defend their ancestral home.

POINTS MATCH

If you want to play this game with other forces, choose at least 700 points for each side.

LAYOUT

The scenario is played on a board 48"/112cm by 48"/112cm. The battle takes place before the gate of the Lonely Mountain. The gate should be in the centre of the board with the mountainside sloping away to either side (see map). The mountainside is passable, but counts as difficult terrain and should be strewn with rocky debris. The River Running flows from the gate and off the opposite board edge. This should be no more than 3"/8cm wide, and counts as difficult terrain. The remainder of the board should be mostly empty, with the odd tree here and there.

STARTING POSITIONS

The Good player deploys his force within the Good deployment zone (see map), the Evil player then deploys his force within the Evil deployment zone.

OBJECTIVES

The Good side wins if it manages to reduce the Evil force to 25% or less.

The Evil side wins if it manages to reduce the Good force to 25% or less.

If both sides accomplish their objectives in the same turn, the game is a draw.

SPECIAL RULES

Traps. The Dwarves have had ample time to plan their defence and have placed a series of snares and deadfalls along the approach to the gate. At the start of the game, before both players deploy, the Good player places three markers anywhere on the board. Each time an Evil model moves to within 3"/8cm of any of these markers, roll a dice. On the roll of a 4, 5 or 6 (Might cannot be used to modify this roll), the model takes a single Strength 6 hit – models with a Strength less than 6 are knocked to the ground. This roll should be made as soon as the Evil model moves to within 3"/8cm. Models who begin their move within 3"/8cm of a marker do not need to test. The Dwarves and Men know the exact location of the traps and so do not have to test.

SCENARIO FIVE – ASSAULT ON LOTHLORIEN

DESCRIPTION

As the War of the Ring rages and the forces of Gondor rally for their final stand, the forest realm of Lothlorien comes under assault by the forces of Mordor. The forest is completely besieged and the Elves valiantly twice repel the foul host as it attempts to pierce the defences. At the height of the third and final assault on Lorien, the Orcs attack on many fronts, stretching the defences to their limits. As Celeborn leads the Elves to repel one force of Orcs, Galadriel takes charge of the struggle against another contingent of the creatures. Can Galadriel's command hold the Orcs at bay long enough for help to arrive?

PARTICIPANTS

The Good side consists of Galadriel, Celeborn, 2 Elf Captains, 10 Wood Elves with armour & Elf bows, 10 Wood Elves with armour & Elven blades, and 20 Wood Elves with Elf bows. Three Elves can be given a banner.

The Evil side has 2 Uruk-hai Captains, 2 Orc Captains, 10 Uruk-hai with Orc bows, 8 Orcs with swords and shields, 8 Orcs with spear, 4 Orcs with Orc bows, 4 Orcs with two-handed weapons, 10 Uruk-hai with swords and shields, 5 Uruk-hai with two-handed weapons, 6 Warg Riders with throwing spear and shield, 6 Warg Riders with Orc bows, and 2 Mordor Trolls. Two Uruk-hai and two Orcs can be given a banner.

POINTS MATCH

If you want to play this game with other forces, choose at least 700 points for each side. The Good side should include at least two heroes.

LAYOUT

The scenario is played on a board 48"/112cm by 72"/180cm. As this scenario takes place in the heart of the forest of Lothlorien, the board should be heavily wooded with a few hills scattered about the board (see map). A river, the Nimrodel, flows through the centre of the board – this is crossable, but counts as difficult terrain. There are two bridges that cross the Nimrodel (see map).

STARTING POSITIONS

The Good player deploys Galadriel, an Elf Captain, and 10 Wood Elves with bows in the Good side's deployment zone (see map). The Evil player then deploys a third of his force within 6"/14cm of the opposite table edge, another third within 12"/28cm of the table edge and the remaining third of his force within 18"/42cm of that table edge.

The Good player then deploys 10 Wood Elves with bows anywhere on the board, but may deploy them no closer than 6"/14cm to an Evil model. The rest of the Good force may be available as reinforcements as the game goes on.

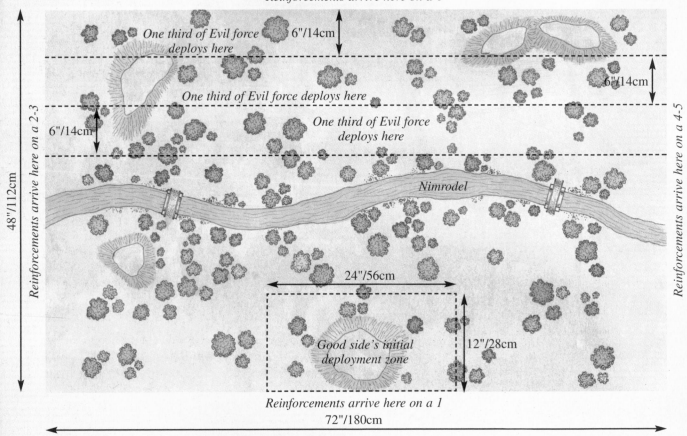

Reinforcements arrive here on a 6

One third of Evil force deploys here — 6"/14cm

One third of Evil force deploys here

One third of Evil force deploys here

6"/14cm

Reinforcements arrive here on a 2-3

6"/14cm

Nimrodel

48"/112cm

Reinforcements arrive here on a 4-5

24"/56cm

12"/28cm

Good side's initial deployment zone

Reinforcements arrive here on a 1

72"/180cm

Vicious hand-to-hand combat in Lothlorien.

OBJECTIVES

The Good side wins if it manages to reduce the Evil force to 25% or less.

The Evil side wins if it manages to kill both of the named Heroes (ie, Celeborn and Galadriel) or reduce the Good force to 25% or less.

If both sides accomplish their objectives in the same turn, the game is a draw.

SPECIAL RULES

Reinforcements. Celeborn has defeated the main Evil force and is leading his survivors back to Galadriel's aid with all speed. From the second turn onwards, the Good player may roll a D6 to see if Celeborn has arrived. On a roll of 4+, the Good player may deploy Celeborn's group (all the Good models that were not deployed at the start of the game) that turn. To see where the group arrives, the Good player rolls a further D6 and deploys them anywhere along the indicated table edge (see map).

Lothlorien. Within the boundaries of the land of Lothlorien, Galadriel's powers maintain the world as it once was. Beyond her own realm her powers are limited, although still strong. Galadriel and Celeborn will pass all Fate rolls on a 2+, rather than a 4 or more.

The Power of Galadriel. The power of the Elven rings is to heal and sustain, not destroy and dominate. With Nenya, Galadriel has woven a powerful enchantment over Lothlorien that protects the Elves from harm. To represent this, whenever an Elf suffers a wound, the Good player may roll a D6. On the roll of a 6 the wound is recovered. This is effectively like using a point of Fate, with the only exception that the wound is recovered only on a 6 rather than on a 4+. Should Galadriel be slain, the power fades and this ability is lost.

NOTES

Again, the Evil player needs to cover as much ground as possible and take the fight to the Elves. With the Elves initially outnumbered, if the Evil player can close the gap before Good reinforcements arrive, sheer weight of numbers will lead to slaughter. Once Celeborn arrives however, things become a little different – the best strategy then is to try to crush one of the groups individually.

The Good player needs to buy time for the reinforcements to arrive, using the infiltrated troops to delay the Evil advance. Galadriel is an incredible asset in this scenario. With her reserves of Will, she can be relied upon to tie up enemy Trolls or Captains with ease, leaving the remainder of the troops to deal with the bulk of the Evil forces.

THE MINIATURES

The Lord of The Rings gaming miniatures are made from either rigid plastic or high quality pewter. The plastic models are an ideal starting point for a collection – they provide the player with a core of warriors at relatively little cost. The metal models are hand-cast pieces available either as boxed sets or in display packs.

All models have separate bases and, in addition, some models have separate shields. All of the plastic models are designed to fit together without glue, but we recommend that plastic models are glued together using polystyrene cement.

ASSEMBLING PLASTIC MODELS

Plastic mouldings are produced as a sprue – just like plastic aeroplanes and other model kits. Before assembling the models it is a good idea to wash the entire sprue in warm water to which a little washing-up liquid has been added. This will remove any residual lubricant left on the sprue.

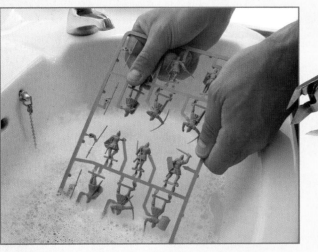

Pieces can be removed from the sprues using modelling clippers or a suitable craft knife. If desired any attachment scars can be gently pared away with a craft knife or filed smooth by means of a file.

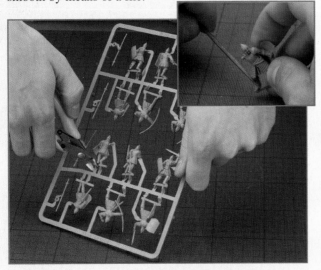

ASSEMBLING METAL MODELS

The Lord of The Rings miniatures range includes both small and large models. Some are cast in a single piece whilst others come as kits of several components. Generally speaking, most of the man-sized creatures are single-piece castings whilst the largest monsters, such as the Shelob, are multi-piece models.

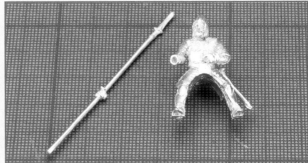

This Knight of Gondor has a separate spear that will need carefully fixing in place with superglue.

Even models supplied as a single metal casting will have a separate plastic base and sometimes a separate shield too. These will need to be attached using superglue or an adhesive modelling putty as described opposite.

Remove any stray metal vents or casting marks from the model before assembling. Vents are cut into the moulds to allow air to escape – this leaves a thin spur of metal that often falls away when the model is removed from the mould. If not this can be removed with a modelling knife or clippers, and any resultant scar can be filed flat using a small modelling file.

If a model comes in two or more metal parts some extra work is required. Test the pieces for fit before assembly and use a file to smooth out any notable blemishes or high points that prevent alignment. Don't worry if the fit is not perfect – hand-cast parts vary slightly and it is usual to find slight gaps that will require filling later. Once you are satisfied with the fit assemble the pieces using superglue.

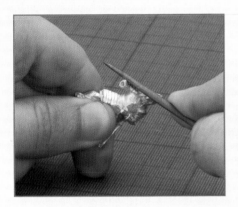
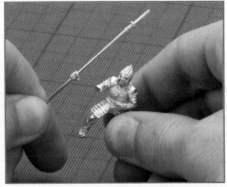

MODELLING TIP

Hand-cast metal models will naturally vary slightly and it is quite common for a model's base rail to sit loosely in the plastic base. This is not usually a problem as the models will be glued to their bases anyway – but a firm fit can be created by taking a small pair of pliers and kinking the base rail slightly.

GLUE

Glues commonly used for modelling include liquid polystyrene, PVA glue and superglue.

FILLERS

Slight gaps and joins will tend to disappear under a coat of paint, or can be filled with a dab of glue. Larger gaps however will need to be filled. There are many types of modelling putty available for this – most come as a two-part epoxy putty that cures once mixed.

These two-part epoxy putties can also be used to fasten shields into place or to fix models onto their slots. They are best employed as adhesive reinforcement where they won't be seen (such as behind a shield).

A good alternative for filling small gaps is ordinary plasticine modelling clay – once painted it will prove quite durable if carefully handled. Plasticine is not suitable for filling larger gaps, but any number of household wood or surface fillers will do the job perfectly well.

You can also use plasticine to weight the bases of plastic models – this makes them more stable and gives a pleasant sense of heft which plastic models otherwise lack. Simply pack plasticine or similar modelling clay or putty under the model's base. As this can sometimes dry out and become dislodged it is worth dabbing a little superglue under the base first to hold the plasticine in place. Some people also use small chips of metal or metal pellets to add weight.

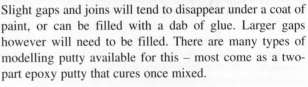

PAINTING THE MODELS

Most players will want to assemble their models right away so that they can learn the game or take part in a new scenario. Other players feel that models are only really 'finished' once painted and would never dream of bringing a warrior to battle without its requisite coat of paint. The Lord of The Rings battle game works perfectly well whether the models are painted or not. If you are learning the game you certainly won't want to wait until you have painted an entire army before playing. On the other hand, most players enjoy the spectacle of painted models and usually get round to painting at least some of their collection.

WHAT YOU WILL NEED

You will need somewhere to paint, such as a desk or table placed by a window so you can see what you are doing. Good lighting is important and if you want to paint in the evenings you will need a desk lamp or something similar.

Once you have cleared a space to paint, put a good thick layer of newspaper onto the surface to protect it from spills and being scratched. It's a good idea to back this up with a piece of heavy card or board on the area where you will be working directly, but an extra layer of newspaper will do just as well.

Finally, make sure your work area is as comfortable as possible. If you can adjust the height of your chair or the table itself so much the better. Put on some music – listen to the radio – relax and enjoy spending time painting.

BRUSHES. Citadel Colour brushes are made specifically with painting our kind of models in mind. They are made from quality sable and sized according to function.

Different painters will favour different sizes of brush depending on their style and subject, but most people find the Standard brush is ideal for most purposes. After that, the most useful is the Detail brush for intricate work, and a Basecoat brush for larger areas. One each of Detail, Standard and Basecoat will provide all you need for most tasks.

If you prefer, other makes of quality sable artist brushes can be used. You can find a selection in any specialist art suppliers. In addition, the The Lord of The Rings paint set comes with a Starter brush which is halfway between a Standard and Detail in size and is an ideal compromise for most functions, especially for beginners who often find a slightly smaller brush easier to handle.

Looking After Brushes – *Brushes are not cheap so it is worth looking after them. They will last longer and serve you better. Try to avoid getting the brush so overloaded that the paint runs into the metal part of the handle (the ferrule) where it will dislodge the glue and unseat the bristles. When you have finished a painting session rinse out your brush carefully in clean, cold water, and repoint the bristles between thumb and forefinger. Store the brushes point-upwards in an old mug or similar container – they will retain their points for longer.*

Old Brushes – As brushes wear they gradually lose their points and develop stray bristles. Pinch off any bristles that become bent or stick out at an angle. Once the brush becomes too worn for general use it can be employed for gluing, painting bases, or for other rough work where it would be a waste to use a good brush.

Old faithful!

Above is a range of paints and brushes available from Games Workshop for painting your The Lord of The Rings miniatures with.

PAINT. Citadel Colour paint is designed for painting plastic and metal miniatures. It is non-toxic and water based but waterproof once dry.

You can also use other water-based acrylic modelling or artists' paints, although you will find colour and consistency varies somewhat from one manufacturer to another.

To begin with you'll need a minimal selection of colours to which you can add different shades as required.

WATER. You will need clean water to rinse brushes off with between colours and to thin down paint. A low, sturdy container is essential to avoid accidentally knocking over your water.

TISSUE. This is useful for wiping paint and excess water from brushes. Also useful for dealing with the occasional spillage.

PALETTE. A fancy word for an old white plate, saucer, glazed tile, or something similar – although an expensive artists' palette is fine too. Whilst it is sometimes convenient to use paint straight from the pots, on the whole it is better to avoid doing so as it is all too easy to mix the colours or introduce dirty paint water. The palette forms a reservoir of colour and a surface to mix paint and water as needed.

PAINT & INKS RANGE

Games Workshop make a range of water-based paints and inks that can be freely mixed to make a huge range of colours.

SHADE & HIGHLIGHT: Recommended colours to be used when shading and highlighting the relevant colour. Where no colour is indicated, we recommend you add some black to the relevant colour to create a shade, or some white to create a highlight colour.

COLOUR	SHADE	HIGHLIGHT	COLOUR	SHADE	HIGHLIGHT
SCAB RED	NONE	RED GORE	BLEACHED BONE	BUBONIC BROWN	SKULL WHITE
RED GORE	SCAB RED	BLOOD RED	DARK FLESH	NONE	TANNED FLESH
BLOOD RED	RED GORE	BLAZING ORANGE	TERRACOTTA	DARK FLESH	VERMIN BROWN
BLAZING ORANGE	BLOOD RED	FIERY ORANGE	VERMIN BROWN	DARK FLESH	VOMIT BROWN
FIERY ORANGE	BLAZING ORANGE	GOLDEN YELLOW	TANNED FLESH	DARK FLESH	DWARF FLESH
GOLDEN YELLOW	FIERY ORANGE	SUNBURST YELLOW	DWARF FLESH	DARK FLESH	ELF FLESH
SUNBURST YELLOW	GOLDEN YELLOW	BAD MOON YELLOW	BRONZED FLESH	DWARF FLESH	SKULL WHITE
BAD MOON YELLOW	SUNBURST YELLOW	SKULL WHITE	ELF FLESH	DWARF FLESH	SKULL WHITE
SCORCHED BROWN	NONE	BESTIAL BROWN	LICHE PURPLE	MIDNIGHT BLUE	NONE
GRAVEYARD EARTH	SCORCHED BROWN	KOMMANDO KHAKI	WARLOCK PURPLE	LICHE PURPLE	TENTACLE PINK
BESTIAL BROWN	SCORCHED BROWN	SNAKEBITE LEATHER	TENTACLE PINK	WARLOCK PURPLE	SKULL WHITE
SNAKEBITE LEATHER	BESTIAL BROWN	BUBONIC BROWN	MIDNIGHT BLUE	NONE	REGAL BLUE
DESERT YELLOW	SNAKEBITE LEATHER	BLEACHED BONE	REGAL BLUE	MIDNIGHT BLUE	ULTRAMARINES BLUE
BUBONIC BROWN	SNAKEBITE LEATHER	BLEACHED BONE	ULTRAMARINES BLUE	REGAL BLUE	ICE BLUE
VOMIT BROWN	VERMIN BROWN	BRONZED FLESH	ENCHANTED BLUE	REGAL BLUE	ICE BLUE

CITADEL INKS

YELLOW   CHESTNUT   MAGENTA   BLUE   BROWN

FLESH   RED   PURPLE   DARK GREEN   BLACK

COLOUR	SHADE	HIGHLIGHT
ICE BLUE	ENCHANTED BLUE	SKULL WHITE
HAWK TURQUOISE	SCALY GREEN	NONE
CATACHAN GREEN	DARK ANGELS GREEN	CAMO GREEN
DARK ANGELS GREEN	NONE	SNOT GREEN
SNOT GREEN	DARK ANGELS GREEN	SCORPION GREEN
SCORPION GREEN	SNOT GREEN	NONE
SCALY GREEN	NONE	HAWK TURQUOISE
GOBLIN GREEN	SNOT GREEN	NONE
CAMO GREEN	CATACHAN GREEN	ROTTING FLESH
KOMMANDO KHAKI	GRAVEYARD EARTH	SKULL WHITE
ROTTING FLESH	NONE	SKULL WHITE
CHAOS BLACK	NONE	CODEX GREY
CODEX GREY	CHAOS BLACK	FORTRESS GREY
FORTRESS GREY	CODEX GREY	SKULL WHITE
SKULL WHITE	FORTRESS GREY	NONE

COLOUR	SHADE	HIGHLIGHT
SHADOW GREY	NONE	SPACE WOLF GREY
SPACE WOLVES GREY	SHADOW GREY	SKULL WHITE
VARNISH	NONE	NONE

METALLIC PAINTS

COLOUR	SHADE	HIGHLIGHT
BOLTGUN METAL	CHAOS BLACK	CHAINMAIL
CHAINMAIL	BOLTGUN METAL	MITHRIL SILVER
MITHRIL SILVER	CHAINMAIL	NONE
TIN BITZ	CHAOS BLACK	BRAZEN BRASS
BRAZEN BRASS	TIN BITZ	SHINING GOLD
SHINING GOLD	BRAZEN BRASS	BURNISHED GOLD
BURNISHED GOLD	SHINING GOLD	MITHRIL SILVER
DWARF BRONZE	TIN BITZ	BURNISHED GOLD

UNDERCOATING MODELS

It is very much recommended that models are primed before painting. This is simply a matter of applying an undercoat – usually white – over the entire model. The undercoat provides an overall surface for the paint itself and ensures that bare metal or plastic doesn't show through.

Even when spraying outside, put plenty of paper down to contain the spray.

There are two basic methods for undercoating. Most experienced painters use a spray can of matt white undercoat or primer such as the Citadel Skull White undercoat. The spray makes an especially good surface finish for the paint.

A more convenient method for beginners is to apply a brush-on undercoat using either Citadel Smelly Primer or Skull White paint. This is nothing more than a coat of white over the entire model.

Colour of undercoat – Some experienced painters prefer to work off a black primer rather than a white base. This can be more difficult to work with because colours always look different when applied over black and coverage may be more patchy. Painters who use this method usually leave the primer uncovered in the deepest recesses of the model, and work up the paint with progressively lighter colours. This can be very effective in the hands of experts but it is by no means a superior method – many experts prefer to work from white.

The defenders of Minas Tirith clash with the forces of Sauron.

MAKING A START

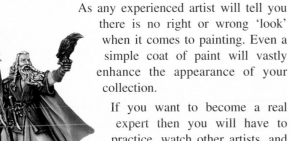

As any experienced artist will tell you there is no right or wrong 'look' when it comes to painting. Even a simple coat of paint will vastly enhance the appearance of your collection.

If you want to become a real expert then you will have to practice, watch other artists, and take the time to develop your skills. Most importantly, don't feel that you have to produce a masterpiece each and every time you paint. Now and again you might want to paint a model specifically as a display piece, but such models are best kept away from the gaming table and preserved from constant handling and wear.

Begin with a model that has been assembled. Make sure any glue used is thoroughly set before applying paint.

Use Clean Water – Each time you sit down to paint get a fresh pot of clean water. At the end of each session throw away the dirty water and clean out your water pot. There is nothing so dispiriting as sitting down to a filthy pot of water!

Some painters routinely use two pots of water instead of one – one pot for general use and the other pot for metallic paint. Metallic paint consists of finely ground metal flakes that tend to float on the water's surface and get into the brush very easily. The metal colour is then transferred to other paint and stands out like a sore thumb on a model. A separate water pot helps to alleviate this problem. In any case, it is a good idea to change the water during a session if it becomes especially dirty.

Paint Pots – Paint will gradually dry out in the pot. Paint left on lids will compromise the fit so that paint dries even faster. To avoid this it is always worth taking the time to wipe the pot lids if they get messy, and add a little clean water to each pot at the end of each painting session.

After undercoating the model a hairdryer can be used to speed the process up if you wish but be careful not to get the model too hot!

FLAT COLOUR

When you apply a single solid colour onto your undercoat, the result is a flat colour – an even coverage with no shading, highlighting or other effects. In some cases two

light coats of paint may be needed to achieve a uniform flat colour – this gives better results than a single very heavy coat, which may obscure detail.

When you're starting out with this hobby painting miniatures in flat colours will be the natural thing to do. However, after you've gained some confidence you might want to start adding little tricks such as a 'wash or 'drybrushing', which will transform a model's appearance dramatically.

WASHES

Traditionally a 'wash' is a mix of usually strongly coloured paint and just sufficient water to give an overall fluid consistency. This mixture is applied over a light base colour and, depending on how much wash is used, will tend to run into the cracks and crevices. The result is an overall 'stain' that is stronger in the recesses where the wash gathers. This introduces a level of naturally gradated shading onto the model and breaks up the overall colour into subtle patches of dark and light. The surface finish will be slightly mottled and therefore appears more natural in the case of organic surfaces such as flesh, leather, and cloth.

Paint the skin Bronzed Flesh.

Apply a diluted mix of Flesh Wash, Scorched Brown and PVA glue to the skin.

Paint the hair Bubonic Brown, leaving the Chaos Black undercoat in the deepest recesses.

Apply the same mix used for the face to the hair.

Paint the cloak Goblin Green.

Apply a dilute mix of Dark Green Ink, Scorched Brown paint, and PVA glue.

To enable wash techniques to be used effectively, the Citadel Colour range includes acrylic inks that are designed to be used with washing and glazing techniques. The darker ink colours are ideal for washes, and black can be mixed in to make them even darker. Because ink contains an intense pigment in a transparent medium, it gives better results than a mix made up of paint and water.

Paint a basecoat of Chainmail over the whole armour.

Apply a wash of Black Ink over the Chainmail areas.

By adding some PVA glue you can change the effect of an ink wash. The PVA glue enhances the gathering qualities of the wash and produces a stronger contrast once dry. You will have to experiment to judge the effect for yourself. Conversely, if you want to reduce the gathering quality of an ink wash, producing a more even overall tone, add a little liquid soap, such as washing up liquid. This breaks the surface tension so the ink stains the surface more uniformly without forming patches.

If you wish to try washing with paint, it is worth experimenting by adding Citadel Colour Varnish to the mix. This makes paint behave much more like ink and strengthens the contrast compared to paint and water alone. Again, as with all wash techniques, you will need to experiment to gauge the result. Some courage is called for!

If you use too much wash, or if the wash is settling where you do not want it, it is easy to draw away the surplus using either a brush or tissue. If bubbles form in the wash they will usually disperse quickly, but sometimes they will dry within the recesses of the model leaving clean patches. Blowing briskly on the model will help to disperse any bubbles whilst the wash is still wet.

Re-undercoat Legolas, hair Skull White.

Paint a mix of Golden Yellow and Bestial Brown over the Skull White.

Apply a watered down wash of Scorched Brown over the hair.

Washes seem to work better over pastel colours as this emphasises the contrast. Add a little white to the basecoat and observe the effect of a wash.

> *The Citadel Colour inks, paints, varnish and PVA glue can be mixed together to vary the properties of a wash. As with all techniques, improvement comes with practise, and in the case of washes it is worth performing a few tests so that you can judge the results for yourself. You can do this by taking a white undercoated figure – like one of the plastic Mordor Orcs – and experimenting with the different effects of using inks, diluted paint, and paint and varnish.*

DRYBRUSHING

A drybrush technique is a fast and attractive way of adding highlights to areas of raised detail. It can also be used to apply a fine texture to large flat areas such as armour plating to create a realistic effect. A light drybrush over an entire model can give it an overall dusting that draws the colours together and gives a natural appearance.

Drybrushing is most easily demonstrated by painting a hair or fur texture. Begin with a suitable base colour that has been shaded with a wash if required – the drybrushing is added at the final stage to provide highlights.

Take the brush (preferably an old brush) and mix up a light shade of the base colour. The paint needs to be fairly dense. If the paint is a little thin, let it dry slightly on the palette. Work the colour into the brush and then wipe any excess back onto the palette.

Now – most importantly – run the brush over a tissue or newspaper, or some similarly absorbent surface, until the strokes leave almost no mark even when applied with pressure. Depending on the effect you want, you can make the brush more or less dry.

Begin by stroking the brush gently over the surface that you wish to highlight. If done properly the brush should leave no discernible strokes, but only deposits a fine, even dusting of colour over the high points on the model.

The drier the brush, the more the effect will appear as a dusting of even colour. Build up the highlights gradually and notice how repeated dusting gives naturally gradated highlights. The longer you work at the result, the more intense the effect.

Several progressively lighter layers of drybrushing can be applied to increase contrast – the final layer can be white. If you drybrush over a fairly bright colour, the result can sometimes look very chalky. If you want to restore colour while retaining the highlighting, apply a wash of ink mixed with a lot of water to bring some of the colour back into it.

Drybrush Scorched Brown straight onto the black undercoated fur.

Apply a lighter drybrush of Snakebite Leather on top.

Give the fur a final drybrush of Bleached Bone.

First, apply a basecoat of Tin Bitz to the Uruk-hai's armour.

Then drybrush over the armour with Mithril Silver.

Drybrush the cloak with Shadow Grey.

Lightly drybrush Bestial Brown on the edge of the cloak to resemble dirt.

LAYERING

Layering is a technique of representing shade and highlights by painting successive gradations of a colour from dark to light. Two-tone layering over a black undercoat provides shading and highlighting and looks effective from any reasonable distance. In principle, the technique can be used with any undercoat and can be refined to the point where individual layers become indistinguishable even from very close up. A multi-tone layering technique taken to its ultimate form gives results that are comparable to a fully blended technique, but there are many situations where an extra layer will help to give definition to a model.

Basic colour   *First colour*   *Second colour*

A sophisticated multi-layer technique relies on mixing the colours together in different proportions to produce intermediate shades. The colour samples shown alongside illustrate this quite well. In our samples the effect is a succession of stripes, but if the stripes are sufficiently narrow then the eye ceases to distinguish the individual shades even from close up.

Dark Angels Green, Scorpion Green, Scorpion Green, & Skull White

Scorched Brown, Snakebite Leather & Bronzed Flesh

Layering can be used to produce a dramatic contrast. Many people find this 'stripy' style very pleasing when well executed. That means choosing colours that work together despite the differences in shade. Dramatic layering rarely uses more than three layers and some examples of useful colour combinations are shown below.

Paint a layer of Dwarf Flesh over a basecoat of Bestial Brown, leaving the deepest recesses dark.

Apply a lighter layer of Elf Flesh over the previous one, concentrating on the highest points of detail.

If you look at the Citadel Colour range you can work out dramatic contrasts by taking a root colour and picking out the midtone and one of the lightest colours in the series.

Many people find it quite difficult to get good results with very bright colours using this technique because the colours are hard to tone together. A way of getting colours to tone together better is to mix a little of the adjoining colour/s into the paint for each layer. Another way to make all the colours slightly pastel is by adding a little of the same very pale neutral colour such as Rotting Flesh, Fortress Grey, Bleached Bone or Skull White – this will draw all the colours together.

Give Saruman's robes a basecoat of Bestial Brown.

Layer Kommando Khaki on top of the folds of the robe, leaving the basecolour in the recesses.

Apply a lighter layer of Bleached Bone over the previous one.

Finally, apply a layer of Skull White on the top of the sharpest folds.

Hair and Fur – *Hair and fur textures can be brought to life by means of brushing a lighter colour over the raised detail to create highlights. The less paint you use the more subtle the effect – experiment to get a look which you like. You may find it helps to actually wipe most of the paint from the brush, leaving only a little dry residue. Then brush over the areas to be highlighted, depositing a fine dusting of paint to the raised areas.*

Base colour

First layer

Final layer

Painting Faces – *Beginners often find faces daunting but it is quite easy to get a realistic effect using the method shown here. In this case the artist is working over a black undercoat – but the technique will work perfectly well over white. The base colour is Dwarf Flesh. Once this is dry, Brown Ink has been painted over and allowed to gather into the creases. Once this is dry, the artist has mixed Dwarf Flesh and Elf Flesh and repainted the face*

Dwarf Flesh

Brown Ink

Mix to finish

but leaving the Brown Ink showing around the eyes, nose, and other recessed areas. Finally, Elf Flesh has been used to paint the high points on the face – the bridge of the nose, cheeks, and brow ridges. This can be seen more clearly in the accompanying diagram.

Detail – *The amount of detail you include is up to you, but don't feel you have to add every fingernail or dot the pupil of each eye. Our models are generally seen at arm's length or greater and will appear very much like real people at 50 to 100 paces away. At those kinds of distances eyes, nails, teeth, and details of clothing don't really stand out. Trying to paint eyes onto models an inch tall is not only taxing, but tends to look unrealistically starey. Such levels of detail are best reserved for those you want to display, where you might happily spend an hour getting the face 'just right'.*

Button, rivets, and small details – *Imagine you are painting a coat with a row of buttons and you have painted the coat colour. Now you want to make the buttons really stand out from the coat. First paint each button black, allowing the paint to cover the entire button and slightly overlap onto the coat. Wait until this is dry and then paint each button with silver, leaving the overlap showing black. Result – a silver button outlined in black. You can use the same technique to outline any small area of raised detail to make it really stand out.*

Varnish – *Some people like to apply a coat of varnish to their model once it is finished. This protects the paint from chipping or wearing away whilst the miniature is being used in a battle.*

Should you wish to varnish your models use either a brush-on polyurethane varnish or a spray can. Some people like the highly shiny finish of protective varnish – but others hate it!

If you prefer a non-gloss finish matt varnishes are available too!

PAINTING DWARVES

Throughout this book there are photographs of superbly painted models on the tabletop. Here we show you how easy it is to get a good result yourself. To paint your models you don't need many tools either; just a few paints, a brush, a space to work on with newspaper to protect the surface and a little patience.

This painting guide shows how to paint a Dwarf. By applying just a few quick and effective techniques, you'll be able to to recreate the same colour scheme we used on Balin's Dwarves.

Q 120%

The model is undercoated Chaos Black.

1

1

1

Textured areas such as metal can be brought to life by brushing Chainmail over the raised detail to create highlights. You may find it helps to actually wipe most of the paint from the brush, leaving only a little dry residue. Then brush over the areas to be highlighted, depositing a fine dusting of paint to the raised areas.

2

Using the same approach as for painting the metal, apply Bestial Brown to the strands of beard and hair. To finish off the beard, paint the clasps with Chainmail.

3

Dwarf Flesh is applied to the face and hands. Try not to paint into the recesses of the eyes and fingers – you want to keep the undercoat showing to define the shape.

3

If you get paint between the fingers or into eyes, slightly thin down some Chaos Black paint and, following the shape of the model, line-in the recesses.

4

Apply a base colour of Snot Green to the Dwarf's tunic and sleeves. To make a solid colour you may have to apply several coats of paint.

5

Bubonic Brown is painted onto the boots.

6

To finish off, an equal parts mix of Flesh Wash and water is applied to the boots to create shading effect.

7

The axe handle and helmet are painted a basecoat of Dark Flesh.

8

Bestial Brown is applied to the belt and pouch.

9

To finish off the Dwarf's tunic, you may want to paint a stripe of Golden Yellow around the hem. You may have to apply several coats of paint to produce a solid colour.

10

Apply a drybrush of Chainmail to the metal on the shield.

11

Re-undercoat the centre of the shield Chaos Black.

12

To finish off the shield, apply a coat of Snot Green over the black undercoat. Apply several coats to get a strong flat colour.

This approach to painting a Dwarf demonstrates how flat colours, when neatly applied to a model with a few painting effects, can really bring a model to life. When painted onto Balin's Dwarves, this simple colour scheme creates a unified look to the force which is effective on the tabletop.

Painting the bases of your models to match each other and your gaming table gives a much better overall effect.

CONVERSIONS

This is not really the place to describe some of the techniques by which ambitious modellers create entirely new miniatures by cutting, transplanting, and remodelling the standard pieces. Hobbyists usually refer to these special models as conversions – you'll find much more about painting, modelling and converting in Games Workshop's monthly magazine White Dwarf.

This nicely converted Gondorian Captain started life as a Spearman – the sword has been carefully cut from another model and repositioned.

The Elven Captain conversion is based on the Elrond model but has been given a different head and a shield slung on his back.

This Rohan warrior has had his spear replaced with an axe.

This Mordor Orc was originally armed with a sword. The hand was drilled through and a piece of wire inserted. An axe head was cut from another Orc and attached to make a long-hafted axe.

This splendid Rider of Rohan started life with a bow but has been converted to carry a sword and shield – his mount has also been changed into a rearing pose.

This Rohan warrior's right arm has been repositioned to make a more dramatic pose.

This standard bearer is converted from an Uruk-hai Pikeman – the crosspiece is brass tubing and the rope binding has been made from cotton. The banner itself is paper stiffened with PVA glue.

Riding down his Uruk-hai foe, this Rider of Rohan was originally converted to feature his spear pointing downwards. Then the modeller decided to add an Uruk-hai being ridden down by the mounted warrior. The final touch was to cut and turn the rider's head towards his victim.

The defenders of Minas Tirith.

ASSEMBLING MULTI-PART MINIATURES

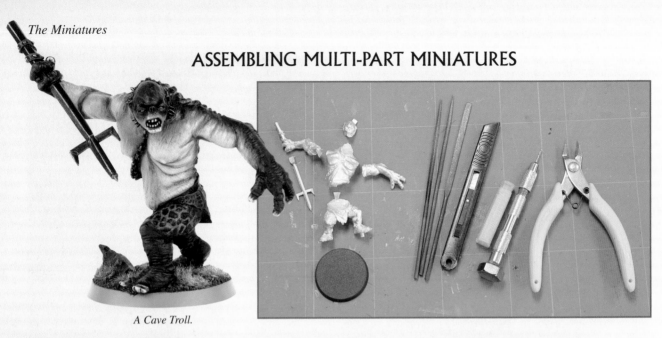

A Cave Troll.

GETTING STARTED

Within The Lord of The Rings range there are a number of large creatures for you to add to your force. These are normally multi-part figures, designed for more advanced modellers, but do not be put off by this. Here are a few of the tools that you'll need to assemble multi-part models:

A craft knife
A selection of needle files
A pair of clippers
A pin vice and drill bits
A cutting board

Safety is a very important consideration when undertaking modelling work of any kind. All of these tools are potentially dangerous and need to be used with care. Blunt blades are dangerous, as far more force is required to make a cut.

1. Using a pair of clippers, carefully remove the tabs from all the component parts.

2. The next stage is to smooth the surface down with a needle file and remove any rough edges.

3. Some multi-part models come with a pin in one of the legs. A hole should be cut onto the base and the pin glued into it. In the case of the 40mm round base, the underside

has a set of specially located holes; turn the base upside down so you can see a suitable hole that matches the model's stance. Drill a small guide hole directly through its centre, using a pin vice.

4. Hold the base firmly and twist the knife gently into the guide hole until it bores through the plastic.

5. The legs are then attached to the base using superglue.

PINNING

In the case of multi-part models, such as the Cave Troll, Balrog and Fell Beast, pinning the different pieces together gives a stronger fit. The model is also less likely to break due to handling during a game. To pin a model, the two joining parts have a matching hole drilled into them into which a small metal rod is glued, adding strength to the joint.

1. Two holes are drilled into the join, approximately 5mm deep.

2. A short length of wire is inserted into each of the holes and a small blob of paint applied to the end of each.

3. Whilst the paint is still wet the two parts are carefully aligned and pressed together. When the two parts are separated the paint leaves two marks where matching holes need to be made. Once they are drilled, slightly longer pieces of wire are glued into the holes and the join completed.

You can pin any parts you feel need strengthening like this.

DETAILING BASES

Larger models naturally have larger bases and it's a good idea to add some scenic decoration such as a small rock, plants or bushes. Bear in mind that one or two well-placed areas of detail will work far better that overloading the base with too much material.

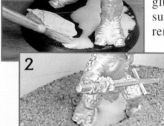

1. A small pebble is first glued to the base using superglue. Once dry, the remaining surface of the base is painted with PVA.

2. Dip the base in sand and, once the material is dry, it is ready for painting.

LARGE CREATURES

Quite often bodies such as the Balrog's come in two halves. To ensure a good join between the two pieces, you may need to file them down a little or fill in any tiny gaps. Apply a thin layer of black paint to the rim of one of the

body halves, and when the paint is dry press the two halves together and give a very slight twist.

When the two halves are pulled apart, paint will have worn away where the pieces need to be filed down. File away small areas of metal, repeating the whole process until a good fit is achieved.

FILLING GAPS

When the model is assembled, some joins may still be

visible. Roll Green Stuff into a long sausage and lay it along the line of the join. Smooth the putty into shape using the blunt end of a sculpting tool dipped in water.

Details such as scales or fur require a little modelling work to blend the modelling putty so that it matches the detail. Using the sharp end of the sculpting tool, follow the pattern and lines of the model as closely as possible.

MAKING FLAGS

You can add a flag to a spear to make a suitable banner or substitute a weapon for a length of wire to make a flag pole. The best material for flag poles is brass rod as this is quite rigid. To add a flag pole to a model it is necessary to cut away any weapon and drill out the fist so that it can carry the wire pole.

A flag can be made from paper. A piece of newsprint devoid of ink, such as can be found along the edges of any newspaper, is ideal for this as it is absorbent but reasonably stiff. Cut the flag shape leaving an extra 5mm towards the pole. Wrap the flag round the pole and check for fit. Using PVA 'white woodworking glue', glue along its extreme edge and allow to dry. Now wrap the flag round the pole and apply more PVA glue thinned with water, allowing the glue to soak into the part of the flag around the pole. Once this is dry paint the entire flag with a mixture of PVA glue and water, arrange into a dramatic shape, and allow to dry. As the PVA dries out it stiffens sufficiently so the flag can be coated overall with white, ready to paint with your preferred design.

Remove the model's weapon with clippers.

File the hand flat.

Drill a hole through the hand with a pin vice.

Cut the flag from a piece of paper.

Push a piece of brass rod through for the banner pole.

Use PVA to fasten the flag.

Fix the flag in place and allow to dry.

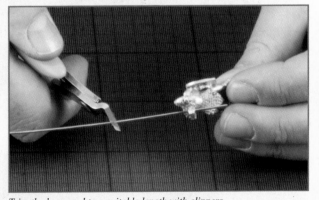

Trim the brass rod to a suitable length with clippers.

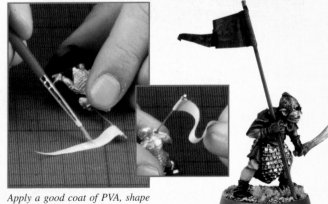

Apply a good coat of PVA, shape as desired and allow to dry.

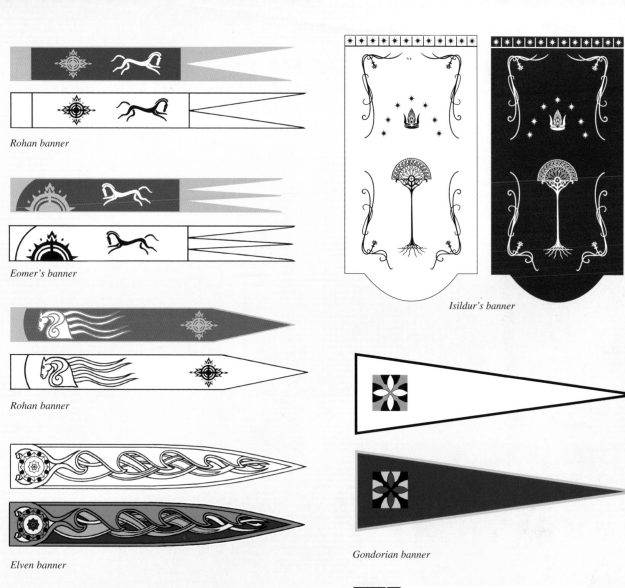

Rohan banner

Eomer's banner

Rohan banner

Elven banner

Gondorian banner

Isildur's banner

Gondorian banner

Aragorn's banner

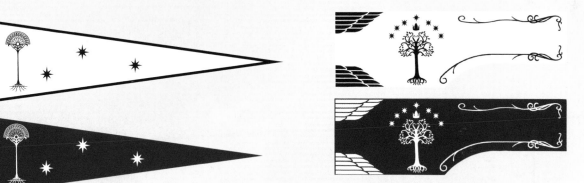

Orc banners

151

MAKING TERRAIN

To fight a battle with miniature warriors it follows that you'll need a miniature battlefield. Some players enjoy creating accurate scale scenes to stage their games, others are happy to improvise around a few basic pieces and let their imaginations do the rest; either way works just as well.

If you enjoy scenery making then you'll probably want to devote more time and attention to the appearance of your battles. If you don't, then you'll still want to know how you can create useful terrain relatively quickly. Whatever your skill level or needs – this section of The Lord of The Rings rules manual is all about making scenery for your battlefield.

THE TABLE

A typical kitchen table will be more than big enough to stage all except the largest battle but a bigger table gives you the flexibility to create grander and more ambitious battlefields. Many enthusiasts make their own dedicated games table by taking a large sheet of chipboard, plywood, or medium density fibreboard (MDF) and fastening it over the top of an old table, desk or cupboard. The standard size for these materials is 8' x 4' (about 240cm x 120cm). This is big enough for staging large battles and about the greatest width that most people can comfortably reach and move models that are in the middle of the table.

Most players don't have the room to leave such a large table set up all the time, so they keep the board separate to the base, storing it elsewhere when not in use. Depending on the material used it may be necessary to provide some bracing underneath to prevent the board bending under its own weight.

If you don't have room for a large table then the kitchen or dining room table can be pressed into service – unless of course your family's needs dictate otherwise. Valuable antiques and prized polished surfaces should be avoided at all costs. If you have no other option there is always the floor – which has the benefit of being flat and large, and should you accidentally drop a model it won't have far to fall!

A CLOTH BATTLEFIELD

One of the quickest and easiest ways of making a battlefield with a landscape of rises and falls is to use a large piece of cloth. You'll need a piece of cloth that's a suitable colour to represent the ground – ideally green or brown – and of a fairly heavy weight. A blanket is ideal.

Spread the blanket over the table's surface and place books, magazines, or something similar underneath to create hills and valleys. With a little care it is possible to make the battlefield interesting by introducing cover that will restrict visibility and provide shelter. With the cloth in place you can add further scenery such as scrub, trees, buildings, and ruins to complete the scene.

COMMERCIAL SCENERY

Most people will be familiar with the kind of detailed scenery available for model railway enthusiasts. A battle scene is very similar in many ways and you can use many of the same items and materials. Most model railway buildings, fences, and actual constructions are a little small, but trees and foliage have no obvious scale and can be used to good effect.

Games Workshop's attractive range of tabletop scenery includes trees, hedges, walling, and various set pieces such as ruins, all of which are similar in concept to those you'll find in railway hobby stores.

The most useful purchase you can make is a bag of lichen. Lichen, or reindeer moss as it is also known, is a natural product that you can buy in model railway stores and sometimes from craft or gift shops as it is also used by flower arrangers (I kid you not!). Lichen can be used to represent scrub, bushes, or any kind of similar vegetation, and can be re-used time and time again to create different layouts.

Lichen, or reindeer moss, makes an excellent hedge or line of scrub.

A few small rocks and a scatter of sand produces an instant scene.

Large rocks doing stierling service as even larger rocks.

SCENERY PROJECT

Terrain models built to represent specific scenes from The Lord of The Rings really create an exciting atmosphere for a battle. Here we show how we went about recreating the wartorn ruins of Osgiliath.

We used polystyrene ceiling tiles and foam card, which is available from DIY and arts & craft stores. The foam card was cut into strips of 30 mm wide and used as the inner walls of the ruins. A polystyrene ceiling tile was used to make the outer brickwork of the walls.

Using a steel ruler and a pen, the windows are drawn onto the strips of foam card and afterward cut out using a sharp craft knife.

The strips of walls were then cut into irregular pieces and glued to a base made from MDF or hardboard.

The brickwork was made from a polystyrene ceiling tile on which we marked out the brick pattern with the help of a pen and a steel ruler.

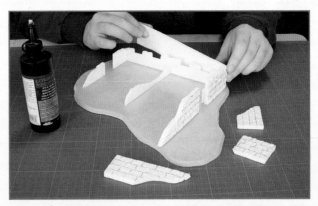

The outer brickwork was then stuck to the inner walls and the windows were cut out using the windows in the inner walls as a guide.

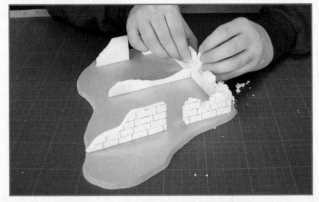

The top of the outer brickwork was crumbled to give it the impression of being in ruins. Leftover pieces of polystyrene were glued onto the base of the model to resemble rubble.

The ruin was then painted with texture paint and undercoated with Chaos Black spray. After the undercoat had dried, the model was drybrushed with Codex Grey, Fortress Grey and finally Skull White. Small tufts of Static Grass were then glued onto the base to add some more detail.

MINAS TIRITH

To capture the towering grandeur of the capital of Gondor, Minas Tirith is a challenge for any modeller. Terrain maker Mark Jones has chosen to focus on a section of the city with a crossroads and fountain.

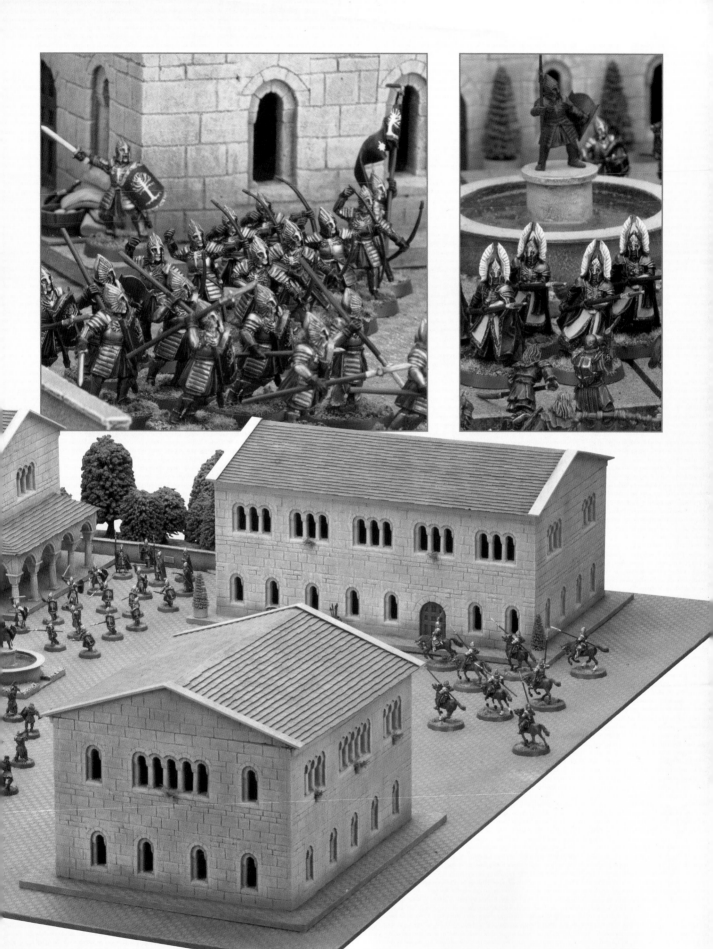

ROHAN

Rohan lies to the west of Gondor, a firm ally and friend in a world troubed by war. The allegiance goes back many years and the the two realms have often stood shoulder to shoulder against the forces of Evil. The Rohirrim are horse-masters beyond comparison, as unmatched in their skill with the beasts as they are in their fiery temper.

Meduseld, the Golden Hall of Edoras.

*"Out of doubt, out of dark to the day's rising
I came singing in the sun, sword unsheathing.
To hope's endI rode and to heart's breaking:
Now for wrath, now for ruin and a red nightfall!"*

- The Return of The King

The Rohirrim charge into a desperate battle with the Uruk-hai.

The Riders of Rohan

HELM'S DEEP

The greatest bastion in the land of Rohan, the castle of Helm's Deep has withstood against the greatest dangers ever to threaten the land of Eorl's people. It was here that the people fled when the land was invaded, first by the Dunlendings in the year 2758 and again in 3019 when Saruman's army swept out of Isengard to destroy the world of Men.

No enemy has taken the Hornburg while men defend it.

The Rohan Royal Guard.

THE GAMING HOBBY

The gaming hobby has grown enormously in recent years as has the variety and quality of games and models available. Where once gamers were few in number and scattered far and wide, now there are few who do not have the benefit of a local club or stockist. Furthermore, the development of the internet has brought the skills and talent of the most creative individuals into the homes of all.

Games Workshop is a specialised company that manufactures and sells fantasy tabletop games and gaming miniatures. The Lord of The Rings battle game is part of a whole range of tried and tested gaming products and is fully supported by Games Workshop's extensive club and tournament program. Every year we hold special events – some of these take place at our Warhammer World exhibition centre in Nottingham, England; whilst our biggest and most popular Games Days are held annually, usually in Birmingham in England and Baltimore in the USA. More recently we have started to hold Games Days in France, Spain, Australia and Canada.

GAMES CLUBS

Gaming is a sociable hobby and you will not be surprised to hear that there are many clubs that cater for gamers of all ages and tastes. If you live in a large city, you'll probably find there is a local games club where Games Workshop games are played. You don't need to be part of a club to enjoy gaming, but there are plenty of advantages, and it is always nice to meet people who share your own passion for gaming.

One of the great things about clubs is there's always someone willing to show you how to play a particular game or improve your painting or modelling skills. In particular, clubs always seem to harbour at least one expert scenery maker who will be only too happy to rope you in to whatever huge and ambitious project he happens to be working on. Many clubs also participate in bigger public events, putting on demonstration games or displays and helping to explain about the games and models.

EVENTS

These are the social occasions of the hobby – a chance to meet fellow hobbyists and swap ideas or just to hang out with old friends. As well as the major events of the gaming calendar, such as Games Day and the Grand Tournaments, there are many smaller local or specialist events held by independent groups or sponsored by Games Workshop. Many clubs hold their own events and, though these are usually small, intimate affairs, some of the larger club events attract hundreds of attendees.

TOURNAMENTS

A tournament of The Lord of The Rings Strategy Battle Game is a great occasion to meet other players and spend a weekend gaming and talking about your favourite hobby. Below you will find the rules that are normally used in the Grand Tournament which takes place once a year in our main headquarters in Nottingham. They are a useful example of a set of tournament rules, and the organisers of many events often alter them as they please to try new and challenging formats of engagement.

TOURNAMENT RULES – THE FORCES

Players will enter the tournament with two forces: one Good and one Evil.

They have a total of 1,000 points to divide between both of their forces.

First of all, players must decide what proportion of their points to allocate to each force (for example: 530 Good and 470 Evil), but a minimum of 250 points must be spent on each force.

For each force the following limits apply:

• *Each force can include a maximum of fifty models.*

• *Each force must include a Hero to lead it into battle. There is no limit on the points that can be spent on Heroes.*

• *No more than a third (33%) of each force's models can be armed with bows/crossbows/thrown weapons (IMPORTANT: models that have the Throw Stones special rule do not count as armed with thrown weapons).*

• *Evil forces cannot include Gollum and can only include up to a maximum of two Trolls (of any kind).*

• *Good forces cannot include Tom Bombadil and Goldberry.*

• *Remember that named Heroes (Gandalf, Lurtz, the Witch King and the other eight Ringwraiths, etc.) can only be taken once.*

• *Whenever any rule is repeated in several publications, the most recent version always takes precedence. This will mean that The Return of The King version is the one to be used.*

SCENARIOS

A tournament always consists of an even number of games. These games will use special scenarios written especially for the event by the organisers, or taken from any of our The Lord of The Rings game rules manuals.

• *In the first game, half the players will use their Good force and the other half will use their Evil force. The first game will be played using Tournament Scenario 1 (as decided by the tournament organisers).*

• *In the second game, players will play the same scenario against the same opponent, but players that used their Good force will now use their Evil force and vice versa.*

Note that the players must swap side of the table, so that the Good and Evil forces play from the same table edge as in the first game.

• *The following two games will use Tournament Scenario 2. Once more, players will alternate using their Good force and their Evil force in the two games.*

• *The tournament continues like this until the players have played all the scenarios from both the Good and Evil side.*

• *The time limit for each game is two hours.*

SPECIAL RULES

• *Models are always assumed to carry all equipment that is given as default in their wargear. Any additional wargear that is taken from their options has to be shown on the model.*

• *In all scenarios, unless otherwise specified, Heroes are not allowed to pick up weapons or any other piece of equipment from slain enemies.*

• *The Passengers special rule will not be used.*

• *When a rider is killed, his mount is always removed.*

• *Scenery for the battle will have been set up by the organisers and may not be moved or changed.*

Games Workshop's monthly hobby magazine White Dwarf is a great place to look if you want more information about The Lord of The Rings battle game or the wargaming hobby in general.

To coincide with the release of The Lord of The Rings – The Return of The King game, White Dwarf has loads of articles enabling you to get more out of your battles, including:

> *News on forthcoming releases.*
>
> *A look at the background of both the movie and game.*
>
> *How to play The Lord of The Rings battle game.*
>
> *New scenarios.*
>
> *Campaigns and battle reports.*
>
> *Advice on painting and converting your models.*
>
> *Scenery masterclasses.*
>
> *Gamers' model collections.*
>
> *Features with sculptors, artists and designers.*

White Dwarf is also the place to look if you want to find out where your nearest Games Workshop store or local stockist is.

To make sure that you don't miss out on anything, you can buy White Dwarf from any of our stores or stockists, and most major newsagents. To be absolutely sure that you don't miss an issue, why not give Mail Order a call. They'll be more than happy to send your copy to you each month and if you take up a subscription you'll be able to take advantage of some of the brilliant deals available only to subscribers.

THE RETURN OF THE KING RANGE

The products listed here comprise some of the range to be released for The Return of The King game. Check out White Dwarf magazine or our The Lord of The Rings website at www.games-workshop.com/lotr/ for more details.

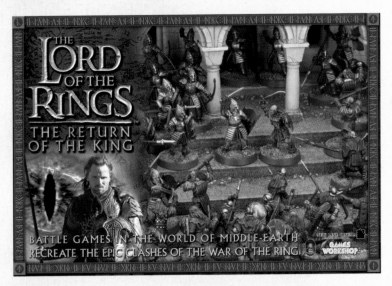

THE GAMES WORKSHOP THE LORD OF THE RINGS WEBSITE

Regularly updated as and when boxed sets and miniatures are released, Games Workshop's The Lord of The Rings website is an ideal place to go to buy your models.

As well as this, the website will link you to the main Games Workshop website where you can find lots of information about painting models, details of wargaming clubs and gaming events in your area and the location of Games Workshop stores and independent stockists.

A large part of the Games Workshop website is dedicated to the wargaming community. This is a major forum which links together thousands of people across the world who are totally devoted to wargaming. Here you will find an abundance of advice written by fellow wargamers on all aspects of the hobby and also links to some of the thousands of websites on the internet written by gamers.

Another great aspect of the site is that it enables players who live near each other to meet up and play a game. So even if you don't have a games store nearby you should be able to find a club near you or join up with someone wanting a battle.

To find out the latest releases and news on The Lord of The Rings releases visit the following website:

www.games-workshop.com/lotr/

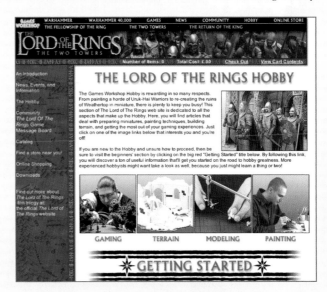

For more details on other Games Workshop releases, general wargaming and hobby information, and links to our wargaming community check out:

www.games-workshop.com

The products shown overleaf are just some of the releases we have planned to coincide with The Lord of The Rings film trilogy. New releases are being brought out each month so make sure you keep up to date by regularly checking out White Dwarf or the website.

The Knights of Minas Tirith assemble for war.

MAIL ORDER

Should you find that you do not have a local store or stockist nearby you can give our Mail Order department a call. Staffed by experienced gamers and collectors, they can supply you with the products that you require, and also help with any questions you may have about The Lord of The Rings hobby. From army selection to rules queries, feel free to give them a call.

If you place an order with us, it will be delivered straight to your door. Call the relevant number below for your country for more details.

UK   0115 9140000

USA 1-800-394-GAME

Canada   1-888-GW-TROLL

Australia   (02) 9829 6111

The Netherlands   ++44115 9168255

Denmark   ++44115 9188506

Sweden   ++44115 9188507

HOW TO USE MAIL ORDER

Ordering by Mail Order is easy. If you have a credit card or debit card you can place your order over the phone.

• **TELL THE STAFF WHAT YOU WANT** – If you are not sure, just ask the telesales staff. They will be happy to help you out.

• **SIT BACK & RELAX** – After you have placed your order, just sit back, relax and wait for your parcel to arrive on your doorstep.

If you wish to pay by cheque (please include your cheque guarantee card number) or postal order, it is just as easy. All you need to do is:

• **FILL OUT AN ORDER FORM** – Printed in the Mail Order section of White Dwarf magazine, with what you would like.

• **COMPLETE PERSONAL DETAILS** – Fill out your name and address in the space provided at the bottom of the form.

• **THEN SIMPLY PLACE YOUR ORDER IN THE POST!**

Shown here are some of the models representing the Free Peoples and Forces of Darkness in The Lord of The Rings strategy battle range. These will be available in boxed sets or as individual miniatures in the case of characters, or as a group of two, three or four warriors, they are an excellent way to add models to your existing force.

THE FREE PEOPLES

Frodo
Sam
Merry
Pippin
Bilbo
Legolas
Gimli
Aragorn
Boromir
Arwen
Elrond
Haldir
Theoden
Eomer
Damrod
Gandalf the White
Treebeard

High Elf Warriors
Wood Elf Warriors
Warriors of Minas Tirith
Warriors of Gondor
Warriors of Rohan
Riders of Rohan
Rangers of Gondor
Citadel Guard
Army of the Dead

Rider of Rohan with throwing spear

Eowyn

Faramir

Tom Bombadil

Aragorn

Ranger of Gondor

Balin

GAMES WORKSHOP STORES

One of the best places to learn more about the game is at your local Games Workshop store. Not only can you find the entire Games Workshop The Lord of The Rings range there but our stores are staffed by experienced gamers who can advise you if you have any questions or wish to take part in an introductory game.

Our stores are also excellent places to meet other gamers. As most will have played other Games Workshop games they're a good starting point if you're new to gaming.

INDEPENDENT RETAILERS

You can also find our great The Lord of The Rings hobby products in a huge network of independent toy, hobby and game retailers across the world.

Many of these stores also offer modelling advice, in addition to stocking The Lord of The Rings range. They may also stock a wide selection of Games Workshop paints and modelling equipment.

If you would like to know where your nearest independent retailer is, you can find a contact number for your area on page 176 of this rulebook. Alternatively, look in White Dwarf magazine or on the Games Workshop web site at www.games-workshop.com.

THE FORCES OF DARKNESS

Sauron
Ringwraiths
Balrog
Shagrat

Shelob
Wild Men Chieftain
Wild Men
Gollum

Easterlings
Moria Goblins
Orc Warriors
Uruk-hai Warriors

Uruk-hai Berserker
The Mouth of Sauron
Cave Troll
Warg Riders

Mordor Orc Standard

Easterling

Uruk-hai Swordsman

Barrow-wight

Mordor Uruk-hai

Gollum

Saruman

CHARTS

MOVE CHART

Type of Model	Maximum move Inches/cms
Man/Woman/Wizard	6"/14cm
High Elf/Wood Elf	6"/14cm
Gwaihir	12"/28cm
Ent	6"/14cm
Hobbit	4"/10cm
Dwarf	5"/12cm
Gollum	5"/12cm
Orc	6"/14cm
Moria Goblin	5"/12cm
Uruk-Hai	6"14cm
Cave Troll	6"/14cm
Balrog	6"/14cm
Ringwraith	6"/14cm
Sauron	6"/14cm
Shelob	10"/24cm
Fell Beast	12"/28cm
Horse Rider	10"/24cm
Warg Rider	10"/24cm

JUMP CHART

Dice	Result
1	Stumbles and fails. Halt at obstacle.
2-5	Success. Cross obstacle and halt.
6	Effortlessly bounds across. Cross obstacle and complete move.

CLIMB CHART

Dice	Result
1	Fall to the ground.
2-5	Continue to climb up/down. If top/bottom reached model halts.
6	Continue to climb up/down. If top/bottom reached complete remaining move.

THROWN RIDER CHART

Dice	Result
1	Knocked flying. Rider placed lying by mount and moves no further that turn.
2-5	Rises from the dust. Rider placed standing by mount and moves no further that turn.
6	Leaps into action. Rider placed standing – no further penalty.

BOW RANGES

Weapon	Range	Strength	Move Penalty
Orc bow	18"/42cm	2	Half
Bow	24"/56cm	2	Half
Elf bow	24"/56cm	3	Half
Dwarf bow	18"/42cm	3	Half
Uruk-hai Crossbow	24"/56cm	4	All
Throwing weapon	6"/14cm	3	None
Rock	*18"/42cm*	*10*	*All*

Wound Chart

DEFENCE

Strength \	1	2	3	4	5	6	7	8	9	10
1	4	5	5	6	6	6/4	6/5	6/6	–	–
2	4	4	5	5	6	6	6/4	6/5	6/6	–
3	3	4	4	5	5	6	6	6/4	6/5	6/6
4	3	3	4	4	5	5	6	6	6/4	6/5
5	3	3	3	4	4	5	5	6	6	6/5
6	3	3	3	3	4	4	5	5	6	6
7	3	3	3	3	3	4	4	5	5	6
8	3	3	3	3	3	3	4	4	5	5
9	3	3	3	3	3	3	3	4	4	5
10+	3	3	3	3	3	3	3	3	4	4

RECORD SHEET

WARRIOR	Move	F	S	D	A	W	C	Notes	M/W/F

THE LORD OF THE RINGS GAME AT A GLANCE

In this section of the manual we've summarised the game rules in a format that is more suitable for reference than the rules section of the manual itself. As such the summary is devoid of explanation and examples and has been presented in as compact a manner as possible. In all cases, the actual rules section of the manual is definitive – refer to the main part of the rules for a full explanation.

1. TURN SEQUENCE

Each turn is divided into phases as follows:

1. Priority
2. Move
3. Shoot
4. Fight
5. End

2. PRIORITY PHASE

2.1 Both sides roll a dice and the highest score has priority that turn.

2.2 In the event of a tie, the priority changes.

2.3 Unless specified otherwise, the Good side has priority in the first turn.

3. MOVE PHASE

3.1 The side that has priority moves its models first. Move one model at a time until all models that intend to move have done so. The other side moves its models once the side with priority has completed its moves. Heroic moves are taken out of sequence before other movement (see Heroic Actions). Courage tests must be taken by individual models before they move in some situations (see Courage).

3.2 A model can move up to the maximum distance indicated on the Movement chart for its type.

3.3 Movement over difficult terrain counts as twice the actual distance.

3.4 If a model has magical powers these can be used at the same time as the model is entitled to move and at any point during its movement. A model must be free to move in order to use a power and must be able to see the target. Models already fighting enemies cannot use magical powers. (see Heroes).

3.5 A model cannot move to within 1"/2cm of an enemy model unless it intends to charge. A model already within 1"/2cm at the start of its move cannot move closer unless it intends to charge.

3.6 A model that moves into touch with one or more enemy models has charged. A model must be able to see its enemy at the start of its move to charge. Once opposing models are touching they cannot move further that Move phase.

3.7 Models cannot move through other models as they move – each model's base defines the ground space it occupies.

3.8 Models are not allowed to leave the gaming area unless retreating from the battle or fulfilling an objective.

3.9 A barrier or object that is at least half the height of the model and up to and including twice the height of the model is considered to be an obstacle. Models can jump obstacles. Refer to the Jump chart. Lower barriers are no hindrance to movement. Higher barriers or barriers broader than double the model's height are impassable.

3.10 A model behind a barrier can defend it – its zone of control extends to the barrier in front of it up to 1"/2cm either side of its base. No enemy can cross this section of barrier.

3.11 Climbing sheer surfaces is treated as difficult terrain with the addition of a Climb test. Refer to the Climb chart.

3.12 A warrior on the top of a wall/cliff can be placed immediately behind its edge and can then defend the edge immediately in front of him and 1"/2cm to either side exactly as if he was defending a barrier

3.13 Falls of more than twice the model's height inflict one Strength 3 hit per 1"/2cm of fall.

3.14 A warrior can lie down or get up once lying down – costing half the model's move in each case.

3.15 A lying down warrior can crawl at 1"/2cm per turn.

3.16 A lying down warrior cannot shoot.

3.17 A lying down model is assumed to be able to see as if standing.

3.18 A lying down model which is partially obscured can only be seen on the dice roll of a 4, 5 or 6.

3.19 A lying down model can fight in combat but cannot strike. If it wins the combat it automatically stands. If it loses it backs away on the ground and counts as trapped.

3.20 A lying down model cannot defend a barrier.

3.21 A lying down model can be jumped over by friends and foe alike as if it were an obstacle.

3.22 At the end of the Move phase, combatants are paired into one-on-one fights where possible, or into one-on-multiple fights where individuals are outnumbered. Spear-armed warriors fighting through friends simply add to one or both sides – they are not counted when dividing into combats.

3.23 Where combats can be divided more than one way the side with priority that turn decides how the combats are formed.

4. SHOOT PHASE

4.1 In the Shoot phase, the side with priority shoots with its models first. Shoot with one model at a time until all models that can do so have shot. Remove casualties as they occur. The other side shoots once the side with priority has finished. Heroic shooting is taken out of sequence before other shooting – see Heroic Actions.

4.2 The maximum range of a shot and Strength value of any hits is indicated on the Missile chart.

4.3 Models that have moved in the Move phase may not shoot in the Shoot phase, depending on the type of ranged weapon they are equipped with.

4.4 An appropriately armed model shoots once in the Shoot phase (note that some Heroes shoot more than once).

4.5 Roll a dice for each shot. A model needs to roll its Shoot value or greater to score a hit.

4.6 If a hit is scored on a partially obscured target roll a dice for each obscuring feature or model that lies in the way of the missile – starting with objects closest to the shooter. A dice roll of 1, 2 or 3 indicates the object/model has been hit and the missile is stopped.

4.7 A model shooting from behind cover does not count his own cover as in the way of his shot.

4.8 A model shooting from behind a friend can do so without penalty provided the friendly model is in base contact and has a base size equal to or less than the shooter.

4.9 If the target is fighting in combat roll a dice: 1, 2 or 3 the shot hits the closest model from its own side; 4, 5 or 6 the shot hits the intended target.

4.10 If a shot is directed at a target which has a combat in the way, roll a dice: 1, 2 or 3 the shot hits the combat, resolve the hit as if it were directed at the combat.

4.11 Good models cannot shoot at an enemy if there is a friend in the way of the missile or fighting the target in combat.

4.12 Work out the effect of hits on targets or models struck in combat or because they are in the way of the shot. Roll a dice and consult the Wound chart. Cross reference the weapon's Strength with the target's Defence value. If the roll is enough to inflict a wound, the target is removed as a casualty if it has 1 wound on its profile, or its Wound value is reduced by -1 if it had 2 or more wounds to begin with.

4.13 Heroes with multiple shots can divide their shots between different targets if desired.

5. FIGHT PHASE

5.1 Combats are resolved one at a time. The side with priority decides which combats to fight first. Heroic combats are fought out of sequence before other combats – see Heroic Actions.

5.2 To determine which side wins a combat, roll one dice for each model fighting or, if models have more than 1 Attack, each model rolls as many dice as it has Attacks. Pick out the highest dice roll on each side. The side that has the highest roll wins the combat.

5.3 Where models score equally, the side whose model has the highest Fight value wins the combat. If this is equal, roll a dice – 1, 2, 3 the Evil side wins; 4, 5, 6 the Good side wins.

5.4 Heroic models may add one or more points of Might to their dice rolls up to a maximum score of 6. If both sides wish to do this they secretly indicate how much Might they are using (minimum of 1).

5.5 All models on the losing side must back away 1"/2cm from the enemy or, if fighting two or more enemies, through any gap large enough for them to move through.

5.6 Models unable to back away because of interposing enemies, friends or terrain are trapped.

5.7 All models on the winning side can strike against their enemy once they have been beaten back. Models strike once for each Attack on their profile. Victors with 2 or more Attacks can divide their strikes between different defeated enemies if they want. Double the number of strikes when striking against a trapped enemy.

5.8 Resolve the effect of each strike on the Wound chart. Cross referencing the striker's Strength with the target's Defence to find the dice score required. Where wounds are inflicted remove casualties or record wounds inflicted where these are insufficient to cause a casualty.

5.9 When a combat is fought across a barrier, models are assumed to be touching even though the barrier divides them. Only one enemy at a time can fight a defender across a barrier.

5.10 A model defending a barrier does not back away if defeated. If neither model is slain as a result of combat, the attacker must back away 1"/2cm regardless of which side won.

5.11 If the model that is making the attack across the barrier wins, then each strike will be deflected by the barrier on the roll of a 1, 2 or 3.

5.12 If the defender of a barrier is killed his attacker moves over the barrier to take his place.

6. CAVALRY

6.1 A cavalry model comprises a rider and his mount, and therefore has two separate sets of characteristics.

6.2 A cavalry model's 'eye view' is always taken from the point of view of the rider.

6.3 Mounted warriors can move through difficult terrain at 2"/4cm per turn, regardless of their normal Move value, climb, lie down, crawl or willingly jump down a drop of more than twice the mount's height. They cannot move up or down ladders and narrow steep stairs, nor can they carry siege equipment.

6.4 Mounts can re-take a failed Jump test – re-rolling 1s.

6.5 Mounting is treated as a jump – dismounting is automatic.

6.6 Cavalry models may carry a passenger, see page 34 for rules about moving and fighting with passengers.

6.7 When shooting at mounted targets, successful hits are randomised: the mount is hit on the roll of a 1,2 or 3 – the rider is hit on the roll of a 4,5, or 6.

6.8 Should a mount be killed, the rider must roll on the Thrown Rider chart. If riders are killed, their mount is also removed as a casualty (for an exception see 6.15).

6.9 If a cavalry model charges into combat against enemy infantry it receives two advantages, even if it is subsequently charged by other enemy on foot. The advantages are lost if the model is subsequently charged by a mounted enemy. These two advantages are: 'Extra Attack' and 'Knock to the ground'.

6.10 'Extra Attack' means the cavalry model gets an extra Attack.

6.11 'Knock to the ground' means that if the cavalry model wins the fight, all his opponents are knocked to the ground. This does not apply to enemies with a Strength 6 or more, unless the mount also has Strength 6 or more. Each strike directed against models knocked to the ground is doubled.

6.12 If a cavalry model is defeated, its opponent can direct their strikes at mount or rider as they wish.

6.13 Mounted models can defend barriers as normal.

6.14 If mounts are killed, their rider is thrown and the model is replaced with an equivalent model on foot.

6.15 If riders are killed, their mount is also removed as a casualty, unless it is important for the scenario for the models to be able to re-mount. If this is the case, follow the rules for loose mounts on page 40.

6.16 Mounted models cannot 'defend by shielding'.

6.17 Cavalry do not receive their charge bonus when fighting infantry that are defending a barrier against them or when in difficult terrain.

7. MONSTROUS MOUNTS

7.1 When shooting at a monstrous mount with a rider, successful hits are randomised: the mount is hit on the roll of a 1, 2, 3 or 4 – the rider is hit on the roll of a 5 or 6.

7.2 Monstrous mounts and their riders never get the Extra Attack bonus when charging.

7.3 Monstrous mounts may knock cavalry to the ground.

8. END PHASE

8.1 The End phase is an opportunity to check whether objectives have been met and make sure all necessary recording has been done before going on to the next turn. It is also a good time to check for 50% casualties if one side is looking a little worn down.

9. COURAGE

9.1 A warrior must test his courage in three circumstances:
1) Attempting to charge a terrifying enemy;
2) At start of a move once half of his force is destroyed;
3) At the start of a move if he is on his own.

9.2 When attempting to charge a terrifying enemy the test is taken once the model moves to within 1"/2cm of the enemy. In other situations, the test is taken before the model moves in the Move phase.

9.3 Models wishing to support a friend who is fighting a terrifying enemy does not need to take a Courage test, as they are not going to charge the terrifying enemy.

9.4 Models are considered to be on their own if there are no visible friends within 6"/14cm and at least two visible enemies within 6"/14cm for every remaining wound the model has.

9.5 Models already fighting an enemy at the start of their move do not have to test.

9.6 To take a Courage test roll two dice, add the scores, and add the model's Courage value. If the total score is 10 or more the test is passed. If it is less than 10 the test is failed.

9.7 Models that pass their test are unaffected. Models that fail their test must retreat immediately.

9.8 Retreating models turn away from the nearest visible enemy and move their full move distance. They will move as directly away as possible, diverting round other models, terrain and obstacles where they are in the way. Retreating models will not move to within 1"/2cm of enemy, or closer if already within 1"/2cm when they start to retreat.

9.9 Models that retreat from a terrifying enemy will effectively move twice – once to within 1"/2cm of the enemy and then a full move away.

9.10 Models unable to retreat because their route is blocked will retreat as far as they can. They still count as having moved full distance for other purposes (eg, shooting).

9.11 If a retreating model can reach the table edge within its move it will do so regardless of direction. The model leaves the battle and does not return.

9.12 Only one Courage test is taken in a turn because of half the force destroyed or being on your own. The first result stands for all.

9.13 If testing because half the army is destroyed, models within 6"/14cm of a Hero who has already tested his courage and passed do not have to test. They automatically stand fast so long as the Hero stands.

9.14 Models that have retreated are not penalised in subsequent turns. The failed Courage test results in a retreat, after which the model is treated as any other. Models will only retreat over successive turns if they fail successive tests.

10. HEROES

10.1 Heroes have three additional characteristics on their profile – namely Might points, Will points and Fate points. Not all Heroes have all three. Might, Will and Fate differ from ordinary characteristics in that they are expendable. Once a point of Might, Will or Fate has been used it is removed from the model's profile.

10.2 Might is used either to modify dice rolls made on behalf of the Hero or to take heroic actions. When modifying dice rolls, each point of Might expended adds or subtracts 1 from the dice roll (minimum score 1, maximum score 6). These additions/subtractions are made after the dice have been rolled and the score is known. Might can be used to modify Will dice rolls or Fate dice rolls, and is most commonly used to boost rolls to hit whilst shooting, rolls to see which side wins a fight, and wound rolls either from shooting or fighting. It is also useful for Courage tests.

10.3 If opposing warriors both wish to use Might to boost their scores in a fight then each must secretly note how much Might they wish to use.

10.4 Where players wish to use Might to make a heroic action they must declare they are doing so at the start of the relevant phase. If both players wish to make heroic actions in the same phase, they nominate which Heroes will act alternately, starting with the player indicated by a dice roll: 1-3 the Evil side goes first; 4-6 the Good side goes first.

10.5 There are three types of heroic action – heroic move, heroic shooting, and heroic combat. Each type of heroic action costs 1 Might point.

10.6 A Hero making a heroic move moves before other models in the Move phase. Friends within 6"/14cm move at the same time.

10.7 A Hero who is making a heroic shot shoots before other models in the Shooting phase. Friends within 6"/14cm shoot at the same time. A Hero does not need a bow or other missile weapon to call a heroic shoot action.

10.8 If a Hero makes a heroic combat action, work out the fight he is engaged in before other fights. If the Hero wins his fight and if all of the enemy in base contact with the Hero are killed, then the Hero and all other models in the same fight can move again immediately. Models moving in this way can charge enemies they can see, initiating new fights or joining old ones if they wish. Models cannot fight more than one heroic combat in a turn.

10.9 Will is used in the Move phase to employ magical powers or to resist those of the enemy. To use a magical power roll one or more dice. Each dice rolled expends 1 point of Will. Pick the highest dice roll. If the score is equal to or more than that required to use the power then work out the result as described for the Hero's power. Might can be used to boost this score if required.

10.10 To resist a magical power roll one or more dice, expending 1 point of Will for each dice rolled. If the score equals or beats the dice score of the model using the power, the power has been successfully resisted.

10.11 Fate is used when a Hero suffers a wound. The model gives up 1 Fate point and rolls a dice. If the score is a 4, 5 or 6 the Hero has miraculously survived and the wound is ignored. This roll can be boosted by Might. If the roll is failed, the Hero can use another point of Fate, and can continue to do so until he has no Fate points left.

11. WEAPONS

11.1 Warriors armed with swords, axes, clubs, maces and similar hand held weapons are considered to be armed and able to fight as described in the main rules. The same is true of bow-armed models armed with bladed bows. No special rules apply.

11.2 **Spears.** A spear-armed warrior can contribute one attack to a fight if he is in base contact with a friend who is touching an enemy. The friend must have a base of the same size as the spear-armed warrior, or smaller, for the spear-armed warrior to be able to support him.

A spear-armed warrior who is supporting a friend as described is not part of the combat for all intents and purposes. The friend supported in this way by a spearman gets one extra attack for that combat.

Only one spear-armed warrior can support one friendly model at a time.

11.3 **Two-handed swords/axes.** Warriors armed with big, heavy swords or axes that require both hands to use are said to have two-handed sword/axes or two-handed weapons. Halberds, glaives, and other axe-like pole arms that need both hands to use can also be considered to be in this category. Models armed with two-handed swords/axes suffer a -1 dice penalty when working out which side has won a fight, but add a +1 bonus to their dice roll to score a wound. In both cases the worst result is a 1, and the best result is 6.

11.4 **Elven blades.** Elven blades counts as hand weapons. An Elf armed with an Elven blade can declare at the start of any Fight phase that he is going to use it with two hands. For the duration of that Fight phase, the Elven blade will count as a two-handed weapon. If the warrior also carries a spear, shield or Elf bow then he may not use the Elven blade as a two-handed weapon.

11.5 **Lances.** A cavalry model with a lance receives a +1 bonus to his roll on the Wound chart if it has charged that turn – even if it was subsequently counter-charged. If two rolls are normally required to inflict a wound (eg, 6/4+) the bonus is added to both rolls. The maximum score on a dice is 6, so a roll of 6 still counts as a 6.

11.6 **Knives/Daggers.** Warriors that have no visible armament are assumed to have knives or daggers tucked into boot tops or hidden under clothing. Models armed with daggers suffer a -1 dice penalty when working out which side has won a fight. The worst roll is a 1.

11.7 **Shields.** Models armed with shields have a Defence value that reflects the added protection of the shield, plus they may defend by shielding. A shielding model rolls two dice per Attack when working out who wins the fight, but cannot strike if it wins. In a multiple combat, all models on the same side must use the shielding rule or none.

11.8 **Pikes.** The same rules for spears apply to pikes as well, with the exception that models armed with pikes can support through two friends instead of just one.

11.9 **Throwing weapons.** Throwing weapons can be thrown normally in the Shoot phase (see the Shoot section). They can also be thrown in the Move phase. Models can throw these weapons during a charge against the model charged. If the target is killed, the charger can choose to complete his charge move against another suitable target.

11.10 **Volley Fire.** A group of six or more bow-armed models in base contact with at least one other member of the group at the start of the Shoot phase can declare they are going to fire a volley. See page 54 for details.

12. BANNERS

12.1 Warriors carrying banners may ride horses but may not use any other equipment apart from armour or heavy armour.

12.2 Warriors carrying banners count as wielding daggers in combat.

12.3 If a warrior carrying a banner is killed, a friendly warrior in base contact can drop all his equipment and pick up the banner. If the banner is not picked up, it is lost.

12.4 All models within 3"/8cm of a friendly banner bearer are in range of the banner. If a fight is in range of a banner, the player who owns the banner may re-roll a single dice when rolling to determine who wins the fight.

GETTING STARTED

If you have never played The Lords of The Rings strategy battle game before, the best way to learn is by setting up your models and starting to play. Below you will find an encounter we have created which is a simple example of the game's mechanics and should help you pick up the basic rules.

CLOSE ENCOUNTER

In this example, a valorous Warrior of Minas Tirith has spotted an Orc scouting ahead of a raiding party. As the Orc rushes towards him, the Warrior of Minas Tirith carefully takes aim with his bow. Can the Orc reach the Man and cut him down before he gets shot?

Place a Warrior of Minas Tirith armed with sword and bow, and an Orc armed with sword and shield 12"/28cm apart, facing each other over a level table.

WARRIOR OF
MINAS TIRITH

12"/28cm

ORC WARRIOR

TURN 1

PRIORITY
At the beginning of each turn, the players must roll a dice to determine who has priority (ie, who is going first) in all three phases of the turn. Winning this roll is therefore very important. The Good side always has priority on Turn 1, so in our example the Warrior of Minas Tirith has priority.

MOVE PHASE
In this phase, the models can move. The Warrior of Minas Tirith moves first because the Good side has priority this turn. He decides not to move and remains stationary, preparing to fire his bow at the enemy.

Now it's the Evil side's turn to move. The Orc has a maximum move of 6"/14cm, and decides to use all of his move to rush towards the Man. Move the Orc 6"/14cm towards his opponent.

SHOOT PHASE
In this phase, the models can shoot their bows. The Warrior of Minas Tirith gets his chance first because his side has priority. He takes aim and shoots the Orc as he runs towards him. The player rolls a dice, needing a result of 4, 5 or 6 to hit the target. He rolls a 2 and misses. In the Evil side's turn to shoot, the Orc cannot do anything because unfortunately he has no bow to shoot!

FIGHT PHASE
Since no models are touching base-to-base, there will be no Fight phase this turn.

TURN 2

PRIORITY
Both players roll a dice, the Good side's result is a 5 and the Evil side's is a 3. The Good side has scored the highest and will therefore have the priority for Turn 2.

MOVE PHASE
The Warrior of Minas Tirith decides to move back half his normal move (3"/8cm). The Orc moves again at maximum speed towards the Warrior of Minas Tirith, but is unable to reach him and engage him in combat. He ends his move 3"/8cm away from the Warrior of Minas Tirith.

SHOOT PHASE
Models that have only moved up to half of their maximum move distance can still use their bows, so the Warrior of Minas Tirith can shoot and this time his dice roll is a 6. The Orc has been hit!

Now we must determine whether the arrow kills the warrior or is stopped by his armour or shield. To find out, the Good side's player rolls a second dice, needing a 6 to eliminate the Orc (he is very well armoured!). The Warrior of Minas Tirith rolls a 5 and the Orc survives, the arrow has been stopped by his armour or shield, or has caused just a superficial wound – the battle continues.

FIGHT PHASE
As in Turn 1, there will be no Fight phase this turn.